U.S. LABOR RELATIONS, 1945–1989

GARLAND REFERENCE LIBRARY
OF THE HUMANITIES
(VOL. 1180)

U.S. LABOR RELATIONS, 1945–1989
Accommodation and Conflict

edited by
Bruce Nissen

GARLAND PUBLISHING, INC. • NEW YORK & LONDON
1990

Library of Congress Cataloging-in-Publication Data

U.S. labor relations, 1945–1989: accommodation and conflict / edited
by Bruce Nissen.
     p.   cm. — (Garland reference library of the humanities ; vol.
1180)
ISBN 0–8240–7141–7 (alk. paper)
    1. Industrial relations—United States. I. Nissen, Bruce, 1948– .
II. Series.
HD8072.5.U19   1990
331'.0973'09045—dc20   89–35964
                                       CIP

Printed on acid-free, 250-year-life paper
Manufactured in the United States of America

To Karen, Jared, and Leif -- B.N.

CONTENTS

CONTRIBUTORS

Solomon Barkin is Professor Emeritus of Economics at the University of Massachusetts at Amherst. He was Research Director for the textile Workers Union of America for 26 years, and held a major post with the Organization for Economic Cooperation and Development (OECD) for a number of years prior to entering academia. He has published numerous articles and several books, the most recent being Trade Union Militancy and Its Consequences: The Changing Climate of Western Industrial Relations (New York: Praeger Publishers, 1983).

Charles Craypo is Professor and Chair in the Department of Economics, University of Notre Dame. He also has been a faculty member and labor educator at Michigan State University, Pennsylvania State University and Cornell University. He has published books and articles on the economics of collective bargaining, unions and industrial change and union structure and government.

Ronald Filippelli is professor and head of the Department of Labor Studies and Industrial Relations at the Pennsylvania State University. He is the author of Labor in the USA: A History (New York: Knopf, 1984), American Labor and Postwar Italy: A Study in Cold War Politics (Stanford, CA: Stanford University Press, 1989), as well as a number of articles and book chapters. He is currently editing the Encyclopedia of U.S. Labor Conflict for Garland Publishing.

Bruce Nissen is Associate Professor of Labor Studies at the Indiana University Northwest campus in Gary, Indiana. He is co-editor (with Simeon Larson) of Theories of the Labor Movement (Detroit: Wayne State University Press, 1987), and has published articles in the field of labor studies.

Paul K. Rainsberger is Associate Professor of Labor Studies at the Indiana University Division of Labor Studies. He serves as the Statewide Program Coordinator for Labor Studies on the Bloomington campus of Indiana University. He is the author of a variety of curricular materials on labor law including a computer-based reference program. Prior to joining the faculty of Indiana University, he was employed as an attorney for the Indiana State Employees Association.

Peter Seybold received his Ph.D. in sociology from the State University of New York at Stony Brook in 1978. He is currently on the staff of the Division of Labor Studies at Indiana University. Among his research and teaching interests are the sociology of work, labor and the political economy, and the structure of power in America.

INTRODUCTION

Labor-management relations in the United States during the decades immediately following World War II were unique in many respects. For one thing, unions were more firmly established in major industries than at any time previous or since. Unlike some other advanced industrial economies, unions never represented a majority of the workforce in the United States; at its height in the early-to-mid 1950s, the unions represented approximately one third of the relevant labor force. Yet, unions exerted an influence well beyond their own membership. The patterns of industrial relationships in the postwar era in the basic manufacturing, transport, and construction industries were clearly set by the terms established in union contracts negotiated between employers and unions.

This book concentrates on the fate of the United States labor movement and the relationships it established with management in the four and one half decades from 1945 to 1990. Unions in the United States have suffered dramatic declines in virtually every measurable way in the 1980s. How this occurred, the pre-conditions in the earlier period which allowed such a dramatic reversal, and prospects for the future are three major concerns of the authors of this book. Because the fate of the labor movement is of such importance for the future of labor-management relations, organized labor's recent setbacks make this an appropriate time to assess the present and recent past.

The chapters in this book attempt to present brief but comprehensive analyses of the post-World War II years from distinct perspectives. In Chapter 1, Charles Craypo utilizes an institutionalist economic framework to examine and explain the decline in organized labor's bargaining power. Operating within a "productive systems" analysis, Craypo carefully dissects the changes in the bargaining environment and bargaining structures which have undermined union bargaining power in the 1980s. One of the many strengths of this chapter is the careful attention to the many different ways labor is being weakened, depending on the particular industry involved. Craypo moves well beyond the usual superficial explanations so common in many analyses of the same subject. In the final section, Craypo contrasts his analysis with that of conventional neoclassical economic theory and of mainstream industrial relations theory. He concludes with a brief sketch of the tasks the labor movement must undertake if it is to recover.

In Chapter 2, Peter Seybold looks at the political fortunes of the United States labor movement in the postwar years. In the United States, unions (especially industrial unions) have always been very dependent on political trends. Unfavorable political developments have always been devastating for organized labor. Seybold argues strongly that the United States labor movement has taken too narrow a view of its political objectives and roles. He argues that this has led to a loss of momentum and ever greater dependency on forces which are not fundamentally favorable to the interests of workers and unions. Seybold concludes his chapter with a prescription for a new political direction within the labor movement and an assessment of likely scenarios for the political future of organized labor.

Chapter 3 looks at the same time period from a legal perspective. Author Paul Rainsberger argues that the legal tradition in this country has been overwhelmingly hostile toward organized labor, with one exception: the 1935-47 period. Beginning with the passage of the Taft-Hartley amendments to the Wagner Act in 1947, Rainsberger demonstrates how each legal change or, more importantly, each reinterpretation of existing law has constrained labor's ability to act effectively while management gets a progressively freer hand to thwart labor. Through a careful exposition of various important legal issues in labor-management relations, Rainsberger demonstrates the degree to which legal doctrine has changed from equivocal support for unionism to a major bias toward capital.

In Chapter 4, Ronald Filippelli views postwar industrial relations in historical perspective. He argues that the long run historical tendencies in the United States have been inhospitable to organized labor. Seen this way, the unusual period is not the decline in union power since the mid-1950s, but the major growth in union power from the mid-1930s to the mid-1950s. Filippelli argues that too many historians have seen the relative good times for organized labor in the 1933-1953 period as the culmination of a steady ascent to its rightful place of power and influence on the American scene. Developing a convincing synthesis of American labor history, the author shows that this interpretation is not tenable. Rather, it was the joining together of unusual events such as the 1930s depression and World War II which made the rapid growth of the late 1930s and the 1940s possible. Filippelli concludes the chapter by tracing the factors which have been weakening organized labor since the middle of the 1950s.

In Chapter 5 I examine the concept of a "social accord" between organized labor and big business in the postwar years. A number of different versions of this accord are given, and some are criticized for historical inaccuracy or overly broad and vacuous terms. However, the terms of a more restricted social accord analysis are examined in light of a struggle over "management's rights" in the years immediately following World War II. The basic terms of this accord were operative for many industries for much of the postwar period: management got stability, unions got (conditional) legitimacy, and the union worker got a steadily rising standard of living. However, four major qualifications are found to be necessary for the social accord analysis, and it is pointed out that the "social accord" language can be confusing. Despite these limitations, the social accord analysis points to extremely important features of postwar labor relations. It pinpoints a major weakness of organized labor as it faces the unfavorable climate of the 1990s.

In Chapter 6 Solomon Barkin puts United States industrial relations in a comparative perspective. Utilizing an institutional economic framework, Barkin explicates the main features of the environment in all the advanced industrial capitalist countries within which trade unions operate. Trends and directions of the labor movement in particular countries (England, West Germany, Sweden, etc.) are also explored. Much of the analysis concerns the relationships between trade unions and their political party partners--usually socialist, social-democratic, or labor parties. The very terms of the discussion (socialist party, labor party, etc.) show how different the situation is in much of Europe from that of the United States. Yet despite these differences, Barkin finds a number of problems and issues to be relevant to all labor movements, and finds the European unions to have problems of their own. The chapter ends with a summation of common perspectives across all trade unions and a look at the internal and external issues facing the labor movements in the advanced industrial capitalist countries.

The essays which make up the chapters of this book are serious attempts to understand the evolution of industrial relations and the fate of the United States labor movement in the postwar years. All chapters present a thoughtful and well informed viewpoint. B y approaching the subject matter with economic, political, legal, historical, and comparative analyses, the book attains a depth of perspective which is seldom found in other works on the same topic. And several of the chapters are genuinely original contributions to our understanding of the period. It is hoped that this book will prove useful to scholars and practitioners alike. In labor relations and union matters, as in most other fields, a clear assessment of the past is necessary for wise choices in the future.

U.S. Labor Relations, 1945–1989

CHAPTER 1

The Decline in
Union Bargaining Power

Charles Craypo*

U.S. union power declined dramatically in the 1980s. Membership as a proportion of eligible workers had been shrinking for some time, but after the mid-1970s it began falling in absolute terms. Then, in the midst of economic recession in the early 1980s, traditionally strong unions started to make significant contract concessions. By the end of the decade they had not recouped their losses despite several years of economic recovery. As a result, the living standards and job conditions of both union and non-union workers suffered.

How did this happen? How did one of the strongest labor movements in the industrialized world crumble so quickly? What explains the decline and is it temporary or permanent? To answer these questions unions and labor relations must be located in the productive system which creates and distributes economic wealth. The major components of productive systems interact with one another and with the dominant social and political institutions to determine, among other things, relative bargaining power between labor and capital. Part one of this chapter summarizes the decline in union membership after 1979; part two describes and explains the major elements of the U.S. productive system; part three traces the decline of union bargaining experiences after 1979; part four examines the economic impact of this decline and the prospects for union resurgence.

* The author is indebted to Frank Wilkinson for helpful comments during the drafting of this paper.

1. Declining Union Membership

Union membership in the U.S. dropped from a postwar high of 23 million in 1974 to 17 million by 1985. More important, union density--members as a percentage of potential membership--fell from 28 to 17 percent, continuing a trend that started in 1954. Unions claimed 17 million members in 1953 and again in 1987; the difference was that 17 million workers amounted to 33 percent of labor's potential membership in 1953 but only 17 percent in 1987. Three patterns emerge from the union density figures shown in Table 1. First, the difference between 1985 and the peak year is negative in every industrial sector. Second, union density in high-wage, basic industries peaked prior to the mid-1950s and then fell steadily. Third, ratios have not been high in the service sectors and only moderately so in government and in each instance they peaked more than a decade ago.

Density ratios for industry groups are too aggregated to discern shifts in bargaining power. Membership changes in individual unions are better indicators because they reflect changes within the core industries and occupations after which U.S. unions are named and structured. Even though most unions are less identified now with specific trades and industries than in the past, they still negotiate major contracts and have their membership bases in them.

Table 1
Changes in Postwar Union Density by Industrial Sector

Sector	Postwar Peak	Peak Year	1985	1985-Peak
(percent change)				
All nonfarm industries	33	1953	20**	-13
Manufacturing	42	1953	25	-17
Construction	87	1947	22	-65
Transportation	80	1953	37	-43
Mining	83	1947	15	-68
Services	14	1975	7	-7
Government	40	1975	34*	-6

*1983
**1984

Source: Adapted from Leo Troy, "The Rise and Fall of American Trade Unions: The Labor Movement from FDR to RR," in Seymour Martin Lipset (ed.), Unions in Transition: Entering the Second Century (San Francisco: ICS Press, 1986), Table 7, p. 87.

Table 2 shows reported membership changes during 1955-87 in two dozen AFL-CIO affiliates. [1] Manufacturing unions experienced the greatest declines in membership. Most peaked in the mid-1950s, descended during the next two decades, dropped sharply in the 1982-83 recession and then continued to lose members. Unions concentrated in the other two goods-producing sectors--construction and mining--show mixed patterns. Mechanical crafts like the plumbers and electricians benefit from structural and technological changes in the industry while others like the laborers and carpenters have to organize elsewhere to offset losses in traditional areas. The United Mine Workers, which is excluded from Table 2 because it is not an AFL-CIO affiliate, presently claims about 230,000 members, one third of whom are retirees, compared to more than 400,000 during the Second World War, the result of mine technology, increased nonunion strip-mining and rising coal imports coupled with falling domestic demand.

Unions in nondurable industries all show steady membership decreases as a result of fewer production jobs and growing nonunion sectors. None has successfully compensated by organizing in other industries, and recent mergers among them are likely to continue as one by one they fall below the minimum membership levels needed to function administratively. Membership in transportation and communications unions fell in response to employment reductions and increases in the number of nonunion firms; membership in service sector unions either held steady or rose as a result of union organizing gains and rapid job growth. Public employee unions generally grew in membership along with the growth in public employment, except in the federal sector during the 1980s.

The Steel Workers' union (USWA) is a dramatic example of an important industrial union experiencing serious membership decline. Despite continued organizing activities and merger with a smaller union, USWA membership fell by 44 percent during 1980-87-- from 1.1 million to 618,000, which was its membership size in the 1940s. In 1980 it represented more than 337,000 workers in basic steel; by the end of 1987 it had only 129,000, a 62 percent drop. Steel now accounts for roughly 40 percent of USWA's membership compared with more than 60 percent a decade ago. Thirty percent of the remaining members work in steel-related industries and the other 30 percent in the "non-traditional" sectors which the union has targeted for future growth. To finance stepped-up organizing activities, delegates to the union's 1988 convention approved the first monthly membership dues increase in 20 years.

Table 2
Reported Membership in Selected National and
International Union Affiliates of the AFL-CIO

Industrial Category and Union	1955	1979	1983	1987
Durable Manufacturing				
Auto (UAW)	1,260	N.A.	1,010	998
Electrical	271	255**	N.A.	185
Machinists (IAM)	627	664	596	509
Molders (IMAWU)	67	50	42	32
Shipbuilders (IUMSW)	27	24	21	12
Nondurable Manufacturing				
Clothing-Textile (ACTWU)	413	301	253	195
Paper (UPWIU)	254*	262	241	221
Oil (OCAW)	160	146	124	96
Printing (GCIU)	143*	N.A.	154	136
Rubber (URW)	163	158	108	97
Chemical (ICWU)	79	50	43	35
Non-Manufacturing				
Communications (CWA)	249*	485	573	515
Airline Pilots (ALPA)	9	44	54	31
Maritime (NMU)	37	30	20	18
Transportation-Communications				
(BRAC)	264	160**	102***	113*
Carpenters	750	619	609	609
Electricians (IBEW)	460	825	820	765
Food and Commercial (UFCW)	522*	1,076	993	1,000
Office Employees (OPEIU)	44	83	89	86
Service Employees (SEIU)	205	528	589	762
Public Sector				
Letter Carriers (NALC)	100	151	175	200
State, County (AFSCME)	99	889	959	1,032
Federal Employees (AFGE)	47	236	204	157
Teachers (AFT)	40	423	456	499

    *   Combined membership of two or more unions that later merged to form the designated organization.

    **   1975

    ***   1985

Source: Courtney D. Gifford, <u>Directory of U.S. Labor Organizations</u> <u>1988-89 Edition,</u> Bureau of National Affairs, Washington, D.C., 1988.

2. Unions and Productive Systems

Figure 1 shows the various elements of the U.S. productive system and how they interact in the production and allocation of wealth. The principal components are competition, industrial organization and labor market structures. A fourth element, the social and political environment, pervades the system but directly affects the supply of workers and the bargaining power of unions. The arrows in Figure 1 indicate major directions of influence among the dominant elements but in reality they all interact to some degree. Unions normally have a leveling effect. Groups of workers form protective segments within which they defend themselves against the superior market power of employers. On the job they insulate production workers and preserve group earnings and conditions; in the economy they make wages insensitive to employment cycles and inflationary pressures. Industrial unions consolidate bargaining units and negotiate company wide contracts that narrow differentials within bargaining units and among plants and industries through pattern settlements.

Interaction of competition and industrial organization has consolidated, diversified and internationalized the ownership and control of productive assets by combining previously competitive firms, bringing unrelated businesses under common control and integrating corporate operations globally. Firms are more mobile than before the current wave of mergers and acquisitions. They also are more likely to become targets of hostile takeovers and to increase their debt obligations to dangerous levels when they resist; then they look to labor as a source of cost reductions and improved cash flow. Operationally, established firms in basic industries follow the leads of their dominant rivals in decisions involving product lines, production processes, financial tactics and labor relations. In practice, this often includes low-wage, nonunion strategies which they hope will put them on a par with the new competitors.

Industrial structures also affect labor market structures. Labor supply interacts with labor demand to determine pay, benefits and job conditions. It adapts readily to the quantity and quality of jobs available. Employers have market leverage over employees because there are fewer of them relative to the supply of workers and they offer work on a take-it-or-leave-it basis. Workers can reject the terms in theory but not often in practice because they must work to subsist. Unions therefore play a crucial role in mediating labor market outcomes in favor of workers. This is especially important in the U.S. where no comprehensive government regulation of labor markets exists to protect workers.

Figure 1
"Productive Systems"

A. COMPETITION
1. Foreign trade

2. Domestic industry

B. INDUSTRIAL ORGANIZATION
1. Existing Firms

 a. Corporate reorganization
 b. Imitative behavior
 c. Low-wage strategies
 d. Product and production
    strategies

2. New Firms

C. LABOR MARKET STRUCTURE
1. Labor Demand

 a. Primary and secondary job mix
 b. Labor processes
 c. Skill and experience criteria

2. Unions and collective bargaining

 a. Unionization levels
 b. Bargaining structures
 c. Bargaining standards

3. Labor supply

 a. Participation rates
 b. Contingency workers
 c. Skill and experience levels

D. SOCIAL AND POLITICAL EVIRONMENTS

 a. Government deregulation of product and labor market
 b. Intensified social stratification

Changes in industrial organization and labor processes have decreased the ratio of good to bad jobs and weakened the bargaining position of workers holding the good jobs. Primary (good) jobs are high-paying, progressive, unionized and secure; secondary (bad) jobs are low-paying, dead-end, nonunion and risky. The current trend is away from manufacturing and towards service, trade and finance, which together accounted for 85 percent of net job growth during 1979-87. Primary jobs have disappeared and been replaced by secondary employment. During 1981-85, 10.8 million manufacturing workers lost jobs in plant closings and phasedowns; 5.1 million of them experienced above average unemployment levels and durations and eventually had to go into different industries, usually at lower pay. Forty percent lost their health insurance in the process. (GAO 1987)

In 1985 average weekly earnings were $402 in industries that declined during 1979-87 and $258 in those that expanded, meaning that it took 1.6 jobs in the expanding sector to compensate in terms of family income for one job lost in the declining industries. Moreover, the number of jobs in highly unionized industries declined by more than 1.3 million during 1979-87 and increased by 12.5 million in industries with low union densities. (Mishel and Simon, 1988) By 1988 one in every four American workers was in a "contingent" job category: part-time, temporary or fixed-term contract. For many this status was consistent with their reasons for working, but for many more it was not. Some 5 million persons were working part-time although they wanted full-time work. The average worker among the more than 5 million earning federal minimum wages in 1987 was a white, unmarried woman under 25 years of age working part-time in a service industry job. Because the minimum wage had not risen since 1981, its real value was 30 percent lower by 1989.

Labor demand trends also reflect new technologies and production processes. Traditional ways of doing things give way to new methods and established job classifications and work hierarchies are replaced. Some jobs are upgraded under the new technology while others are diminished or abolished. Labor-operated cell manufacturing, for example, could account for as much as 70 percent of U.S. metal-manufacturing in the future. This is a process which upgrades individual worker skills and responsibilities and replaces assembly operations with team methods. It also creates segmented, elite work groups which have the potential to subordinate union bargaining units to employer objectives and sets the stage for eventual micro-electronic displacement of some production labor. (Knauss and Matuszak, 1989) Nevertheless, technology displaces traditional work processes gradually rather than suddenly, and union concessions which erode existing job classifications and unilateral increases in work organization by management are more likely to affect worker rights and security in the short run than is new technology.

Labor stratification patterns in changing industries benefit some workers and hurt others because they create two-tiered systems of job access and compensation. Some workers obtain long term, core employment with opportunity for individual training and advancement and higher pay because employers are dependent on labor in core production processes; others are relegated to ancillary employment status which offers neither security nor opportunity. In the absence of unions and government regulation the labor force becomes increasingly stratified and unequal. Employee training and craft apprentice systems are downgraded or eliminated and replaced by on-the-job training and the use of composite crafts. Employers try to train workers only for tasks related to their own production processes rather than pay for generic skills and knowledge. This practice economizes on labor costs for the firm but diminishes the productive capability of the nation's work force.

On the labor supply side, families adjust to changes in labor demand with higher female participation rates and contingent employment. The current increase in multiple wage-earner households in the U.S. follows from the unavailability of goods-producing jobs and the need for two or more members of the household to work, often in secondary jobs, to maintain living standards. Among these new entrants are the most disadvantaged members of the labor force in terms of formal job credentials, alternative employment opportunities and institutional protections. These workers are the least likely to organize unions and the most likely to accept low pay and bad job conditions. Average real family income in the U.S. in 1987 was about the same as in 1979 and 1973, peak years in the two previous expansionary periods, but to maintain real income levels more household members had to work and work for more hours than they had in 1979. Those that could not or would not experienced falling real incomes. Despite modest inflation rates, adjusted wages for all industries decreased 7 percent during 1979-87: 10 percent for male and 1 percent for female workers. Finally, the jobs of more than 3 million U.S. workers dropped from middle to low-level earnings and 38 million Americans presently have no health insurance coverage. (Mishel and Simon 1988)

Concurrent changes in social and political trends resulted in labor market deregulation and made disadvantaged workers vulnerable to market discipline. Since 1981 the Job Training Partnership Act has been the only federal labor market program. Essentially it subsidizes selected in-plant job training programs and assists the reemployment of displaced workers. But no more than 7 percent of the latter were enrolled by 1987 and fewer than half of those received training; older, less educated workers were neglected and successful enrollees got jobs paying below average earnings. In addition, the emergency funds Congress made available in 1983 were only partially spent and created few jobs. Moreover, unemployment insurance coverage was reduced from 50 percent of the unemployed in 1980 to less than 30 percent in 1988. Government labor market policy thus eased the transition of new workers and those displaced from primary industries into the expanding low-wage industries.

Government also can diminish union power indirectly. Deregulation of transportation and telecommunications undermined bargaining strength in those industries. Deregulation of labor relations weakened unions in organizing drives and contract negotiations by allowing employers to push unions into making concessions under the threat of job losses and by narrowing the scope of bargaining to exclude critical issues of work retention and union representation. Finally, government commitment to free trade policies made it possible for foreign exporters to more than triple their share of U.S. markets for manufactured goods during 1963-1980. [2]

A shift in social attitudes after the 1960s further damaged unions. Earlier in the postwar period Americans had been determined to avoid another Great Depression like that of the 1930s. Unions therefore were seen as beneficial economic institutions responsible for the high wages and earnings which promoted strong purchasing power. But in the 1970s and 1980s public concern shifted from economic depression to inflation, foreign trade deficits and industrial decline. Living standards gave way to higher productivity as the chief policy objective and unions received much of the blame for rising production costs and America's inability to compete globally. They had become part of the problem rather than the solution--they represented special interests instead of the national interest.

Moreover, many new workers were exhibiting the same anti-union individualism that had characterized the labor force prior to the rise of the CIO. Along with increasingly aggressive anti-union initiatives by employers, the effect was to reduce significantly the number of union certification elections and union win ratios. Unions seemed confounded by the hostile environment and unable to carry out effective organizing drives to compensate for membership losses in the declining sectors.

In sum, union and nonunion workers alike experienced hardship as a result of union decline and labor market deregulation. Weakening unions undermined earnings without improving job opportunities and deregulating labor markets undermined both earnings and jobs.

3.   The Decline of Union Bargaining Power

Strong unions get "fair wages" for workers in competitive labor markets. Frank Taussig, an early American market economist, argued that union power is the best assurance that workers in capitalist economies will be paid the full value of their product.

> Labor organizations are thus effective toward securing 'fair wages'; that is, the current or market rates determined under the conditions of competition. They aid in enabling the laborers to get, in each particular case, the wages determined by the full competitive demand for the special sort of service; and they aid in bringing the general rate of wages to the full discounted value of the product of labor in general. (Taussig, 1917: 265)

Employers have market power over individual workers, he observed, and as a result they can and will pay them less than they are worth. Union power is necessary to redress the inequities.

Relative union bargaining power rests on two conditions: employer ability to pay higher labor costs and union ability to make employers pay. Employer ability to pay depends on the ability to pass on labor cost increases in higher prices, to take them out of profits or to recover them through productivity gains. For unions to make employers pay they must: (1) organize all of the workers who make or are capable of making products that compete in the same market; (2) establish bargaining structures that match industry structures so that union negotiators can confront management decision makers and engage in effective job actions in the event of bargaining impasses; (3) link negotiated pay increases to economic trends: cost-of-living, productivity and industry settlement patterns; (4) either organize their industrial jurisdictions completely or develop operating agreements with other unions that prevent them from being whipsawed against one another by common employers. [3]

If unions establish conditions in industries that can pay they usually have bargaining power. But this power is subject to evolutionary erosion because it is rooted in a specific industrial structure and behavior pattern and to a particular time and place. Changes in the industry and its institutional environment ordinarily undermine labor's power because they make the original bargaining structures and relationships obsolete. Such changes involve industrial organization, labor processes and public policy. Unions in every basic manufacturing and service industry in the U.S. have experienced harmful environmental changes of this sort. (Craypo, 1986)

Union Bargaining Power Before 1979. The collective bargaining system developed during and after the Second World War stabilized labor relations in the U.S. for more than three decades. Organized labor had emerged from the war in a strong tactical position. Total membership was up two thirds as a result of war-time expansion of basic industry and favorable treatment given unions. Together the National Labor Relations Board and the War Labor Board strengthened industrial unionism, secured union representation rights in basic industry and institutionalized national contracts and pattern bargaining. (Moody, 1988; Glyn, Lipietz and Singh, 1989) [4]

Industrial unions were strongest in basic industries dominated by a few large firms. These oligopolists routinely set or "administered" product prices according to full-cost pricing formulas designed to achieve target profits at predetermined levels of production. A profit markup was added to the combined cost of labor, material and overhead. At General Motors, for example, the markup on new car prices gave the company an average net profit rate of 15 percent annually on investment at an operating level of 80 percent of production capacity. Similar markups delivered 8 percent profit rates at U.S. Steel and 12 percent at Standard Oil. The administered price system was both stable and effective: actual rates of return in most oligopolized industries approximated their target rates during the postwar decades. (Blair, 1972; Wachtel and Adelsheim, 1977)

Market power insulated firms from foreign or domestic competition but it also made them vulnerable because it discouraged product quality and production efficiency. Large producers invariably found ways to jostle one another for greater domestic market shares without disrupting the industry. Significant improvements in product quality by one firm (performance, reliability, design and engineering, service and delivery) were seen as an aggressive act inviting retaliation by rivals; and cutting prices to raise individual profit margins could trigger mutually destructive behavior. They were avoided by price leadership in durable consumer goods like autos, uniform pricing systems in wholesale commodities like steel, and deliberate price-fixing arrangements in bid-priced products like power transformers. Product quality was standardized among major sellers by imitative behavior, patent pooling and suppressed product innovation. Competitive selling practices were aimed at building consumer brand loyalty: saturation advertising, product style and design changes, full-line product marketing, and national dealer and finance systems.

Differences in market power and ability to pay among smaller firms depended on their relationships with primary firms, the conditions of production and prevailing labor market structures. Some operated as secondary suppliers to oligopolized manufacturers. Ability to pay rested on the terms and conditions set for them by these primary producers. Most were organized by the same unions which represented workers in the oligopolized sector and generally came under pattern bargaining settlements although they did not have to match fully the standards of the large firms. Firms in service industries often enjoyed local and regional monopolies because of geographic limitations on production and distribution. They had the ability to pay but unions seldom had the ability to organize them. Other employers had the ability to pay because the product could be made in only one place, as in building construction, or the service was provided in a limited number of places, as in longshoring. (Levinson, 1967)   They tended to be unionized within the spatial areas and negotiated master contracts which paid high wages and benefits. Secondary employers often were profitable and paid low wages because their labor markets were unregulated. In the absence of government standards and union contracts they controlled the labor process and had access to disadvantaged workers who were easily exploited. Gaps between their value and their pay could be greater than in the primary industries. These workers occupied the lowest rungs of the industrial stratification ladder, existing largely outside the postwar labor relations system and benefiting only marginally from the high-wage, high-consumption productive system that was developing.

Financial and structural power made oligopolies hard to unionize but, once they were, unions could exploit their ability to pay in wage bargaining. By the 1950s labor was organized in all but a handful of basic industries. In his classification of U.S. unions during the 1920s, Robert Hoxie observed that most unions imitate the structures and standards of the industries they represent. This clearly was the pattern after World War Two. Labor secured centralized bargaining structures to match the horizontal and vertical integration of oligopolies, something they had not done since amalgamated craft unions were ousted by U.S. Steel in 1901 and the Chicago meat packers a few years later. Unions thus had bargaining power but it was derived at least in part from employer control of product markets, which left labor vulnerable to adverse trends in competition and industrial structures. High standards and labor relations stability thus were linked to continued market control by core employers.

Once these structures were in place the parties negotiated on the basis of mutual dependence and conflict. Strikes were frequent but confined to immediate employers by law and industrial relations custom. Firms accepted the institutional system and seldom tried to displace established unions or replace striking workers. Labor and capital were dependent on each other for production and jobs and shared the benefits of employer market positions, but they also contested one another over relative income shares and argued grievances arising over the extraction of labor in the work place. (Moody, 1988) Negotiated master contracts typically lasted three years and pattern bargaining extended pay increases and benefit improvements within and among industry groups.

High earnings and job and income security solidified union members in the primary sector. Employers found they could not erode standards or refuse to make regular improvements without inviting costly strikes. Confrontation simply was not worth the price. Centralized contract negotiations and formal work stoppages gave an appearance of ritual and ceremony which has obscured the presence and importance of labor relations power and inspired observers to mistake the appearance for the reality and conclude that " big labor" and "big business" made an accord in which unions stopped challenging capital in exchange for high wages. In fact, unions and employers had not reached an accord as much as a stalemate which neither side had the resources or inclination to break.

Unions also negotiated job security and progression into master and supplemental contracts. They accepted existing job classifications and pay grades--legacies of the scientific management era--and made them negotiable items subject to restrictive contract language and enforcement procedures. At the plant level the effect was constant tension and conflict between local unions and supervisors on the shop floor. Supervisors were under pressure to meet production quotas and standards and union members were resolved to fight work intensification efforts. Unsettled grievances accumulated and intractable differences persisted when national negotiators were unable to resolve local disputes involving jobs and standards.

In principle the union wanted to remove workers from arbitrary rules and decisions in these matters; the effect however was to link

work intensity, job security and earnings potential to established
product lines and familiar production processes. This gave organized
labor a vested interest in the industrial status quo. Having wrested
exclusive control from management in work classifications and
assignments, incentive pay systems and supervisory procedures--
industry's traditional methods of work intensification--workers did not
want to see the system changed. Now, however, unions are considered
dysfunctional institutions for trying to preserve the rules and practices
associated with an uncompetitive mode of production.

        Union Bargaining Power After 1979.   Postwar union power
depended on continued U.S. economic expansion and supremacy in
world markets, prevailing technologies and production systems, and
secure markets in the basic industries. Each of these came under attack
in the 1970s and by the end of the decade relative bargaining power had
shifted back toward industry. Managers started coming to the bargaining
table saying they were under increased competitive pressures and needed
labor cost reductions in order to survive. Unions were in no position to
resist because employers in fact were closing and relocating production
facilities and diversifying operations. Large numbers of veteran union
members in primary industries were displaced, workers who had formed
the backbone of the industrial labor movement. Creation of new
production units widened the relevant labor force to include unfamiliar
work groups which unions could not organize, dismantled the
established bargaining structures and sometimes pitted units of the same
employer against one another, removed corporate decision makers from
bargaining responsibility and accountability, and placed established
firms in precarious financial settings. (Craypo, 1975)

        It is important to distinguish between competition from
overseas and from domestic sources. Foreign competition was an
important factor in the decline of steel, for example, but so were
domestic mini-mills. Union losses in tires, meat packing, construction
and airlines did not originate in foreign trade but instead from internal
industry changes. Experiences in these industries illustrate the
interactions in Table 1 between competition and corporate structure and
the subsequent impact on relative bargaining power.

        Events in steel typify the two main responses of basic industry
to increased competition: industrial restructuring and labor cost
reductions. In 1950 the U.S. was the world's leading steel producer and
exporter; by 1986 it was the fourth largest producer and the biggest
importer. Integrated steel closed about a third of its total capacity,
shifted production from the East and West Coast mills which were most
vulnerable to foreign steel shipments to new and refurbished facilities in

the Midwest and from heavy to light steel products, including galvanized sheet and strip steel for the auto and appliance industries and tin plate for food containers. They also entered into various joint arrangements with foreign companies at the same time they successfully lobbied Washington for quota restrictions and "trigger price" protections against imports. The goal was to reduce domestic steel supply relative to demand in order to support rising domestic prices and to lower Big Steel's "break-even" point of production at 50-60 percent. Finally, they diversified into unrelated industries. As early as 1981 nonsteel operations accounted for 38 percent of company assets, 27 percent of revenues and 34 percent of profits. In 1983 U.S. Steel acquired Marathon Oil, the nation's fifth largest petroleum producer, for $6 billion and afterward changed its name to USX. [5]

Labor cost reduction began with the marginal producers. Wheeling-Pittsburgh Corp. broke industry patterns in the 1970s when it demanded and received special terms from the USWA. Other major producers retaliated by expelling Wheeling-Pittsburgh from the industry bargaining group, whereupon the company promptly negotiated additional union concessions in exchange for an employee stock ownership plan financed from cost savings. Smaller steel producers also got union concessions on hardship grounds. Led by U.S. Steel, the main bargaining group then proposed a multi-billion dollar concession package to the union but the locals voted it down. When their contracts expired in 1983 the same companies came back with even greater concession demands and this time persuaded labor to give wage cuts, benefit reductions and other changes worth an estimated $3 billion. (Hoerr, 1988)

Foreign tire producers, by contrast, affected U.S. firms by their domestic presence. Michelin brought radial tires to this country in the 1960s and when U.S. producers did not respond to the competition Michelin built integrated, nonunion plants here and in Canada. Domestic firms then either got into radial production or began leaving the industry. Goodyear, which was determined to maintain its dominant market share and had been forced to divest its non-tire holdings while resisting a hostile takeover attempt, entirely phased out tire production at its unionized Akron plants and built new radial capacity in the South and Southwest. Firestone cut production in half, General sold its U.S. tire holdings to Continental, a German company, and Uniroyal got out of the business. Meanwhile, Continental and Bridgestone (Japanese) also built and acquired U.S. plants. Thus the domestic oligopoly which once negotiated auto-based pattern agreements with the Rubber Workers Union has virtually disappeared.

Prior to industry bargaining in late 1981 Uniroyal negotiated separate wage and benefit concessions worth about $55 million, which saved the company less than one percent of its total production costs, hardly enough to rescue a firm whose real problems were in product line and quality and which eventually abandoned tire production despite the concessions. (Slaughter, 1983: 54) The other companies later settled for wage freezes, except at B.F. Goodrich's Akron plant, where employment was down more than 80 percent and the local union took a pay cut and suspension of COLA in exchange for a company promise to continue operations and a profit-sharing plan. Eventually it, too, was closed. (Jeszeck, 1986)

Market changes in meat packing, however, have had almost nothing to do with foreign trade or producers. Each of the old-line companies was acquired during the conglomerate wave of the 1960s and was in varying degrees treated as "cash cows" and allowed to deteriorate operationally. Aggressive new companies, led by Iowa Beef Producers, meanwhile revolutionized the industry. They relocated slaughtering and processing plants closer to cattle ranches and feedlots, shipped final beef cuts directly to metropolitan retail outlets rather than semi-dressed carcasses to wholesale butchering warehouses, and built new nonunion plants and paid substandard rates at their older unionized operations.

The other packers closed and sold plants, shifted operations from fresh to packaged beef products and forced substantial union concessions. Base rates in union plants were driven down by as much as one third, but the disadvantaged companies still wanted more. Armour and Co., a subsidiary of Greyhound, established a pattern of concessions covering most of the industry. Greyhound had closed several Armour plants and threatened to close more on grounds of uncompetitive labor costs. Wages were frozen and COLA payments deferred and the industry agreed not to close additional facilities for at least 18 months. The promise did not hold however, and one by one the marginal firms came to the union for additional cuts.

Union decline in construction followed deterioration of the unionized sector and the production conditions that had bolstered high union earnings. During the 1970s the ratio of nonunion to union work rose sharply as union contractors joined the open shop movement, either by operating nonunion or establishing nonunion subsidiaries to bid on jobs against other open shop contractors; in addition, some of the large nonunion contractors expanded their operating jurisdictions into traditional union areas. Union contractors, which accounted for 80 percent of industry revenues twenty years ago, today get less than one third, and only one in five construction workers currently is employed under union contract. The Associated Builders and Contractors, the principal organization of open shop employers, claimed 3,000 members in 1970 but today boasts 20,000. Moreover, although small firms (less than 50 employees) still dominate construction employment, giant contractors are increasingly mobile, pervasive and nonunion. (Erlich, 1988)

Air transportation illustrates the effects of government deregulation on union power. In this case it opened the way for competitive fares and routes among airlines and encouraged the formation and expansion of low-cost, non-union carriers like Texas Air and People Express. Starting as a small regional carrier known for its stormy labor relations, Texas Air was reorganized as an airline holding company by chairman Frank Lorenzo. It began acquiring other airlines, including People Express, Continental and Eastern, until it had become the nation's largest carrier and its most anti-union. It also was heavily in debt. Lorenzo made huge concession demands from the unions and when they resisted tried to break them, as he did at Continental by declaring bankruptcy during a labor dispute. He then headed for a showdown with union mechanics and pilots at Eastern over similar demands. This was after he had sold several profitable segments of Eastern's holdings, but the carrier still was losing money and making daily interest payments of nearly $900,000. In self-defense the rest of the industry had conformed to Texas Air's low-fare, low-wage strategy and airlines labor relations had become less stable and more confrontational. (Cf., McKelvey, 1988)

These cases show how increased competition, industrial restructuring and new management strategies destroyed the postwar foundations of union bargaining power in key manufacturing and service industries. Combined with economic recession and unfavorable shifts in the social and political environment, they produced the most sustained period of union concessions in the postwar period. The frequency of major work stoppages declined sharply, from 235 in 1979 to 96 in 1982 and 54 in 1985, reflecting a new dichotomy in labor relations. Where production methods and product markets enabled firms to make and sell products almost anywhere, strikes are no longer frequent because employers get the concessions they want by threatening to relocate operations. But where firms do not have operating mobility and want to reduce labor's share in order to meet competition or simply increase profit margins, they have to confront unions directly and either back them down in concession bargaining or take a strike in which they hire strikebreakers and eventually debilitate or decertify the union. Widely publicized examples are Greyhound, Phelps-Dodge, Hormel, and International Paper. (Birecree, 1989) [6]

Union Bargaining Concessions. The American economist Carter Goodrich observed years ago that "a union's strength may be roughly gauged by the issues on which it fights." (Goodrich, 1975: p.16) If that is so, then the strength of U.S. unions declined seriously during and after the 1970s, judging from the contract concessions they made. By the late 1960s unions already had established good terms and conditions of employment and now were challenging employers to make the work itself more humane and tolerable, negotiating additional paid-time away from the job and exploring ways to make jobs less monotonous and onerous. By the mid-1980s, however, after years of dislocation and recession, unions had completely abandoned work reform and instead were trying to protect   previously established standards -- and often their own institutional security.

Union bargaining concessions occur when unions accept freezes or reductions in negotiated wage and benefit levels or modifications of work rules and production standards. Such concessions are not unique to the 1980s. They appear historically during economic recessions, as in 1962-63 when nearly one quarter of the workers covered by major contracts accepted wage freezes, and when firms have operating difficulties in specific plants, as in the 1970s at GM's Dayton, Ohio Frigidaire plant and Firestone's Akron tire plant.

During the 1980s, however, the frequency and intensity of concessions were unprecedented. Virtually every union representing production workers in manufacturing and basic services gave up established economic standards and protective language.   These concessions occurred in three stages. They started in the late 1970s in firms threatened by product competition and involved specified cuts in wages and benefits, usually with the promise of reimbursement if and when the employer became profitable. The second stage occurred before and during the severe recession of the early 1980s when work rule and economic concessions spread to industries where unions were vulnerable. The third stage began in the mid-1980s and undermined or eliminated the economic bargaining standards responsible for the postwar increases in living standards: cost-of-living, productivity and comparability among bargaining units.

The 1970s concessions occurred first in construction and then sporadically among basic industries where recession and poor operating performance caused large producers to ask for and get temporary labor cost freezes and reductions in order to improve their cash flow. The difference between the recessions of the 1970s and those of the 1980s was that the first occurred in the absence of imports and deregulation and therefore did not impair administered price practices in the concentrated industries. After the 1974-75 recession it was business as usual and most wage and benefit levels were duly reinstated.

The second stage occurred in an environment of intense competition. This time domestic firms could not manipulate products and prices to meet profit targets. The goal instead was to reduce labor costs. If total revenues could not be increased satisfactorily, then total costs might be reduced enough to still make money at lower levels of employment and output. Low wage strategies dominated this phase of the concession trend: wage freezes and work rule changes by both flight and ground crews at Braniff, Continental, Eastern, Pan Am and United; work rule changes in six Ford Motor plants and wage cuts in another; work rule modifications and wage cuts at 23 plants operated by major tire producers; wage cuts at selected mills of Wheeling-Pittsburgh, U.S. Steel and others; and wage reductions of up to 20 percent for at least 30 trucking firms in the nation's largest employer association. Wage cuts and freezes also were made in retail food stores, packing plants, machine tool companies, health care facilities, print shops and lumber and paper mills. Further concessions occurred in each of the eight basic manufacturing and service industries whose contracts expired in 1982. Negotiated wage settlements that year were the lowest ever recorded by the BLS. Nearly half the workers covered by major collective bargaining agreements received no first-year raises and about one third none over the life of the contract. Whereas contract concessions in 1981 involved an estimated 3 percent of the negotiated contracts covering fifty or more workers, during 1982 the ratio jumped to 12 percent and to 28 percent in 1983 and 1984. Every sector of the economy in which unions enjoyed postwar bargaining power was now "concession-prone" in wages. (Mitchell, 1986) [7]

The effect on traditional bargaining units was enormous. Unions lost millions of members to plant closings and relocations to nonunion areas and by the emergence of nonunion employers, events which not only eroded the organizational base but weakened tactical union power and worker militancy in the remaining units. In autos, for example, UAW-Big Three master contracts covering 675,000 workers in 1978 covered only 508,300 in 1988, a decrease of nearly one fourth due to plant closings and layoffs, job reductions and job combinations. Continued disintegration of its bargaining units did not prevent the UAW from making concessions and from entering into cooperative union-management programs with each of the Big Three companies.

Workers covered by UAW contracts with the three largest farm machinery makers fell by nearly two thirds between 1979 and 1987 and by more than one third in those between the electrical workers union (IUE) and GE, Westinghouse and RCA. Bargaining units also were slashed in telephones following deregulation and corporate reorganization. Unions avoided making contract concessions in negotiations following the breakup of the AT&T holding company in 1983 but they lost thousands of jobs to operating and cost-cutting measures. In 1988 CWA revealed that 78,500 jobs had been cut nationally since 1983 and that AT&T had notified the union that another 16,000 would be eliminated. These cuts represented more than half the number working under the master contract in 1988.

Concessions spread within and among industries through pattern bargaining. In autos it began in 1979-80 with the federal government's financial rescue of financially troubled Chrysler Corporation and the estimated $1 billion in scheduled wage and benefit increases the UAW surrendered in order to win Congressional approval of two Chrysler loans totaling $1.07 billion. Ford and General Motors then demanded similar givebacks when their contracts expired in 1982. In return, the firms promised not to close plants by purchasing parts from non-union suppliers. GM, which stood to gain $3 billion in union concessions, also agreed to keep open four plants it planned to close.

Employer associations in non-manufacturing industries demanded concessions on grounds their members faced product market competition from non-union firms and would eliminate jobs if they did not get cost reductions. As in manufacturing, the threats usually followed actual shutdowns and layoffs. Major intercity truckers and the Teamsters union negotiated a national pay freeze, diversion of COLA payments to maintain worker pension and health benefits and work rule changes. This was in response to industry recession, entry of some 3,000 low-cost carriers following industry deregulation, and a 20 percent unemployment rate among union drivers. Employers agreed not to sell or lease assets to nonunion operators or to subcontract work.

Did such widespread concessions represent a temporary shift in relative bargaining power or changes in industry competition, structure and tactics? A survey of unionized employers showed that structural changes were more responsible for bargaining concessions than the 1982-83 recession. More than half the companies said they needed union givebacks to be competitive and many tried to reopen existing labor agreements in order to get them. One fourth either had negotiated concessions or were doing so at the time. Building contractors and trucking companies asking for concessions all cited competition from nonunion competitors as the major reason for their demands; but fewer than half the durable goods producers gave that reason, instead citing imports as the competitive problem. In exchange, unions overwhelmingly wanted some kind of job security. (Mills, 1983)

Factors in addition to the business cycle, import pressures and deregulation were responsible for union givebacks. Concessions spread from one firm and industry to another with little distinction between profitable and unprofitable performance and often independent of the employer's competitive situation. Indeed, 81 percent of the companies which obtained concessions in the survey cited above were profitable at the time, which suggests that concessions had the effect of maintaining profit margins rather than saving threatened firms. Pattern bargaining was beginning to work against rather than for unions and the ability and willingness of employers to relocate production and replace striking union workers had shifted bargaining initiatives and momentum from unions to employers. By 1985 it was clear that structural and behavioral changes had redefined the standards or "norms" associated with wage bargaining. (Mitchell, 1985)

Despite the uninterrupted economic expansion after 1983, two million workers were being permanently displaced a year (half of them in manufacturing) and large numbers of employers still were asking for and getting concessions. Millions of new jobs were created but most of the net gain in employment during 1979-87 involved dead-end, low-wage jobs in the service industries, especially retail trade and personal services. (Bluestone and Harrison, 1988.) Moreover, hourly employment within manufacturing had shifted from durable to nondurable goods production, from industries such as steel and machinery, where unions were strongly represented, to those like plastics and micro-electronic components, where they were not.

Among the more serious and perhaps long-term casualties of labor's decline were the economic bargaining criteria that had been so important to rising living standards during the postwar era. COLA clauses, for example, were being eliminated or weakened as employers sought to rid themselves of large and automatic adjustment payments. During the inflationary 1970s the ratio of workers covered by cost-of-living clauses rose above 60 percent (in 1977) but by the end of 1985 it had fallen below 50 percent and by 1988 to 40 percent. [8] Concession bargaining put caps on or reduced benefit formulas in existing COLAs and deferred or canceled scheduled payments. This is important because it allows firms to tailor wage costs to their individual production and product market situations.

A major change in standards involved elimination of deferred increases in hourly wages and substitution of annual lump sum cash payments. These are not incorporated into hourly wages and therefore do not improve workers' long-term compensation . Lump sum and bonus payments, which occurred rarely before the 1980s, affected 6 percent of major contracts in 1984, 19 percent in 1985 and 36 percent by 1988 (excluding the construction industry, where they did not occur). Most were in manufacturing industries previously dependent on formula bargaining.

The old standards were thus replaced by wage criteria fundamentally different in design and purpose. The new standards allowed employers to impose bargaining objectives consistent with employer strategies which reflected management's perception of changing competition and the appropriate responses. Second, they shifted the rationale for pay improvements from equity, living standards and other matters external to the firm to production, financial performance and other internal concerns. Union negotiators were taken out of the familiar environment of industry wide bargaining norms and patterns and placed in unfamiliar surroundings in which they could neither verify nor dispute employer claims on the basis of available information--a problem compounded by the frequent devolution of concession bargaining from national and regional levels to local bargaining tables. Not only did union negotiators have incomplete knowledge of operating conditions, they also had no control over decisions on how the money that was saved as a result of concessions should be used to secure jobs. Typically they made concessions without reasonable assurances they were needed or expectations they would work. Firms seldom divulged their strategies and financial accounts at the bargaining table.

What did union workers get in return for their concessions? Did they preserve their living standards or guarantee jobs? Did they save threatened plants from being closed? No significant relationship exists between making concessions and achieving any of these union objectives. In order to maintain living standards unions agreed to give up deferred increases and automatic wage adjustments in return for bonus payments contingent on future productivity gains, employer profits or production cost-savings. High wages no longer forced managers to use labor efficiently; low wages simply reflected the fact that they were not efficient users of labor.

Bonuses actually received in major industries represent a fraction of hourly wage increases that were being negotiated prior to the concessions. In the auto industry, for example, bargaining unit members got modest profit sharing and performance bonuses during 1985-88 which also widened hourly earnings differentials among competing firms, which the UAW had diligently tried to avoid over the years. Ford workers received more than $8,000 in profit sharing payments during 1986-88, which is the equivalent of about $1.30 an hour over the three year period (although base wages were not increased by that amount); Chrysler workers got at least $2,000 in bonuses during 1985-88, or the equivalent of $0.25 an hour, and GM workers got about $530 in profit sharing for 1985-88, the same as $0.07 an hour. Big Three contracts also contained COLA clauses and guaranteed wage increases based on productivity gains.

Payment formulas negotiated in other basic industries had not improved much by the late 1980s. Forty-three month long contracts for 1988-91 in aluminum called for a $4,500 bonus payment (the equivalent of about $0.60 an hour) to each member for ratifying the contract and in anticipation of industry performance, plus a $0.50 an hour increase in base wage rates. The combined $1.10 an hour will keep workers about even with inflation at 1987-88 levels but will decrease real hourly earnings if inflation accelerates. Aluminum workers had made substantial concessions to employers in 1986 contract negotiations and expected this to be the catch-up round of bargaining. [9]

A second type of bargaining tradeoff involves promised job security for money and work rule givebacks. Negotiated employment guarantees are discussed often by the parties and the media but occur infrequently. Most employers will not agree to contract terms that restrict future production decisions or require them to retain workers they do nor want. Moreover, membership support for tradeoffs has waned as a result of unsatisfactory experiences. Thus only 7 percent of the contracts negotiated in 1986 and 1988 contained job security provisions, and most of those were severance pay and other benefits aimed at cushioning the impact of job losses rather than preventing them. (Uchitelle, 1989)

Unions in electrical products, tires, meat packing, steel, and telecommunications, among others, were unable to negotiate widespread job guarantees despite the many closed plants in those industries. The UAW is an exception to this trend, having negotiated temporary prohibitions against plant closings in master agreements with auto and farm machinery firms. But these were agreed upon only after the companies had closed numerous plants and appeared to have stabilized domestic plant operations; but additional phasedowns and relocations occurred nevertheless, in part because the prohibitions had not been intended to protect union jobs against changes in product markets.

Concessions will not save threatened plants because such decisions seldom depend on increases or decreases in direct labor costs but instead, according to the author of a study using nation-wide data on closures, "appear to reflect the strategies and idiosyncrasies of individual firms." Closings are as likely to occur in nonunion as in union settings, in southern as in northern locations, and in nonimport as in import-sensitive industries. If anything, ownership by a diversified parent corporation increases the chances of local plant shutdowns. (Howland, 1988) A survey of more than two dozen plant closings in a medium-sized Midwest factory town during 1953-84 shows no relationship between union refusal or willingness to make concessions and the magnitude of the concessions, for example, and management decisions to close plants. (Craypo, 1985) Moreover, in some instances management experimented with new standards and work organization in unionized plants before extending them to their nonunion facilities and closing the former. (Knauss and Matuszak, 1989)

Union concessions thus failed to protect living standards, jobs and establishments and instead contributed greatly to two trends in bargaining outcomes: overall union-nonunion earnings differentials narrowed and negotiated wage increases were lower than those in preceding rounds of bargaining. By 1988, however, unions began to make bargaining gains. The ratio of major contracts containing both wage increases and lump-sum increases in the first year rose from 11 percent in 1987 to 85 percent in 1988, even though the average wage increase was only 1.1 percent or $0.11 an hour. These gains also occurred disproportionately in industries experiencing labor shortages. Negotiated increases were above average in health care, for example, because employers were having difficulty finding qualified workers and had to offer higher earnings to fill job vacancies. But some profitable manufacturing industries did not have to negotiate commensurate pay increases and imposed below average raises. Indeed, average real earnings for all workers continued to decline in 1987 and 1988.

Thus, after a decade of union concessions the trend may be less intense and perhaps even reversed in some quarters, but it certainly has not disappeared. It may in fact eventually end the way it started, industry by industry, beginning with those experiencing profits and labor shortages. A shift also may occur in bargaining standards--away from plant and firm performance and back to postwar compensation formulas and settlement patterns. This could include a union revitalization in basic manufacturing, albeit with scaled-down negotiating units. Nevertheless, many unions have been organizationally damaged, and it remains to be seen whether they can regain their former structural power.

4. The Economic Impact of Declining Union Power

Apart from the benefits unions provide for individual workers and working class families, they perform two important and interrelated functions in the economy. They sustain high levels of economic demand and they force managers to work harder to achieve higher levels of productivity. High demand and productivity promote industrial competitiveness. And increased industrial competitiveness in turn creates high levels of demand. This interaction of aggregate demand, industrial productivity and market competition is characterized as the principle of "cumulative causation." An evolutionary and progressively more powerful cause-and-effect relationship occurs among these three factors but the cumulative effect can be positive or negative in terms of growth.

It can produce successively higher or lower living standards depending on the direction in which the economy is headed: demand, efficiency and competitiveness can be steadily improving or deteriorating. Plant and equipment, industrial skills and knowledge, social and physical infrastructure can be constantly maintained and enhanced or neglected and eroded. When they are nurtured, they contribute to sustained growth; when they are not things may get progressively worse. For example, profits can be invested in productive assets or in corporate takeovers, and inventions can be turned into useful products or discarded and subsequently developed by other nations. Enhanced productive wealth accompanies the first set of choices and deindustrialization the second. Either way, once in progress, the trend gathers momentum and is increasingly difficult to reverse. (Eatwell, 1982; Singh, 1977)

Unions and bargaining have a positive and active role to play in the principle of cumulative causation and in the accompanying increases in growth rates and living standards. Negotiated wage increases make domestic firms and industries more competitive: when unions push up direct labor costs they make employers find ways to improve unit labor output by using workers more efficiently and getting the most out of available technology and capital resources. In this way, wages can be said to determine productivity; but when the direction of causation is reversed, that is, when wage raises are made to

depend on prior productivity improvements, there is no guarantee that
such improvements will occur in the first place.

High wage patterns have another positive effect on the
economy because when increases are distributed evenly and widely
across the industrial system they raise the level of net consumption and
equalize the gains from greater unit labor output than when they are
concentrated in certain occupations, industries and regions. Equitable
distribution of productive wealth promotes long-term economic growth
and social stability and unions are the most important non-
governmental institution for this purpose. Union workers employed in
primary industries purchase the goods and services made by union
workers in other primary industries and high wages and wage increases
in primary manufacturing, where increases in unit labor outpour are
greatest, become the benchmark for wages in secondary industries.

Economic history justifies union bargaining power in Western
capitalist societies. It is important to remember that the advanced
capitalist countries, including the U.S., enjoyed a "Golden Age" of
rapid economic growth and rising real incomes from the early 1950s
through the mid-1970s. America was in the forefront of this historic
expansion during the early years but later gave way to the Japanese and
West Europeans. Even so, the U.S. experienced rapid rates of increase
in unit labor output and the stock of productive capital. The same
things had happened in the 1920s but ended in the Great Depression of
the 1930s; this time, however, strong unions and liberal governments
prevented industry from absorbing most of the productivity gain in
higher profit margins and choking off the expansion through inadequate
consumer purchasing power. Instead, a demand-investment-
consumption-demand cycle evolved during the Golden Age in which
rising real earnings fueled demand during the upswing and high "social
wages" (wages and benefits plus tax transfers) put a floor on the decline
during recessions. (Glyn, Hughes, Lipietz, and Singh, 1989)

But in the conventional economic theory of growth, profits,
investment and accumulation are independent and dynamic variables and
wages and living standards are dependent on them. Therefore, in theory
earnings should adjust to changes in the more conventional engines of
growth. In other words, if investment and productivity should decline,
then high wages and wage increases can no longer be supported, and
living standards must be reduced in order to accommodate the lower
level of investment activity. Human behavior contradicts the theory,
however. Wages are not conveniently flexible because of social
customs and trade unions, both of which naturally resist downward
erosion of real earnings. (Wilkinson, 1988)   Indeed, by the 1970s

U.S. unions had reversed the theory: established living standards determined wages instead of it being the other way around. The established criteria in wage bargaining--cost of living, productivity trends and comparable settlements-- protected living standards against inflation and recession and automatically lifted them during periods of economic expansion and rising productivity. (Craypo, 1986)

Union bargaining power raised aggregate demand because it gave greater purchasing power to those with the highest propensity to buy the goods and services that kept labor employed and plants and equipment running. The greater the degree of union density and the spread of high-wage settlements across industries the greater the union impact on labor's share, aggregate demand levels and efficient utilization of capital and labor. The lower the density of unionization and the greater the exclusion of non-elite labor groups from negotiated wage patterns the lower the spread of union benefits within the labor force and the beneficial impact of unions on the economy. The postwar performance of the U.S. industrial system was mixed in this regard. Real earnings and aggregate demand levels rose steadily but much of American industry did not maintain its competitive edge beyond the 1960s and millions of low-paid workers remained unorganized. The decline of basic manufacturing and the union movement thus was simultaneous and interactive.

This happened in part because in the U.S. industrial setting high wages and negotiated wage increases did not force managers to manage more competitively. Primary firms did not have to economize on labor even though it became more expensive. Not being under serious price and quality competition from foreign or domestic rivals, they incorporated labor costs into pricing formulas and substituted non-price, non-product forms of competition, which, in turn, discouraged product improvement and innovations. Meanwhile, the steady flow of imports into home markets turned into a flood of goods in the 1980s.

Established domestic firms had lagged behind the design, production and marketing developments occurring at home and abroad. This left them unprepared for the industrial crisis of the 1980s and instead of concentrating on products and markets they instinctively compensated by dismantling production facilities and lowering the total wage bill and unit labor costs, although the principle of cumulative causation would have indicated to them that the real problems lay elsewhere, in their inability to maintain product and production supremacy (Lieberman, 1988) and in the failure of the U.S. productive system to generate institutions which promote industrial research, planning and investment, as do the German and Japanese systems.

Figure 2 illustrates these interactions. Union power and collective bargaining outcomes interact with relative income shares and aggregate demand. When, for example, trends in competition, industrial structure and social and political environments put unions at a bargaining disadvantage and encourage employers to adopt low-wage, anti-union strategies, the effect is to reduce labor's share of income in the productive system. The broadest statistical measure of income shares, which actually understates the share received by hourly workers and non-managerial salaried employees, shows a steady rise from 65 percent after World War Two to 76 percent in 1982, followed by a sudden drop to 73 percent in 1986, when a one percent change represented more than thirty billion dollars.

As a result of the competitive decline of the American productive system union workers are being asked to give up a labor relations system which worked in their behalf for decades in exchange for an industrial experiment that gives every outward sign of subordinating their interests and making them the prime risk-takers. The solution being offered them reduces labor's share of income and the overall level of consumer demand on grounds that labor has priced itself out of competitive markets and Americans are living beyond their means. As Figure 2 indicates, however, these policies are likely to aggravate the problem. Driving down wages does not necessarily improve long-term unit labor output, even though that is the stated objective. Unit labor output normally increases fastest during periods of continued economic expansion when plants are operating at or near capacity levels. This occurs independently of changes in direct labor costs. Unit output also may increase moderately during severe recessions and when individual firms are phasing down their operations because less efficient resources are being taken out of production and workers laid off faster than output is reduced. But the latter is a perverse measure of productivity because it bodes ill for long-term industrial performance and income shares. It also masks the rundown that is occurring in the nation's production base, which in turn makes the system prone to imports and high-cost production because of low levels of capacity utilization.

Individual employers, however, are interested in reducing short-run unit labor costs in response to competition because normally that widens profit margins. Unit labor costs can be reduced either by increasing unit labor output (productivity) or by reducing worker compensation. In the 1980s employers found it quicker and easier to cut wages than to increase unit output. Cutting wages may improve the employer's profit position but by itself does nothing to improve

Figure 2
"Union Power in the Macro Economy"

Competition	Employer Strategies: 1. low-wage		Labor Supply	Income Shares	Competition
	2. R & D		Unions and Collective Bargaining		
Industrial Structure			Labor Demand	Aggregate Demand	Industrial Structure

productivity--and in addition introduces the macroeconomic disadvantages discussed above. Also there is a limit to the amount of labor cost reductions that can be achieved through wage cuts.

A low-wage strategy therefore is not necessarily a recipe for better performance in the product market. [10] In specific instances it may be nothing more than a formula to raise profit margins long enough to finance the firm's exit from its traditional product market. The union of course has no way of knowing which scenario is in progress. A national industrial strategy of depreciating its currency and lowering unit labor costs in order to make manufactured products more competitive at home and abroad is a formula for surrendering the living standards of domestic workers to those of the lowest-wage competitors in the field. In our case, we have to ask whether the wages of Detroit auto workers and the investment strategies of General Motors, Ford and Chrysler should be determined by industrial policies in Tokyo, Seoul and Mexico City and, if they are, what will be the effects in this country?

Contrary to this analysis of union impact, conventional economic theory concludes that unions have made themselves obsolete and suggests that this is good for the nation's long-term competitiveness in both domestic and foreign markets. Market theory explains union decline as the direct result of large union-nonunion compensation differentials which over time make union employers uncompetitive. This infers a direct cause and effect between labor costs and competition and between competition and union membership; it shows little regard for the complex interactions among direct costs, unit labor costs and unit labor output, and between unit labor costs and product price. Existence of a direct and negative link between changes in hourly compensation costs and union membership is a purely theoretical proposition that in recent years is counterfactual to the failure of American industry to become more competitive in global markets despite years of falling real wages and the recent narrowing of union-nonunion differentials. It is also unsupported by union wage and membership experiences in specific industries. In construction, for example, the union-nonunion wage differential remained constant between 1973 and 1978 and even narrowed after 1978, which should have increased the competitiveness of union contractors and encouraged union growth, yet union density in construction fell from 39 to 22 percent during 1973-86. (Allen, 1988) Anti-union structural and institutional forces would seem to explain more of the decline in this instance than does the theory of union wage differentials.

The industrial relations analysis of union decline is more influenced by factual trends and institutional relationships than is the theoretical neoclassical explanation, but it, too, shows a tendency to accept the presumption that U.S. firms have not been able to sustain high labor costs and adversarial labor relations in the face of intense competition. [11] Employers, government and the academic community alike tell unions that they should abandon the adversarial role and accept a more passive, cooperative relationship with individual firms and plant managements. The model they advocate resembles Japanese-style fragmentation and company unionism and is based on the proposition that long-run worker interests are closely identified with the profit performance of the immediate employer. Part of the union function therefore is to assist the firm in its response to intensified product competition.

But precisely how the competition arose and persists and exactly what the threatened firm should do in response to it are seldom discussed. Competition is treated instead as an external constant, a given variable which by its very presence justifies the need for changing contract terms and adopting a new kind of labor relations. Industrial performance, employment and income levels are said to depend on lower unit labor costs and greater employee involvement and union-management cooperation. But industrial performance, or competitiveness, involves not only reducing labor costs and achieving shopfloor cooperation but also developing genuine union participation in long-term strategies concerning capital investment, production process and location and product quality. In practice, however, current union-management cooperation programs usually are limited to cost reduction efforts and profit sharing schemes. Advocates of simultaneous union concessions and union-management cooperation have to justify this approach in view of the problems that are occurring in labor relations today because employers promote increased labor participation but simultaneously pursue unilateral management control over critical operating decisions and low-wage, job-reduction strategies in the production process.

A productive systems analysis argues, in contrast to market theory and industrial relations explanations, that manufacturing decline and the erosion of union bargaining power originate in the interaction of opposing and unequal forces in the creation and distribution of wealth. Interaction among productive components makes key firms in basic industry uncompetitive in product markets for reasons both related and unrelated to the labor market effects of unions, and which left untreated can lead to downward cumulative causation. In this view, organized labor lost power not because it is a market imperfection or an adversarial agent but because it became structurally and institutionally vulnerable to employer strategies and reorganizations made in response to changes in foreign and domestic product markets. Labor's decline mirrors the emergence of changed forms of competition and industrial structures, changed labor strategies by employers and the state, changed labor forces, and changed social and political environments.

Under what conditions could there be a resurgence of American unions that is consistent with a competitive, equitable and expanding national economy? The answer is suggested in the historical accomplishments and failures of the union movement. The respective success and failure of craft and industrial unions in the last century showed the ability of trade unions to organize and mobilize workers around the common trade and the corresponding inability of class-based industrial and national labor movements to organize workers of diverse origins and experiences around the concept of class exploitation and to overcome the growing power of large corporations in America. The result was a small, fragmented and elite union movement of skilled craftsmen who looked after their own interests quite effectively but for the most part refused to open their ranks to the lowest-paid, most exploited workers and consistently opposed the formation of independent industrial unions. The decline of the trade union movement in the 1920s and its utter defeat during the 1930s demonstrated the short-sightedness and narrowness of craft unionism in a mass production economy where craft and industrial workers alike suffered the consequences of labor's inadequate income share and insufficient demand levels in the economy.

The CIO industrial union movement rescued American business and business unionism from themselves by extending high wages and income security to millions of working class families and mobilizing labor political activity. But the benefits that accrued to workers as a result of the expanded labor movement fell short. Large segments of the labor force were excluded geographically, industrially and demographically on the basis of social stratification, race and sex. CIO unions and some AFL affiliates tried but failed to broaden union influence and support, for example by directing the legislative fight for a national health insurance system and by committing time and resources to the unsuccessful bid to organize Southern textile mills. After several vain attempts to extend organized labor into new arenas, individual unions turned to issues affecting their respective industries and to the job of independent negotiation and administration of contracts, essentially leaving unfinished the business of transforming the union movement into a labor movement. As in the 1920s and 1930s, however, unions and union workers again paid a heavy price for their complacency and satisfaction with a partially organized work force, this time in the 1970s and 1980s when employers seized upon union fragmentation to deregulate labor markets and utilized the increasing pool of disadvantaged workers to accomplish their industrial restructuring and low-wage strategies.

The history of the American labor movement is thus a story of arrested development. Craft unionism gave the movement its impetus but never took it beyond fragmented, occupation-based business unionism; the CIO widened labor's structure and vision but in the end got no further than pattern-bargaining, product-based business unionism with a limited social agenda. Both proved exceedingly vulnerable to changes in the industrial and social order and their eventual decline demonstrates the need for another kind of unionism, one which organizes the unorganized, which finds the legal and institutional mechanisms to extend favorable terms and conditions of employment from advantaged to disadvantaged work groups and which finishes labor's unfinished social agenda. For these things to happen there will have to be a resurgence of union representation and bargaining power. And for that there must be a burst of union activity in the service sectors. Revitalized unions in basic manufacturing can be expected to set the pace for wage and benefit improvements, but the large and growing service industries must provide the membership base for an expanded labor movement and bargaining system.

Unions will have to learn on their own how to organize low-wage workers. One thing is certain, however: successful organization will require unions to come to terms with who these workers are and where they reside in the social hierarchy in addition to knowing what they do and where they work, because who they are and what they are explain why they took those jobs in the first place. As in the past, union growth in new areas is both essential and difficult because labor's decline cannot be reversed in the present environment without opening the movement to everyone. And unions cannot do that without changing the way they and their members perceive disadvantaged workers.

Endnotes

     1. These figures are based on per capita payments to the Federation and therefore are not always reliable; but they are internally consistent over time and therefore sufficient for our purposes.

     2. A $5 billion surplus in 1967 in the country's merchandise trade balance (manufacturing plus oil and food) turned into a $27 billion deficit in 1979 and a colossal $153 billion deficit in 1987, $60 billion of it in autos alone. By 1987 every product category except military hardware had turned negative--even agricultural produce.

     3. Union power also depends of course on less tangible and uncontrollable factors: e.g., member militancy, levels of unemployment, negotiating skill and tactics. Only the immediate structural and institutional determinants of union bargaining strength are included in this discussion.

     4. Organized labor's power following the two world wars differed substantially. AFL leaders supported America's entry into World War One and the Wilson Administration reciprocated with policies which helped unions win recognition and negotiated benefits in a number of key industries. After the war, however, leading firms in steel, meatpacking and other basic industries engaged union workers in lengthy strikes and succeeded in reversing labor's wartime gains. (Larson, 1975; Brody, 1980) After the Second World War unions not only maintained representation in the basic industries but consolidated the primary bargaining units and expanded into secondary industries.

     5. USX-U.S. Steel's reorganization typified the industry during this time and was characteristic of the extensive corporate restructuring by leading firms in other durable manufacturing industries. By 1984 it had closed 11 mills nationwide; early that year it announced it would close 13 more, representing one-fifth of its remaining steel capacity, at a time when it was buying rival firms and mill properties in order to get updated capacity in alternative product lines. One month later, as part of its shift from capital to consumer steel products, U.S. Steel disclosed plans to acquire National Steel, the sixth largest producer which had just been reorganized as National Intergroup after selling its tin plate works to employees and investing into financial services and aluminum. The announcement meant USX was scrapping plans to build a huge "greenfield" mill on the shores of Lake Erie. When the Justice Department prohibited the acquisition on anti-trust grounds USX revitalized flat-rolled sheet steel at its Gary Works. National Intergroup subsequently formed a joint venture with the Japanese producer Nippon Kokan which acquired half of National's domestic steel

capacity and agreed to oversee operating improvements in National mills scheduled to supply Midwest auto plants.

6. International Paper, the leading firm in that industry, locked out union workers who rejected concession demands in early 1987; local unions at three other mills struck following contract expirations and similar concession demands. IP's justification for the concessions was the need to raise its annual net profit rate to 15 percent over the business cycle. The company continued operating profitably with nonunion employees, strikebreakers and a handful of former strikers who crossed picket lines. As other local agreements expired union workers either accepted the concessions or worked without contracts. After 16 months, with 21 of the 27 IP locals without contracts and many threatened by decertification proceedings, the international union called off the three strikes and made an unconditional request for the remaining 2,300 strikers to return to work. IP rejected the offer and instead rehired workers on an individual basis. (Birecree, 1989)

7. In some metal mining and primary metal industries unions made concessions in exchange for future earnings payments linked to relevant ore and metal prices. Silver miners and smelter workers in Idaho, for example, ratified a concession contract that links wages to current silver prices and worker productivity; average hourly wage rates fluctuate with silver prices ranging from a low of $8.15 to a high of $17.50--compared to a straight $14 per hour average under the old agreement. In return, and in view of rising silver prices, the Sunshine Mining Company agreed to reopen several mines which had been closed for more than a year, although production employment was expected to reach only about one-third of its previous peak level.

8. Two thirds of the increase in wage rates in basic steel during 1972-82 were from COLA adjustments.

9. Data for contract settlements in public sector employment reveal no similar concession trend. Lewin however found that substantial concessions were being made by state and local government employees and teachers in regions and communities hard hit by manufacturing dislocation and recession, e.g., Detroit and the state of Michigan, and where governments were in fiscal crisis, although the cuts were not as sharp then as they were in New York during the 1979-80 crisis. (Lewin, 1983)

10. The experience of the British iron and steel industry is indicative. Union wage concessions during the 1920s in response to increasing global competition simply compensated for the industry's underlying production inefficiencies and did more to aggravate than solve the problem. (Wilkinson, 1989)

11. This theme dominates the current industrial relations literature, but the most informed and comprehensive argument is made by Kochan, Katz and McKersie, 1988.

References

Allen, G., "Declining Unionization in Construction: The Facts and the Reasons," Industrial and Labor Relations Review, Vol. 41, No. 3, April 1986.

Birecree, A., "Labor Relations at International Paper Company in the 1980s: A Preliminary Analysis" (unpublished paper). Second Annual Labor Market Segmentation Conference, University of Notre Dame-St. Mary's College, Notre Dame, IN, April 1989.

BNA, Labor Relations in an Economic Recession: Job Losses and Concession Bargaining, Washington, D.C.: 1982.

BNA, Changing Pay Practices: New Developments in Employee Compensation, Washington, D.C.: 1988.

Blair, J., Economic Concentration: Structure, Behavior and Public Policy, New York: Harcourt Brace Jovanovich, 1972.

Brody, D., Workers in Industrial America: Essays on the 20th Century Struggle, New York: Oxford University Press, 1980.

Craypo, C., "Collective Bargaining in the Conglomerate, Multinational Firm: Litton's Shutdown of Royal Typewriter," Industrial and Labor Relations Review, October, 1975.

Craypo, C., "Experiences in the Deindustrialization of a Factory Town," in Betty G. Lall, editor, Economic Dislocation and Job Loss, New York: NYSSILR, Cornell University, 1985.

Craypo, C., The Economics of Collective Bargaining, Washington, D.C.: Bureau of National Affairs, 1986.

Eatwell, J., Whatever Happened to Britain?, London: Duckworth, 1982.

Erlich, M., "Who Will Build the Future?", Labor Research Review, Vol. 2, No.2, Fall, 1988.

GAO, Dislocated Workers: Local Programs and Outcomes Under the Job Training Partnership Act, Report to the Congress, United States General Accounting Office, Washington, D.C.: 1987

Glyn, A., A. Hughes, A. Lipietz, and A. Singh, "The Rise and Fall of the Golden Age," in Marglin, S., editor, The End of the Golden Age: Lessons for the 1990s, Oxford: Clarendon Press, 1989.

Goodrich, Carter, The Frontier of Control (1925), London: Pluto Press, 1975.

Grabelsky, J., "Bottom-Up Organizing in the Trades," Labor Research Review, Vol. 12, No.2, Fall 1988.

Harrison, B. and B. Bluestone, The Great U-Turn: Corporate Restructuring and the Polarizing of America, New York: Basic Books, 1988.

Hoerr, J.P., And the Wolf Finally Came: The Decline of the American Steel Industry, Pittsburgh: University of Pittsburgh Press, 1988.

Howland, M., Plant Closings and Worker Displacement: The Regional Issues, Kalamazoo, MI: W.E. Upjohn Institute, 1988.

Jeszeck, C., "Structural Changes in Collective Bargaining: The U.S. Tire Industry," Industrial Relations, Vol. 25, No 1, 1986.

Knauss, K. and M. Matuszak, "The Implications of Cell Manufacturing for U.S. Factory Workers and Their Unions," Labor Studies Journal, Vol. 14, No. 1, Spring 1989.

Kochan, T., H. Katz and R. McKersie, The Transformation of American Industrial Relations, New York: Basic Books, 1986.

Larson, S., Labor and Foreign Policy: Gompers, the AFL, and the First World War, 1914-1918, Rutherford, N.J.: Fairleigh Dickinson University Press, 1975.

Lewin, D., "Public Sector Concession Bargaining: Lessons for the Private Sector," Industrial Relations Research Association, Proceedings, December 1982 Meetings, New York: 1983.

Lieberman, E.D., Unfit to Manage!, New York: McGraw-Hill, 1988.

McKelvey, J. T., Cleared for Takeoff: Airline Labor Relations Since Deregulation, Ithaca, N.Y.: NYSSILR, ILR Press, 1988.

Mills, D. Q., "When Employees Make Concessions," Harvard Business Review, May/June, 1983.

Mishel, L. and Simon, J., The State of Working America, Washington, D.C.: Economic Policy Institute, 1988.

Mitchell, D.J.B., "Recent Union Contract Concessions," Brookings Papers on Economic Activity, I, 1982.

Mitchell, D.J.B., "Shifting Norms in Wage Determination," Brookings Papers on Economic Activity, II, 1985.

Moody, K., An Injury to All, London: Verso Press, 1988.

Singh, A., "U.K. Industry and the World Economy: A Case of De-Industrialization?", Cambridge Journal of Economics, Vol. 1, 1977.

Slaughter, J., Concessions: And How to Beat Them, Detroit, MI: Labor Education and Research Project, 1983.

Taussig, F.W., Principles of Economics, Vol. 2, New York: Macmillan, 1917.

Uchitelle, L., "Job Security a Mirage for Unions Despite Wage Concessions of 80s," New York Times, January 9, 1989, p. 25.

Wachtel, H. and P.D. Adelsheim, "How Recession Feeds Inflation: Price Markups in a Concentrated Economy, " Challenge, September-October 1977.

Wilkinson, F., "Productive Systems," Cambridge Journal of Economics, Vol. 7, 1983.

Wilkinson, F., "Where Do We Go From Here? Real Wages, Effective Demand and Economic Development," Cambridge Journal of Economics, Vol.12, 1988.

Wilkinson, F., "Industrial Relations and Industrial Decline: The Case of the British Iron and Steel Industry 1870 to 1930" (unpublished paper), University of Notre Dame, 1989.

BIBLIOGRAPHY

1. The Bureau of National Affairs, Labor Relations in an Economic Recession: Job Losses and Concession Bargaining, (Washington, D.C.: BNA, 1982). Documents the adverse effects of economic recession during the early 1980s on union bargaining power and production employment in basic industries. Disaggregates data by industry and in some instances by major firms. Numerous bargaining case studies demonstrate the impact on unions.

2. The Bureau of National Affairs, Changing Pay Practices: New Developments in Employee Compensation, (Washington, D.C.: BNA, 1988). A useful review of the effects of union decline and changing competitive environments on industrial pay policies. Emphasizes "new compensation" practices that are being substituted for standard formulas and deferred increases in hourly earnings, including bonus payments and variable earnings systems based on performance levels of individual employees, work groups and plants or firms. Numerous case studies of union and nonunion settings illustrate these trends.

3. Craypo, Charles, The Economics of Collective Bargaining: Case Studies in the Private Sector, (Washington, D.C.: Bureau of National Affairs, 1986). Describes standards used in postwar economic bargaining and develops a framework for estimating and explaining union bargaining power. Uses detailed case studies of craft and industrial bargaining to illustrate negotiating processes and outcomes. Discusses the decline in union bargaining power after 1979.

4. Edwards, Richard, Paolo Garonna, and Franz Todtling, editors, Unions in Crisis and Beyond: Perspectives from Six Countries, (Dover, MA: Auburn House, 1986). Comparative studies of the economic crisis affecting advanced capitalist economies in the West and their labor movements. Case studies of the United States, United Kingdom, Italy, France, Austria, and Sweden vary in approach and findings but reveal certain common experiences: increased postwar

41

acceptance of unions and collective bargaining followed by declining union power linked to declining national economic performance, greatest in the United States and the United Kingdom and least in Austria and Sweden.

5. Goldfield, Michael, The Decline of Organized Labor in the United States, (Chicago: University of Chicago Press, 1987). Analyzes union membership losses and failure to win recognition elections. Concludes that the events of the 1970s and 1980s do not explain union decline satisfactorily; argues instead that business initiated an unrelenting offensive against organized labor in the 1950s and union failure to respond effectively has altered the power relations between classes and weakened unions in the long-run.

6. Harrison, Bennett, and Barry Bluestone, The Great U-Turn: Corporate Restructuring and the Polarizing of America, (New York: Basic Books, 1988). Examines the characteristics of jobs created in the U.S. economy after 1979. Concludes that corporate restructuring has had a drastic effect of the kinds of jobs being made available and that the ratio of high-paying production jobs in the labor market is declining as a result.

7. Hoerr, John P., And the Wolf Finally Came: The Decline of the American Steel Industry, (Pittsburgh, PA: University of Pittsburgh Press, 1988). A well-written account of the deterioration of the domestic steel industry based on extensive observation of events and interviews with industry and union officials. Graphic descriptions of corporate decision-making and the impact of industrial decline on communities and workers. Blames the inability of Big Steel to adjust to competition largely on inflexible and adversarial relationships in collective bargaining and advocates greater union-management trust and cooperation which links labor relations to investment and other development strategies.

8. Kochan, Thomas A., Harry C. Katz and Robert B. McKersie, The Transformation of American Industrial Relations, (New York: Basic Books, 1986). The most informed and comprehensive treatment of changes occurring in U.S. labor relations from an industrial relations perspective. Describes and analyzes these changes on the basis of strategic choices made by firms in response to increased competition and identifies the emergence of an increasingly nonunion industrial relations system in place of the conventional postwar practices. Supports increased union participation and joint labor-management planning to achieve the production flexibility that is needed for improved industrial competitiveness. Proposes labor law

reforms to facilitate the rise of industrial relations practices more consistent with the changed environment.

9. Lieberman, Ernest D., Unfit to Manage!: How Mis-Management Endangers America and What Working People Can Do About It, (New York: McGraw-Hill, 1988). A critique of American business practices in a time of increased product competition. Argues, mainly from anecdotes in the commercial and business press, that industry loses more by fighting unions than it would cost to pay high wages and benefits and to establish cooperative relations with organized labor and implement participatory systems involving production workers.

10. Lipset, Seymour Martin, editor, Unions in Transition: Entering the Second Century, (San Francisco: ICS Press, 1986). Historical and reflective essays and empirical studies on the declining state of organized labor in the United States. Contributions by academic and practitioner authors vary considerably in subject, purpose and point of view. Addresses recent union decline in membership density, representation elections, political influence, and bargaining strength and the likelihood of resurgence based on the experiences of unions in other industrialized countries.

11. Mishel, Lawrence and Jacqueline Simon, The State of Working America, (Washington, D.C.: Economic Policy Institute, 1988). Documents changes in living standards of working Americans in the 1980s. Regardless of which measurement is used--real income, income and job distribution, income security--the average worker was worse off in 1987 than in 1979 despite the significant increase in employment and relatively modest inflation levels. Contains nearly one hundred statistical tables showing these trends.

12. Moody, Kim, An Injury to All: The Decline of American Unionism (New York: Verso, 1988). The best and most comprehensive critique of postwar U.S. labor and industry from a leftist perspective. Attributes labor's decline to centralized union administration, consolidation of industry at home and overseas, the debilitating effect on labor of the postwar "social accord" between unions and managers and the combined efforts of big business and government to cripple U.S. unions. Advocates greater rank-and-file activism and control in unions and a broadening of the organizational base to include previously unorganized workers.

13. Slaughter, Jane, <u>Concessions--And How to Beat Them</u>, (Detroit, MI: Labor Education & Research Project, 1983). Presents the case against union concessions based mainly on collective bargaining experiences in manufacturing during 1981-83. Argues that concessions were neither necessary nor successful in saving jobs and threatened plants. Written for trade unionists but is useful for the general reader.

14. Wilkinson, Frank, editor, <u>The Dynamics of Labour Market Segmentation</u>, (London: Academic Press, 1981). Comparative studies showing the differences among alternative interpretations of labor market segmentation. Emphasizes the role of unions and other institutional structures in the determination of wealth distribution, worker living standards and job conditions. Views labor markets as being stratified along numerous lines including diverse forms of trade union organization and bargaining effectiveness rather than being divided directly between primary and secondary segments. Available in a U.S. edition.

CHAPTER 2

American Labor at the Crossroads
Political Resurgence or
Continued Decline?

Peter Seybold*

I. Introduction

At a recent conference in Canada (1988) an AFL-CIO official was asked whether the American labor movement had considered forming its own labor party. "Why should we?," he replied, "we already have tremendous access to the Democratic party."

This exchange captures in a nutshell the dilemma facing the American labor movement in the 1980s as well as the strengths and weaknesses of the American labor movement in the period after World War II. Wedded to the Democratic party and a narrower conception of politics than most labor movements in other countries, the labor movement in the United States was moderately successful in terms of electoral politics in the 1950s and 1960s. But labor's commitment to mainstream politics and to the Democratic party had a number of contradictory aspects which by the 1980s had stripped labor of its character as a social movement and reduced it to just another special interest group.

* Special thanks to Lee Balliet and Bob Higgins for their editorial suggestions and comments.

As we move toward the 1990s, the American labor movement finds itself at a crossroads. Should it continue down the path it chose immediately after World War II, which stressed becoming a major player in a political system dominated by political parties firmly committed to business dominance? Or should it examine its previous course and choose instead to recapture its essence as a broad social movement committed to social justice and open to questions regarding the fundamental nature of the economic and political system?

Unfortunately, the choices facing the American labor movement in the 1990s have been considerably narrowed by the global economy and the labor movement's own postwar political legacy. Had it adopted a different set of policies in the 1940s and early 1950s it may not have been confronted with such difficult choices thirty-five years later. However, for a variety of reasons which we will examine below, it chose a relatively restricted role for itself both in domestic and international politics. By the 1980s, the labor movement was struggling to retain its status as a major player in American politics. Too often it was ignored or simply treated as an artifact of history.

To be sure, the reasons for the labor movement's relative decline in political influence in the post World War II era were only partially its own doing. Throughout this period labor was locked into a bureaucratized and institutionalized mode of conflict with a built-in bias in favor of capital. The labor movement struggled, valiantly at times within this framework, to create a more just system which provided an adequate social wage for all citizens; but the cards were stacked against it. Failing to press the case for society-wide social reforms after the war and to further organize the workforce, it was content just to be recognized as a major player. The consequences of setting such limited goals for the labor movement and the failure to encourage rank and file activism in the 1940s and 1950s would only become clear when the labor movement was put on the defensive in the 1970s.

In contrast to the 1950s and 60s, the American economy failed to continue its impressive growth in the 1970s. By the middle of the decade, the labor movement was confronted with a hostile political environment in which many of its fair-weather friends turned against it. The cruel lesson for labor, driven home again and again in the 1980s, was that liberal Democrats were not committed in principle to the labor movement. Rather, they were supportive of labor's political goals only when the economy was growing at a fast enough rate to finance the cost of labor-backed social legislation. In a period of slow growth or no growth the terms of public discourse were transformed from a debate over increasing the social wage (1950s, 1960s, early 70s) to a debate over reducing the social wage in the 1980s.

Caught off guard, the American labor movement was unprepared to face either the rapidly changing international economy or the drastically altered political atmosphere in the United States. By the 1980s, it was apparent that the combative spirit of the 1930s and the visionary goals of social unionism had been lost among the present generation of labor leaders. Instead, their instincts told them to turn inward and to protect what they had. Feeling betrayed by their political allies and by the American public, which had absorbed more than thirty years of anti-union propaganda since World War II, the labor movement had its back to the wall.

The decisions made by American labor leaders in the late 1940s and early 1950s concerning the tactics and goals of the American labor movement began to haunt it by the 1980s. With only 17% of the workforce organized in 1988, the union movement gave the appearance of a special interest group. Moreover, among younger workers and students in secondary and post-secondary schools, the history of the labor movement and the benefits of unionization went unappreciated. The grim reality confronting labor was that young people, even from union households, could not be convinced by their parents of the importance of holding a union card. Nor were many young people aware that the standard of living they enjoyed and its resulting life-chances could be directly traced to their parents' membership in a trade union.

In a cruel paradox of history, the children of workers who experienced plant closings often blamed the union rather than the company for the closing of the plant. With the assistance of an uncritical press, community members were typically bombarded with accounts of greedy union members' demands which forced the company to close its doors and flee in search of a more favorable business climate. The constant exposure to only one side of the story (the corporate side) eventually took its toll, even, and perhaps with greater impact, in blue collar towns. The stage had been set for a corporate-generated "blame the union campaign" which deeply penetrated the consciousness of Americans. Tragically, such a message rang true to a surprising number of community members raised in the era of postwar prosperity.

The willingness of average Americans to embrace a virulent anti-union message can only be understood in the context of a post World War II social, political, economic and educational milieu in which unions and their goals became increasingly invisible. Just as blaming the union worker for a stagnant mid-1970s economy makes no sense, blaming average Americans for being pro-business and anti-union sheds hardly any light on a complex social process. Support for the status quo by most Americans is not surprising since mainstream U.S. institutions continually work to reproduce opinions that reinforce the existing structure of power. Despite the prevailing bias in favor of business interests, corporate ideology never completely dominates the social outlook. It needs constant reinforcement because the every-day life experience of non-elites calls into question the basic fairness of American institutions. As a result, a disjuncture often occurs between what people have learned on the abstract level (in schools and other institutions) and what their real- world experience tells them.

If anything can be said about the attitudes of Americans after World War II, it is that they have consistently exhibited a fragmented and contradictory social consciousness. (Gramsci, 1971; Parkin, 1971) Lacking access to an oppositional framework which can put into perspective their discontent, Americans are prone to repeat corporate ideology when asked abstract political questions. More concrete political questions usually elicit a different response from working-class Americans, ranging from distrust and cynicism about the system to gut-level hostility towards big business. What is noteworthy, however, is that anti-big business, populist sentiments remain part of the American political landscape despite a long-term trend towards depoliticization among non-elites since World War II.

In the 1980s, populist appeals to anti-elite sentiments only occur as a last-ditch campaign tactic of floundering Democrats. With the exception of Jesse Jackson (Collins, 1986), even the most liberal Democratic party politicians have repudiated class-based, anti-business political appeals. As a result the theoretical framework for such appeals, if not the vocabulary, has been relegated to the margins of American politics. Democrats and Republicans alike have found it uncomfortable to talk about social class in a time of economic stagnation.

Since the mid 1970s when the American economy came grinding to a halt, the terms of political debate have been drastically altered. Political discussion shifted from expanding the welfare state to decimating it, from toleration of unions to resistance to even business unionism, from the appearance of racial tolerance and support for affirmative action to overt manifestations of racial hatred and talk of reverse discrimination, from passive support for women's rights to active opposition to gains made by women. This sea change in

American politics can be seen as the beginning of the politics of stagnation and the end of the business/labor accord. Liberal programs and unions could be tolerated only when the economy was growing and the pressure from social movements was intense. From the mid 1970s, American corporations and their political allies mounted a sustained corporate offensive against federal social programs and against the labor movement. Corporate elites sought not only to gain increased leverage over fundamental sectors (economic, political, social, knowledge-producing) of American society, but also to immobilize and render impotent their opposition. The goal of corporate elites was nothing less than to regain the initiative by reversing the gains made by working people in the 1930s and the 1960s.

The bitter irony for those who still subscribed to the ideals of the civil rights, labor, women's and environmental movements was that capital was on a mission that had as its goal a union-free, regulation-free, civil rights-free, social justice-free America. Moreover, big business and its allies had appropriated the zeal and the utopian vision previously reserved for progressive social movements. Progressive social movements were not only on the decline in the 1980s, they were also confronted with right-wing social forces which threatened to become a reactionary mass movement.

Corporate elites then had a direction in which they wanted to move, a plan (devised by conservative think-tanks), and a way of packaging this plan which had visceral appeal to the American people. (Clawson and Clawson, 1987) In addition, they had another advantage because they did not have to deal with the disunity and fragmentation that poor peoples' movements usually encounter. Cementing the alliance between American businesses was the nightmare, which was becoming reality, of increasing challenges to the hegemony of U.S. capital by foreign competition and by social movements in less developed countries that threatened to nationalize U.S. assets.

Just at the moment (late 1970s) that corporations and their allies were gearing up for a major offensive, the American labor movement had become isolated and was out of step with other progressive social forces in the U.S. Labor's declining political influence was signalled by its failure to win labor law reform in 1978, despite having both a Democrat in the White House and a Democratic Congress. Corporate lobbying had turned the tide especially among southern Democrats who now felt free to ignore the labor movement's pleas for support. This defeat, as well as relentless economic pressure from corporations facing foreign competition, ushered in an era of concessionary bargaining for American labor unions. As Americans witnessed the inability of the labor movement to stem the concessionary wave, it reinforced the notion that labor unions were helpless in the face of a changing political economy.

The hard times for labor continued in the remaining Carter years and reached their apex with Ronald Reagan's smashing of the air traffic controller's union (PATCO) and the devastating depression of 1981-82. Although the AFL-CIO tried to regroup its forces with a series of Solidarity rallies following Reagan's election, there was little grassroots follow-up to these media events. The right-wing was on the move and liberalism, even of the corporate type, was fast becoming politically irrelevant.

When it became apparent to the labor movement that the corporate siege would continue, especially after Reagan's reelection in 1984 and a "recovery" which left many behind, the AFL-CIO initiated changes. After much soul-searching, AFL-CIO leaders initiated plans for a study of the changing situation of workers and their unions, beefed up media and public relations efforts by the labor movement, and sought to bring back into the house of labor unaffiliated unions. In order to better fight large conglomerates, smaller unions merged with each other or with bigger unions within their sector of the economy. As the service sector continued to grow, increased organizing efforts in this area became a focus for even industrial unions such as the auto workers, steel workers, and the machinists.

While the efforts of the national AFL-CIO in the 1980s were commendable, if very late in coming, these efforts remained top-down in character and relatively unconnected to either grassroots unionists on the local level or other progressive social movements. Again, it was not that the national AFL-CIO did not seek to turn around its situation, but rather that it chose a familiar and very narrow framework in which to carry on its fight. The leadership of the AFL-CIO simply could not return to a broader social unionism, and despite its militant rhetoric, the AFL-CIO could not transcend the limits of its postwar political legacy.

Even more debilitating was the adherence of the national AFL-CIO to an outdated and morally bankrupt foreign policy. (Cantor and Schor, 1987) This pledge of allegiance by the AFL-CIO to an unsophisticated and dogmatic cold war ideology (free trade unions vs. communist trade unions) distanced itself further from its potential allies in the religious community as well as the peace and anti-intervention movements. Within the labor movement, the heavy-handed suppression of dissenters from the AFL-CIO foreign policy line created even more distance between the rank and file and the national federation.

It was almost as if the leaders of the AFL-CIO expected elites to call off or moderate the corporate offensive against labor, once they could conclusively prove to business that the labor movement was thoroughly committed to anti-communism. Despite labor's continued support for Reagan's foreign policy line, American capital continued to be exported abroad, and with it American jobs. The AFL-CIO was powerless to stop the flow.

Labor was left with the hope that corporate excesses would generate enough backlash among the American people to enable a more unified, stylized, neo-liberal Democratic party to regain political control. (Ferguson and Rogers, 1986, 1981) The conventional wisdom in the 1980s, for both the Democratic party and the labor movement, was that changes were necessary but not drastic changes; top-down decision-making would still work, if the decision makers would refine their message. According to this view, the Democratic party and the labor movement needed to be retooled, but not radically changed. Victory was at hand for both labor and the Democrats, once Reagan retired. All the Democratic party had to do, it seemed to party leaders, was to make it clear to the American people that it was again safe to be a Democrat. The party had to assure the American people that it had learned the lessons of the 1980s, by abandoning any pretense of defending the interests of poor and minority people.

A political change would occur, the Democrats hoped, because the American people were tired of the Republican product, especially if Reagan was not there to sell it. All the Democrats thought they had to do was to repackage basically the same product and convince the American people that they could better manage Reaganomics in the absence of Reagan.

Completely tied to the Democratic party and the two party system, the leaders of the American labor movement could do nothing but fine-tune their efforts. However, their efforts were appreciated only by Democrats in districts where labor support was still crucial. National Democratic leaders maintained considerable distance from the labor movement in order to avoid the charge that they were beholden to special interest groups. As the 1990s approached, the question of independent political activity was not even in the minds of most American labor leaders or members. Thus, the reply from labor officials that they were pleased with their access to the Democratic party.

As this overview of the American labor movement's declining political fortunes has made clear, there are many issues which need clarification. Among the questions that will be addressed in the remainder of this chapter are: 1) Why did the American labor movement take the path outlined above after World War II? 2) Was there another path that it could have taken in this period? 3) Will the American labor movement grow even weaker in the future and truly become irrelevant to the modern era?

As always, it is difficult to speculate about how things could have been if the American labor movement had taken a different road. It is important to recognize, however, that in analyzing labor's political fortunes we can not remove it from its larger social, political, and economic context. After 1945, the American labor movement developed within the world's most powerful capitalist society and thus was subject to its dynamics. At the time there was talk of an "American Century" in which the United States would totally dominate world affairs. By the 1980s, it was clear that America's ride at the top of the world lasted approximately twenty-five years.

Certainly, the American labor movement shared some of the benefits of the country's twenty-five year domination of the world. It also shared the contradictions of this period and was shaped by larger social forces. The postwar history of the American labor movement, however, was not predetermined. History is made by people working within an institutional framework that shapes their choices. Yet, they do make choices.

Is it fair to ask why American labor leaders did not question the larger institutional framework in which they operated after World War II? Or why the American labor movement took the path that it did? The answer is yes. In raising questions about the historical development of the American labor movement, we are not questioning the motives of American labor leaders. Quite the contrary, this chapter takes as an article of faith that labor movements play a crucial and indispensable role in a democratic society. However, this chapter also adheres to another fundamental principle put forward by C. Wright Mills-- social critics abdicate their responsibility if they take for granted the structure of society and its institutions. (Mills, 1959)

In the discussion that follows we will develop an interpretation of American labor's shifting political fortunes that depends heavily on the work of others. In measuring labor's political influence we will examine three levels of political activity: 1) capacity to project its political strength in the collective bargaining process, 2) ability to influence national legislation and national elections, 3) power to alter the larger political environment by shaping the limits and terms of debate. If it is true that as the American labor movement approaches the 1990s it is at a crossroads, only an open discussion can clarify which fork in the road it should take. It is in this spirit that I will develop a critical analysis of the American labor movement after World War II which will likely produce more questions than answers. In so doing, this chapter seeks to contribute to the debate on the current state of the American labor movement.

II. The Crucial Decade (1945-1955)

> In January 1946, 174,000 United Electrical Workers, 800,000 Steelworkers joined the 225,000 G.M. auto workers already on strike, creating the greatest work stoppage in U.S. history. More was to come. In total, four industries experienced general strikes and a total of 4.6 million people engaged in nearly 5,000 work stoppages, costing employers a staggering 116 million work days. (Green, 1980: 194)

Against this backdrop, the worst fears of corporate elites seemed to be coming true; open class conflict had not been suppressed. In the period immediately after World War II, business leaders sought to heal the wounds of the depression era and stabilize the social system. With America's industrial capacity untouched by the ravages of war and other major industrial powers in ruins, American business saw a great opportunity to supply the world with goods and services. To accomplish this task would require industrial peace at home, a peace which appeared threatened by the wave of strikes in 1946 and the possible reemergence of class-based politics.

Although the job actions and strikes of 1946 were largely defensive in character, they nevertheless were very unsettling to business elites. Militant action by workers, even if only to retain their existing rights, served as an example to other groups fighting for their fair share in postwar America. For corporate elites, the New Deal reforms had gone far enough and it was time for them to actively intervene to prevent the further extension of citizenship rights in the United States.

Business leaders were especially troubled by the discussion within Congress in 1946 of an Economic Bill of Rights, which would guarantee to all Americans who wanted to work the right to a decent-paying job. In their worst nightmare, corporate elites were haunted by the prospect that the basic rights of American citizens would be broadened to include: the right to a job, to health insurance, to pension benefits, and to other social entitlements. A political environment which included these issues could only lead to additional questions about the relative proportions of the economic pie controlled by various segments of the population. Therefore, although they were never really in danger of losing control of American society, even during the Depression, corporate elites wanted to permanently eliminate social class as a category of political analysis after World War II.

As David Eakins has shown, the problem of how to stabilize the economy and the polity without granting further concessions to American workers was discussed in corporate liberal policy circles well before the war ended. (Eakins, 1966; Shoup and Minter, 1977) A consensus developed among government officials and business leaders that sustained economic growth was the key to forestalling class conflict. Questions about the relative proportion of the economic pie controlled by the upper class could be sidetracked, if everyone could be promised a better standard of living in a growing economy. Combined with the attack on social class as a category of analysis, this domestic equivalent of containment sought to put a lid on social conflict.

If this strategy was indeed successful it might also help to restabilize the political process in the United States. A 1948 report by the Study Committee of the Ford Foundation indicated that many citizens were alienated from the basic political institutions of American society. Increasingly, they regarded the principles of American democracy as a set of cliches which did not apply to their lives. Such attitudes, combined with a very low voter turnout in the 1948 presidential election (51.1%), raised fears among elite members of a possible legitimation crisis. How could corporate elites and their political allies go forward with their postwar plans if disaffection was widespread among the population? The prospect that disaffected Americans might find an alternative political framework to express their discontent was even more troubling.

Finally, in the period immediately following World War II there was considerable uncertainty about the economic direction America would take. Without the stimulus provided by the war, would it fall back into depression thereby raising again class-based political questions? Or would it prosper and thus provide the economic foundation for a politics which submerged issues related to social class?

The course taken by American society in this era would not be determined solely by the plans of corporate elites. It would also depend on the ability of social movements, such as the labor movement, to put pressure on the political process and to formulate an alternative approach. As Mike Davis has shown (1986), the American labor movement was facing major obstacles, some of its own making and others which were imposed by larger social, political, and economic forces. In order to better understand the politics and economics of this era, we will examine below the state of the American labor movement between 1945 and 1955.

Demobilizing the Rank and File

In light of the dramatic upsurge in unionization from 1933 to 1941 (the number of unionized employees tripled from 2,805,000 to 8,410,000), it is clear that the American labor movement was in a position to become the leader of a progressive coalition after World War II. (Green, 1980:173) In terms of its political influence, labor's strength was exhibited in the organized industrial sector through the collective bargaining process and within electoral politics in areas that were union strongholds. However, in the postwar period the labor movement's influence over relevant national legislation and its ability to shape the terms of political debate were severely limited by its lack of political unity and its bureaucratic organization.

Before reviewing the period between 1945 and 1955, it is important to note that the seeds had been sown for the integration of the American labor movement into postwar capitalist society prior to 1945, both inside the labor movement and within corporate liberal policy circles. For example, the process of coopting the Congress of Industrial Organizations (CIO) had received a big boost when President Roosevelt was able to prevent it from bolting the Democratic party in the late 1930s. This insured that the militant wing of the labor movement would be firmly tied to the existing two-party system. In addition, the CIO's efforts to gain independence were further weakened by the cooperation between business, labor, and government during World War II. This included joint planning boards that laid the basis for future cooperation between these groups as well as organized labor's adherence to a no strike pledge during the war.

The experience of the labor movement during the war was particularly crucial because it was here that the basis for a government/business/labor accord was established. As a result of wartime measures such as the maintenance of membership clause, and the weakening of the shop floor power of stewards by formal rules for mediating disputes, workers were both organized into unions by government and subsequently limited in their actions by an increasingly bureaucratic system of labor relations. (Davis, 1986; Green, 19´   ) The federal government became the primary arena for struggle, which muted the effect of rank-and-file militance. It should also be pointed out that the war broke up the small work groups within the major industrial plants, and their cultures of solidarity, which provided the core of support for militant action within the CIO. By disrupting the way of life of workers whose identity was forged in the late 1930s and by diluting union sentiments with nationalistic appeals, the war greatly affected the union movement. In addition, the war introduced new workers into the workforce and fundamentally altered the political climate by providing an all purpose justification (the war effort came first) for putting union concerns on hold.

The strike wave of 1946, while massive, and certainly an unpleasant reminder of the power of organized workers for the corporate elite, was not characterized by the same level of rank and file militance and direction as pre-war outbreaks. The top-down leadership style of many of these job actions foreshadowed a tendency which would become dominant within the labor movement as a whole over the next four decades. The leadership of many of the major AFL-CIO unions seemed to be almost as concerned about containing rank and file insurgency as were the business leaders they encountered in their negotiations.

The relative inability of the labor movement to transfer the power which they displayed in collective bargaining into the national political arena was confirmed by the passage of the Taft-Hartley Act by Congress in 1947. This act, which institutionalized a legal framework for labor relations that has permanently haunted the labor movement, severely restricted workers' right to strike and limited other forms of militant action. The National Labor Relations Board (NLRB) under Taft-Hartley could now be used against workers and their unions as well as against employers. As James Green put it, the pendulum was swinging against workers in 1947 and administrative law as well as judicial law reflected the alignment of class forces. (Green, 1980:198)

Internal divisions within the labor movement over strategy and goals and over the existence of left-wing militants in their midst prevented a united front from developing against Taft-Hartley. While John L. Lewis of the Mineworkers and the United Electrical Workers (UE) encouraged an all out fight against Taft-Hartley, other labor leaders were reluctant to support the mobilization of the rank and file. By this time the internal battle lines within the labor movement had been drawn, between those who supported business unionism characterized by top-down bureaucratic control, those who retained top-down organizational control but took a more militant stance, and those who wanted to return to militant mass action and social unionism of the type displayed in the heyday of the CIO.

Of critical importance to the resolution of this question was the labor movement's attitude towards its left wing and more generally its receptivity to anti-communist appeals. As the corporate offensive gathered steam in the late 1940s it nurtured anti-communism within the political sphere both to divide the labor movement and to justify its plans for overseas expansion. Initially introduced by corporate elites and picked up by President Truman in the form of a loyalty oath, anti-communism was later adopted by Republicans such as Richard Nixon. Anti-communism reached its height, in terms of public awareness, with the hysterical rantings of Senator Joseph McCarthy in the early 1950s. It is on the issue of anti-communism that the labor movement suffered a failure of nerve and paid for the previous failure of socialist ideals to become part of the political mainstream. The labor movement's inability to come to grips with anti-communism and to grant full participation to its left-wing would all but eliminate its chances to challenge the contours of political debate in the next three decades.

Faced with a choice of repudiating anti-communism, a choice which because of its past political history the labor movement was unprepared to handle, the AFL and the CIO severed ties with their left wing. (Ginger and Christiano, 1987) Not only did the American labor movement do nothing to combat anti-communism, it actively assisted in purging its ranks of radicals.

In the final analysis, the leadership of the American labor movement in the 1940s and a sizeable proportion of the membership simply did not have a political vision beyond becoming a recognized player in liberal capitalism. Since it lacked a conception of an alternative society which transcended the limits of capitalist society, the labor movement's leadership and some of its membership had little sympathy for the left (both communist and non-communist) or inclination to defend it. The pressure of the anti-communist crusade in America was too much to withstand and the labor movement, seeing an opportunity to gain further legitimacy in elite circles, purged itself of its militant left wing.

The effect of the split within labor's ranks between radicals and conservatives was devastating, especially in the CIO. Without even an investigation, the third largest union in the CIO, the United Electrical Workers (UE), was tossed out of the CIO during its 1948 convention. (Green, 1980) In subsequent years, the UE's membership declined drastically as successful raids were conducted against it by other unions. Bargaining within the electrical industry became fragmented, leaving workers open to company attempts to play one union off against another. It also permitted employers to refuse to deal with the UE and to claim that the labor movement fully supported this policy.

By 1950, employer attacks and the purges of left-wing unions from the CIO reduced the CIO's membership from a wartime peak of 5.2 million members to only 3.7 million members. (Green, 1980:203) The more conservative AFL was gaining a stronger footing in the labor movement and the CIO was losing its force and its claim to being a leader of a larger movement for social justice.

Of the many turning points for the CIO, the period of the late 1940s stands out not only because of the internal splits in its organization and its capitulation to anti-communism but also in its failure to go forward with its plans to organize the South. Wracked with internal contradictions, which prevented it from sending radical organizers committed to civil rights to the South, the CIO called off its Operation Dixie campaign in 1947. (Davis, 1986; Green, 1980) This campaign, which was to extend the successful CIO organizing tactics of the 1930s to the southern states could, in hindsight, be seen as pivotal to labor's political fortunes in the postwar era. Failing to go forward with Operation Dixie stripped the CIO of its claim to being linked to a larger social movement and separated the labor movement from the civil rights movement. This left the door open for conservative forces in the labor movement to consolidate control and endorse the Democratic party's truce with southern Democrats. Moreover, the failure to organize the South and fully commit itself to civil rights left the labor movement in a defenseless position when corporations picked up stakes in the North and relocated in southern states.

The goal of organizing a broader movement for social justice with the labor movement as its base was put on hold. If the labor movement had chosen this more progressive direction it undoubtedly would have faced many obstacles. The growing power of American corporations, a Democratic party which was more conservative under Truman, a postwar effort by elites to suppress conflict, and the repression of the American left during the McCarthy era would have made a left turn difficult.

Building a progressive coalition during this period with the labor movement in a leading role constituted an ambitious and risky project. In the short run such an effort probably would have provoked a strong corporate response with negative consequences for the labor movement. Nevertheless, a progressive coalition was not a utopian dream nor did it require a giant political leap. In fact, the basis for a social movement which sought to expand the citizenship rights of all Americans could be found in the Economic Bill of Rights which was at the core of Roosevelt's 1944 State of the Union message. The bill in its purest form guaranteed all citizens such fundamental rights as the right to a job, decent housing, medical insurance, and a good education. This expanded list of the rights of all Americans constituted the potential building blocks for a progressive social movement in the 1940s.

The American labor movement along with other progressive social forces could have made the fight for a more inclusive definition of citizenship rights its focus in the postwar political arena. Rather than take on such a difficult struggle, the labor movement turned inward in an effort to protect past gains and to defend itself from a postwar counter attack by business elites. A potentially powerful popular alliance for an economic bill of rights never coalesced. It fell victim on the one hand to growing corporate power, McCarthy-era political repression, and the ability of elites to define the nation's political agenda; and on the other hand, to the fragmentation of progressive forces, loss of ideals, and the immediacy of short-term political and economic goals.

Although the labor movement in the 1950s and 1960s was the principal backer of almost every piece of progressive legislation, it had lost its vision and its will to challenge the institutional framework of capitalism. Instead, it fought for incremental gains in wages and benefits for its members. The goal of building a society which broadly defined peoples' citizenship rights remained only in rhetoric. The extent to which the labor movement had strayed from its more ambitious goals of social unionism soon became clear in a series of agreements between the auto workers and the auto industry in the late 1940s.

Under the leadership of Walter Reuther, the United Auto Workers (UAW) won an unprecedented cost-of-living escalator clause from General Motors in 1948. (Green, 1980:208) In 1949, the UAW won a supplement to Social Security in the form of pension benefits. Even as these gains were won, working conditions within the auto plants took a turn for the worse and the ability of the rank and file and their stewards to alter the situation was stymied by the now well established grievance system. A system of labor relations which relied on stewards was being replaced in the auto plants by bureaucratic rules and the increased influence of committeemen (a position created within the UAW in 1946). The committeeman position was important because it further diluted the steward's influence by creating another level in the hierarchy as well as more distance between the shop floor and local union officials.

In 1950, Reuther signed what came to be known as the Treaty of Detroit, a five year contract with GM that called for the UAW to suspend the right to strike in return for the continuance of the cost-of-living (COLA) escalator clause and improvements in pension, welfare, and insurance plans. It was this agreement that provided the model for labor relations in the postwar era. Management would unilaterally control the organization of production and in return would assure the union of increases in wages, pensions, and other fringe benefits. (Green, 1980:208; Davis, 1986) While the agreement between the UAW and GM was pathbreaking, it signalled to others in the labor movement that one of the most powerful industrial unions, the UAW, would no longer contest management control of production. Moreover, it indicated to other CIO unions that the possibility of challenging the limits of capitalism and developing a broader social unionism was unrealistic in the climate of the 1950s.

In James Green's words:

> Like the other new men of power in the unions, Reuther accommodated to the post-war context in which the hopes of the 1930s became little more than rhetoric. By 1950, the world of the worker had begun to change significantly. It was the dawn of another era in which even the new unionism of the CIO seemed obsolete. The labor movement entered the 1950s on the defensive. (Green, 1980:209)

The fate of the CIO seemed to be cemented by the UAW/GM pact. Without a militant left present in its ranks to rekindle its activism and renew its dreams of an alternative society, the CIO's cutting edge was lost. The disagreements with the AFL over tactics and goals which seemed so crucial at an earlier time dwindled, and a reuniting of the AFL and the CIO seemed inevitable.

In 1955, the AFL and the CIO merged and in combination advanced the goals of a tightly controlled, bureaucratic business unionism and coupled them with allegiance to cold war foreign policy. C. Wright Mills' prophecy (1948) that the American labor movement would become more bureaucratized and integrated into the capitalist system came true. Mills argued that over time the rank and file of the labor movement would have less and less influence over the labor movement's course. Politics in the postwar era, for Mills, was increasingly becoming a competition between interest groups represented by lawyers and technicians with the masses looking on. Labor leaders during this period, who Mills called the new men of power, assisted in the consolidation of the political and economic system based on a business/labor accord. While they were certainly not arch-conservatives, American labor leaders after World War II had become "managers of discontent" and in so doing they established the limits for legitimate discussion within the labor movement.

The plans of corporate liberal policy groups for post-World War II America seemed to be falling in place as the American labor movement restricted its goals and complied with the new rules of the game. Gone were the questions about the basic structure of the system and the efforts to organize the bulk of the unorganized workforce. The labor movement had matured, at least in the eyes of the corporate elite, and could be relied on to be a predictable player in the political and economic marketplace.

The American labor movement chose its course for the future in the late 1940s and early 1950s. It turned away from its depression-era social movement roots and from a full involvement in the civil rights movement. In moderating its domestic policy goals and embracing cold war foreign policy, the AFL-CIO made peace with existing social institutions. In foreign affairs, it uncritically backed the American government's efforts to assist American business abroad even if it required overthrowing popular governments and giving power to right-wing dictatorships. Labor's desire for acceptance as a full partner in American capitalism led it to curry favor with big business by supporting the subordination of labor movements in less-developed countries (Central and South America for example). In the domestic political arena the labor movement remained a progressive force in the 1950s. However, in its political activities, the labor movement was restricted in its influence over legislative matters and national elections. More importantly, it was unable to shape the larger political environment.

The labor movement had its greatest impact in the early 1950s as a bargaining agent in the core of the industrial economy and as a countervailing force to the power of the business community. While this was not in any way an insignificant role for the labor movement, especially when viewed from the perspective of the 1980s, it marked a significant decline in the scope of its political power.

III. The Politics of Prosperity (1950s and 1960s)

> Why should we worry about organizing groups of people who do not want to be organized? If they prefer to have others speak for them and make the decisions which affect their lives without effective participation on their part, that is their right. Frankly, I used to worry about the membership, about the size of the membership. But quite a few years ago, I just stopped worrying about it, because to me it doesn't make any difference. It's the organized voice that counts--and it's not just in legislation, it's any place. The organized fellow is the fellow that counts. (George Meany, AFL-CIO President, 1972, quoted in Edsall, 1984:151)

In the 1950s and 1960s the organized fellow did count, more so in the collective bargaining process than in the broader political arena. In 1953, 35% of the U.S. workforce, excluding agricultural workers, were union members. This figure was comparable to the level of unionization at the end of the Second World War. In other words, the years following the war produced no new gains in the percentage of the workforce organized. By 1960, union membership fell to 31.4% and by 1970 it was down to 27.3%. (Edsall, 1984:142) In 1988, it is down to 17%.

Viewed from the perspective of AFL-CIO leaders, the period from the end of World War II to the early 1970s was a good time for the American labor movement. The American economy was generally on a roll. There were recessions and periods of slower growth, but in general the economy experienced a long wave of growth. The organized workforce reaped the benefits of an expanding economy, as jobs were readily available, real wages increased, and the standard of living of workers improved.

In terms of dollars and cents, the labor movement in America had little complaint. In the politics of prosperity, the business/labor accord seemed unbreakable because while profits were up, so were wages. Social programs also expanded, especially in the 1960s, and an expanding economy provided the money to pay for them. The bargaining power of the labor movement in the manufacturing sector of the economy remained relatively strong. In addition, the expansion of government programs was also beneficial to the labor movement because with it came a new source of organized strength, the government worker.

By the end of the 1960s, the business/labor accord had existed for two decades. Bigger companies within the manufacturing economy had grown accustomed to dealing with unions and recognized the constructive role they played. Unionism as practiced in the U.S. during the 1950s and 1960s had an added benefit for management: more of the responsibility for keeping the workforce in line could be given to unions. The deradicalized labor unions which many businesses negotiated with were by this time reliable players in the system of industrial relations. As known elements in this system, labor unions functioned to blunt the more confrontational impulses of the rank and file. American labor unions seemed to have won their place in the political economy and appeared to be a fixture in the manufacturing sector. As long as they accepted their place and did not question the terms of the business/labor accord, unions would remain part of the corporate liberal institutional framework.

In the political arena, labor unions exercised power as one of many influential interest groups in the 1950s and 1960s. In regions of the country where labor was strong they were able to promote their political candidates, but they were not able to improve their position or reverse the damage done by the Taft-Hartley Act. Media images aside, the American labor movement experienced a decline in its political clout during this time. To be sure, labor leaders had political influence, but it was largely restricted to collective bargaining in organized industries and to a lesser extent as a countervailing force (through defensive actions) to the power of the business community. While labor's political influence was not insignificant, by the 1950s it was unable to shape the nation's larger political agenda.

The extended period of growth experienced by the American economy from the end of World War II through the 1960s concealed many other problems for the labor movement. The economy changed dramatically during this era both in terms of the movement away from a manufacturing economy and the composition of the workforce. Service jobs were becoming more important, and women workers were playing an increasingly significant role in the economy. The traditional base of support for the labor movement--blue collar, industrial jobs--was eroding, while clerical, technical, and professional jobs were expanding. (Edsall, 1984; Davis, 1986)

The warning signals for labor were already present by the beginning of the 1960s, but they could only be seen if the focus of attention switched from the manufacturing core. George Meany was correct in saying that it was the organized fellow that counted. In the areas of the economy which were organized by the labor movement, the union worker did fare comparatively well in the first two decades after the war. However, the main drift in the economy was away from the most heavily unionized industries. The social, economic, and political environment for labor was changing, but the leadership of the labor movement either was unaware of or unwilling to acknowledge the major transformation of American society under way.

It was easier for labor leaders to focus on the power that they still wielded in the collective bargaining process and to a lesser extent in electoral politics. Their main goal during the 1950s and 1960s was to hold on to their stake in the system and to protect their membership. Without a broader set of goals which connected the labor movement to the civil rights movement and the struggle of unorganized workers for social justice, labor's political influence waned. Within the Democratic party, labor was taken for granted, as pressure was applied by other social movements in the 1960s. Since labor leaders during this period did not articulate any other goals beyond protecting their stake in the system, Democratic party leaders brushed them aside. The labor movement had largely attained the economic goals it originally mapped out in the late 1940s. As a result Democrats could retain the support of labor leaders by simply pointing to labor's gains in real wages and benefits.

The prosperity of the 1960s, coupled with the relative isolation of labor's leadership from other progressive forces, prevented the labor movement from seeing the dangers ahead. Labor's inability to take a longer view was the consequence of its break with its radical wing and with left-wing intellectuals during the McCarthy period. The labor movement in the 1960s simply did not have the resources or the connections to other progressive organizations to understand that the economy was leaving unions behind. Nor could it see the importance of developing more activist links to the civil rights and women's movements. Consequently, labor's efforts to support minorities and women were largely confined to lobbying for common legislative goals.

AFL-CIO's allegiance to cold war politics and U.S. government foreign policy coupled with its ouster of labor's left-wing also made it impossible for labor's leadership to develop any ties to the anti-war or student movements. Moreover, the labor movement's failure to develop any independence from the American government on foreign policy issues caused it to be identified with the forces of reaction in the 1960s. The support of some labor leaders for the backlash against the anti-war and student movements created barriers which stood for years between the labor movement and the 1960s generation. The process was reciprocal as students and members of the peace movement did not have extensive ties to the labor movement nor a sympathetic understanding of blue-collar work lives. The end result of the mutual alienation of students from union workers would later be felt by the labor movement when it tried to win younger workers to organized labor's cause.

With the U.S. economy artificially stimulated by the Vietnam war and the unemployment rate low, the consequences of labor's relative isolation would not become clear until the economy stagnated. The main drift of social and economic forces against the labor movement should have been apparent in the 1960s to the national AFL-CIO leadership. Since the mid-1950s private sector unionism has been on the decline. The absolute number of union members continued to increase, but the relative share of the workforce organized by labor dropped. (Freeman and Medoff, 1984) This was due to the rapid growth of the total labor force and the fact that the expansion was occurring in areas of the economy which were unorganized. Even in sectors of the economy which were union strongholds (construction, transportation, and mining), the percentage of union workers declined. (Freeman and Medoff, 1984:221)

If we confine our analysis to the 1950s and 1960s, we can say that it was clear that the union movement was statistically on the decline. Business opposition was growing to the labor movement in all areas except the industrial core and government. Labor leaders certainly could not have anticipated, in the 1960s, the breach of the business/labor accord that occurred in the late 1970s. Nevertheless, the numbers were running against the American labor movement. As Freeman and Medoff report:

> From 1960 to 1961 unions won over 218,000 members through NLRB elections, but union membership fell by 746,000. From 1967 to 1968 unions won 271,695 members through NLRB elections, but union membership rose by 549,000. Despite increased membership from 1967 to 1968, however, the proportion of workers organized remained virtually constant. (Freeman and Medoff, 1984:240)

There were other indicators of labor's weakening position, such as the rate of union success in National Labor Relations Board (NLRB) elections. As Freeman and Medoff put it, private sector unions in the United States were slowly being strangled. A combination of factors was working against the American labor movement, some beyond their control and others which they could do something about. Among the factors discussed by Freeman and Medoff in their discussion of the decline of private sector unions were: 1) the changing structure of the economy; 2) the decline of union organizing efforts; 3) the growth of managerial opposition; 4) the effect of management opposition on union decline; 5) and the changing context of NLRB representation elections. (Freeman and Medoff, 1984, chapter 15)

Nobody could have accurately predicted the effect of other trends which were apparent in the 1960s, such as the rapidly changing economic structure of the United States or the development of new union-busting tactics by management in the 1970s. However, the point which stands out is that the broad trends were there for the AFL-CIO leadership to see, and they did not respond with a program of analysis and action.

Fundamental changes were occurring in the economy and in the federal government during the 1960s. The labor movement benefited from the pressure placed on the federal government by other social movements, but in a time of change and with the Democrats in their strongest position after the 1964 landslide, labor was unable to win any major new legislation. The leadership role of the progressive forces in the United States had passed from the labor movement to the civil rights movement. Moreover, the plight of the "other America" would not be addressed by a unified movement for social justice. Instead, social movements representing various constituencies would confront social issues in a piecemeal fashion.

While the pressure from poor peoples' movements was intense on the federal government, victories were won. Social legislation was passed to address some of the more blatant injustices (discrimination against minorities, barriers that restricted voting rights), but the structure of the economy remained unchallenged. To be sure, the reforms won in the 1960s by social movements were important, but they failed to address the economic roots of injustice. Moreover, many social movements looked to the federal government rather than to a set of institutions under their own control to remedy inequalities.

In this tumultuous period of American history (the 1960s), the labor movement's isolation and inability to shape the larger political agenda became apparent. The glue which might have brought together various social movements into a unified progressive populist movement was a critique of the basic structure of the American economy. The logical place for this kind of a critique to be generated (even if its content did not go beyond European social democratic principles) would normally be the trade union movement. Yet, during this period the American labor movement was so locked into its position as a responsible player in liberal capitalism that it could not provide the basis for a larger critique of the institutional structure of the United States.

In the midst of the 1960s' wave of popular protest, the labor movement could not offer a vision of a fundamentally different society. The opportunity to launch a major organizing drive to bring the mass of unorganized workers into the labor movement was ignored. Such an organizing drive, while late in coming, could have provided the basis for stronger ties between the labor movement and the civil rights movement. (Davis, 1986) In so doing, it might have rekindled the possibilities among progressives for a broader, more unified political coalition.

In terms of legislative power not only was the labor movement unable to successfully battle back against the Taft-Hartley Act, it was also unable to prevent the passage of the Landrum-Griffin Act in 1959. This act further tightened federal control over the labor movement, by giving the government unprecedented rights to meddle in the internal affairs of unions and by extending prohibitions against secondary boycotts. (Yates, 1987:34-35) The inability of the labor movement to exercise veto power over legislation damaging to its interests gave testimony to its diminishing political power.

With Democrats in office for most of the 1960s, including the Johnson landslide, additional questions can be raised about the political efficacy of the national AFL-CIO leadership. In a period when victories were won by other social movements, the AFL-CIO's political agenda which still rested on reversing Taft-Hartley was buried. In instances when the labor movement benefited from the passage of social legislation (voting rights, welfare rights), the impetus for reform did not come from the union movement although labor's lobbying efforts often played a very significant role. Labor's officialdom had by this time forfeited their leadership position among progressives.

While the labor movement was relatively isolated from certain other progressive groups, particularly those with a more activist orientation, it was not unaffected by the social movements of the 1960s. More workers were influenced by the political climate of the period than is often recognized. A wave of insurgency among rank and file union members in the late 1960s and early 1970s reinforced this point. In 1968, more strikes occurred than in 1946 which was the previous high point. The booming economy of the 1960s also gave organized workers increased bargaining power and in turn encouraged day-to-day shop floor struggles. Militant actions by the labor movement were not halted in the 1950s and 1960s but they were largely confined to the local level and remained unconnected to each other. The national leadership of the American labor movement was at best unsupportive of these struggles and at worst openly hostile to them.

When the politics of prosperity came to an end in the early 1970s, the labor movement was politically unprepared to face new challenges. While it is certainly true that labor fought hard within the rules of the game it had agreed to after World War II, it did not have a plan when the rules changed. As the long period of economic growth came to an end in the early 1970s, business and labor headed in different directions. It took time for corporate elites to refine their strategy, but they were not inhibited by their previous commitment to a business/labor accord. That agreement was forged in an era of sustained growth. As it became clear to business elites that the 1970s would be fundamentally different than the previous two decades, they shifted gears. (Clawson and Clawson, 1987)

Corporate elites entered a period of economic stagnation (post-1973) with several advantages. First, they were operating within a legal and political system which stacked the cards against the labor movement. Second, it was easier for elites to develop a plan and coordinate their interests than for labor which was considerably larger, more heterogeneous and relatively lacking in financial resources. Third, economic downturns traditionally strengthened the corporate hand against working people thus, giving elites added economic and political leverage. Fourth, despite their rhetoric to the contrary, corporate elites were never committed in principle to the agreement between business and labor. For big business, the management/labor pact was always a marriage of convenience. Finally, the labor movement had long since lost its momentum and had been lulled into a sense of false security. It is to the changing political and economic climate of the mid- and late 1970s that we now turn.

IV. The Politics of Stagnation (1973-1988)

The 1970s would mark a critical turning point for American business and labor. The optimism of the past was challenged by a changing international setting. The Vietnam War carried special symbolic significance for America, but there were also other social forces at work in the world which would prove equally important.

Among these were the rise of the oil-producing cartel (OPEC), a synchronized world recession in 1974-1975, the growing power of liberation movements in the less developed countries, and increased intra-capitalist rivalries; especially challenges to U.S. domination by Japan and West Germany. The political and economic rules of the game on the international level, which the U.S. virtually dictated to the world after World War II, were drastically altered in the 1970s. The "American Century," which began after the Second World War, was drawing to a close by 1972 and the world was increasingly becoming economically interdependent.

The oil embargo by OPEC countries brought to public attention other problems (wasteful energy practices, industrial inefficiencies, technological backwardness) which had been bubbling underneath the surface of American society since before the start of the Vietnam war. The artificial stimulation of the American economy by the war had delayed the resolution of a number of important social and economic questions relating to the organization and productivity of American business. While the oil-producing countries were often scapegoated in the American press, the oil crisis was only partially responsible for America's economic problems and in fact, hurt Japan and Western Europe more than the United States. There were deeper historical and structural reasons for America's sudden lack of competitiveness. The recession which hit the U.S. in 1974-1975 was the deepest economic downturn since the 1930s' Depression and unlike other recessions after World War II, it was duplicated in the other major capitalist countries. The oil shock, followed by a world-wide recession, convincingly demonstrated that the United States and the world were entering a decidedly different era. In many respects, the American economy and its working population have never completely recovered from this chain of events.

Corporate elites in America reacted to the changing international business context and the stagnating domestic economy with a vengeance. Once they were convinced that the events of 1973-1975 were not just a temporary aberration, they developed plans to restructure the political economy in order to yield higher profits. From the mid-1970s to the present, business elites and their political allies sought to create the political and economic foundation for almost complete domination of American society. (Edsall, 1984; Lekachman, 1987) Their strategy involved more than just minor adjustments in the system. Instead, they sought to abrogate the terms of agreement between capital and labor and reverse the gains made by poor peoples' movements in the 1960s. By waging a concerted attack on the social safety net of poor and working people (the minimum wage, unemployment compensation, workers' compensation, food stamps) and institutions which working people could use (legal aid, the NLRB, OSHA), corporate elites sought to undercut the ability of workers to defend themselves. (Piven and Cloward, 1982)

The stage was set for conflict between the interests of corporate elites and the interests of American workers. The AFL-CIO's options in the 1970s were severely limited by the declining scope of its political power. For the labor movement, this was not the 1930s or even the 1960s. By 1975, the political environment for the labor movement was completely different. As Thomas Edsall notes:

> In 1975 unions began to lose a majority of their attempts to organize nonunion plants and other facilities; for the first time since the passage of the National Labor Relations Act and the creation of the NLRB in 1935, the victory rate in representation elections--that is, elections in which the employees of any individual workplace vote on whether or not to have union representation fell below 50 percent. In 1976, the percentage of the workforce represented by unions fell below 25 percent, the lowest level since 1938. (Edsall, 1984:149)

Within this context the leadership of the national AFL-CIO embarked on a massive lobbying effort to enact labor law reform in 1977 and 1978. The Labor Law Reform Bill of 1977 sought rather mild reforms which were aimed at strengthening the enforcement of already existing labor laws. (Yates, 1987:151) It is especially significant that this bill left standing the major anti-labor provisions of the Taft-Hartley Act. In other words, the labor law reform bill did not pose a substantial threat to business interests. It did seek to restore more balance to the current system of industrial relations which the business community was in the process of altering to better suit its needs. Consequently, even this very moderate labor law reform bill provoked a strong reaction from corporate elites. Its crime was that it ran up against the corporate tide.

With a Democrat in the President's office and a Democratic Congress, the leaders of the AFL-CIO fully expected to win labor law reform. They knew the fight would be difficult so they mounted a strong lobbying campaign on Capitol Hill. The tactics utilized by the labor movement to win passage of the bill were traditional and familiar. (Yates, 1987) Labor's lobbyists went to Congress to twist the arms of labor's "friends." A great deal of money was spent and many legislators were contacted by the AFL-CIO's lobbyists. The bill, however, never reached the floor of Congress and remained stuck in committee. The standard political practices, which the labor movement had effectively employed in the past, failed to work. When push came to shove, enough Democrats abandoned labor's cause so as to prevent the bill from coming up for a vote.

The failure of the labor movement to win labor law reform clearly reflected a changing political and ideological environment. If labor could not even pass a relatively weak bill with the Democrats in power, what could it expect in the future? The fight over the Labor Law Reform Bill was remarkable for another reason--businesses, both large and small, organized a grassroots national campaign against this rather timid bill.

It was the business community, not the labor movement, which galvanized citizen support in a massive effort to turn back this bill. As Michael Yates reports:

> The National Right to Work Committee mailed out
> an astounding fifty million postcards attacking the
> bill; six million of these were returned to members of
> Congress. (Yates, 1987:153)

The joining of forces of this hard-core right-wing group with more
liberal business groups to block labor law reform showed that the
business community was highly organized and in command of direct-
mail methods for reaching the larger population. It also showed that
the business community was unified and had little to fear in terms of
retaliation by labor.

While labor's national leadership seemed to be mired in the
tactics of the past and unwilling to wage a grassroots campaign, a
different pattern was unfolding in Missouri. Here many of the same
forces clashed in a fight over passage of The Missouri "Right to Work"
Initiative. Although in this case labor fought to defend existing law
rather than advance new legislation, labor's tactics were especially
innovative. The right-to-work movement in Missouri set out to pass
legislation in 1978 which would prohibit unions from negotiating
union security clauses with an employer even if the employer agreed to
one. (Yates, 1987:154) Right to work laws are permitted under Taft-
Hartley and had previously been passed in mostly southern states.

Although Missouri is a highly unionized state, polls indicated
a year before the vote was taken that two-thirds of Missouri voters
favored the passage of a right to work law. Surprisingly, at the time of
the poll even 40 percent of the union members in Missouri supported
such legislation. Organized labor's work was cut out for them. With
their back to the wall the labor movement in Missouri had to go
beyond traditional lobbying tactics. A united labor campaign developed
which mobilized the rank and file in the labor movement, reached out to
grassroots organizations, registered new voters, and educated Missouri
citizens on the dangers of this legislation.

The campaign put on by the United Labor Committee against
the right to work bill stepped outside the traditional boundaries of
labor's political tactics. Labor reached out to other interest groups to
form a broad coalition, it refined its communications techniques,
utilized computer technology and outside consultants, and it turned
loose rank and file unionists who understood what was at stake and took
the campaign to the people. (Yates, 1987:161)

These tactics and others mobilized a broad coalition against right to work legislation and turned a sure defeat for labor into an impressive victory. The labor movement and its allies in Missouri won the battle for public opinion and defeated the right to work campaign.

The contrast between the actions of the national AFL-CIO in its efforts to win labor law reform and what occurred in the Missouri right to work fight illustrate the paradoxical position of the labor movement in the late 1970s. On the national level the AFL-CIO failed to mobilize the labor movement and its allies at the grassroots in the battle for labor law reform. The leadership of the AFL-CIO did not recognize the predicament it was in when the labor law reform bill came up for consideration. Even if they did it is unclear whether the labor movement was actually capable of leading a grassroots fight.

In Missouri, the situation was considerably different. The labor movement effectively overcame the special interest label which has plagued the national AFL-CIO. An aggressive counter attack was waged by the labor movement against the right to work bill in Missouri and it proved successful because labor returned to its social movement roots.

As the Missouri example demonstrates, labor still can lead a progressive coalition. On the national level the leadership of the labor movement in the late 1970s was unable to adapt to a changing political environment. It waited in vain for business to play by the rules of the game which labor had grown accustomed to in the era of prosperity.

This was not to happen. In the last two years of the Carter administration things grew even tougher for the labor movement. Once Carter restarted the Cold War machine (Chomsky, 1979) the remainder of his term was dominated by international politics, leaving the labor movement in the lurch. As Edsall notes, polls taken from March 1978 to November 1980 showed that the level of public confidence in labor leaders fell to an average of 13 percent, down from an already low 21 percent in the mid-1960s.

The last two years of the Carter administration laid the groundwork for the Reagan era. The Democrats abandoned any pretense of being the party of social reform and stepped up the forty-year process of militarizing the economy. Even the largest unions were affected by the rapidly changing political and economic climate. As Edsall reports:

> From 1979 to 1982, the unions that lost the largest
> number of members included the Teamsters, one of
> the most affluent and conservative of unions, losing
> 400,000 members from 1977 to 1983; the United
> Auto Workers, which in just one year, from 1981 to
> 1982, lost 8.8 percent of its membership, dropping
> from 1,107,576 to 1,010,595; and the United
> Steelworkers of America, in which the drop has been
> even more precipitous, with membership falling 25
> percent in two years, from 927,869 in 1980 to
> 692,897 in 1982. (Edsall, 1984:161)

While the Carter administration paid little attention to labor's political agenda in its last two years, it did not openly encourage union busting. This would be left for the Reagan administration, which completely shared the business community's goal of stripping the labor movement of its remaining political power.

From the beginning of the Reagan administration, the tone was set for an all-out attack on labor unions. (Edsall, 1984; Lekachman, 1987) Reagan's busting of the thoroughly middle-class air traffic controllers' union (PATCO) was a signal to business to attack the labor movement. Neither PATCO nor the AFL-CIO could stop the Reagan administration's banning of the air traffic controllers union.

The depression of 1981-1982, managed by the Reagan administration, proved to be the worst blow to the labor movement in the 1980s. The administration stood by and watched as unemployment reached disastrous levels, the highest since the 1930s' Depression. The callous indifference of the Reagan administration to human suffering was made worse by its efforts to tighten eligibility requirements for a whole range of essential social benefits. This included placing further restrictions on eligibility requirements for unemployment compensation, food stamps, disability, and welfare benefits.

From the perspective of corporate elites, the 1981-1982 depression accomplished its main task--it disciplined the labor movement by crystallizing workers' fears of economic insecurity for years to come. While the slow down of the economy from the Reagan administration's perspective was necessary to tame inflation, this was only one aspect of a broader pro-business strategy. In the first term of the Reagan administration, the various ideas of business leaders for restructuring the economy and polity came together. The common thread which tied different parts of the corporate-inspired campaign together was the creation of an economic environment that maximized the power of business. (Piven and Cloward, 1982)

To achieve such an environment would require a full scale attack by corporate interests on the wages, working conditions, political, and legal defenses of working Americans. In the 1980s, the goals of business shifted from working within the guidelines of the business/labor accord for a favorable agreement, to completely subordinating workers by ignoring the rules of the game when more favorable terms for business could be imposed. The attack on the social wage by organized business interests and their White House allies would fundamentally change the social, political, and economic landscape.

By the time of the presidential election in 1984, the economy had experienced a partial recovery. It was unlike any previous postwar recovery in that it was uneven and left many people behind. To use Mike Davis' expression, it was a "pathological recovery," based upon a mountain of debt resulting from a massive peace-time military build-up. (Davis, 1986) Military Keynesianism provided the impetus for economic recovery rather than social spending, and thus the benefits of the recovery reached a far narrower segment of the population. Coupled with creative manipulation of the media by the administration, a bungling Democratic campaign, and a large dose of social amnesia, Reagan won a second term by a landslide. The turnout was very low (53% of the eligible voters); Reagan actually won a smaller proportion of the potential electorate (32.3%) than Eisenhower, Kennedy or Nixon in 1960, Johnson, or Nixon in 1972. (Ferguson and Rogers,1986:29)

In Reagan's second term, business consolidated the gains it won between 1981 and 1984. Taking advantage of an anti-union and anti-liberal climate it tried to lay the foundation for its continued dominance into the 1990s. Secure in its knowledge that the Reagan administration would side with them on every important question, corporate elites sought to institutionalize their gains and acquire even greater political leverage. With the Democrats, the labor movement, and other progressive social movements on the defensive, corporate interests were able to set the agenda for debate on the national level.

During the Reagan era, the labor movement tried to correct some of its earlier mistakes and regain its political clout. In terms of getting its message across, making strategic political decisions, using political contributions to aid candidates favorable to labor, and forging unity among its affiliates, the national AFL-CIO improved its performance. Public opinion polls also showed that the public blamed corporate executives much more frequently than labor unions for a company's troubles. The bad-guy image of labor seemed to be fading, especially in light of the excessive greed displayed by some corporate executives in the late 1980s.

While the public image of labor was improving (Gallup Poll, June 1988) late in Reagan's second term, the larger political climate and the bargaining climate for unions was still terrible. Labor leaders were between a rock and a hard place as the internationalization of the economy took its toll on organized workers in America. The labor movement and its leadership were operating within a political economy that gave more and more cards to management. In the long, but uneven recovery occurring after the 1981-82 depression, the manufacturing sector trailed behind and showed no signs of revival, until the dollar's value dropped far enough to cause American exports to increase. Even with the recovery, workers' real incomes continued to drop and the middle class was divided. The top of the middle class, mostly professionals, did well in Reagan's America, while other segments of the middle class, including many unionized workers, found their standard of living taking a dive. By the end of Reagan's second term, America was polarized. A two-tier society of haves versus have-nots seemed to be more of a reality in 1988 than at any time since the 1930s.

Aside from efforts to improve its public relations image and refine its traditional political efforts, the labor movement was tactically at a standstill. As a result of the anti-union atmosphere nurtured by the Reagan administration and the effect which it had on bargaining, many unions were forced into joint efforts with management. Discussion abounded of team efforts, quality circles, and more generally of a new era of labor-management cooperation. Many unions went ahead with programs that sought to institutionalize what was being called the "new industrial relations." (Parker and Slaughter, 1988) The results of such programs, as of the late 1980s, have been mixed at best for the labor movement.

Another strand of the labor movement, originating in rank and file caucuses and among labor figures who either participated in or have knowledge of the militant activities of the 1930s, advocated a return to more adversarial labor relations. To this date, the efforts of this more activist wing of the labor movement have included: attempts to organize unemployed workers, establish an anti-concessions movement, conduct national boycotts and corporate campaigns, resist plant closings through coordinated activities, build international labor solidarity, and challenge official AFL-CIO foreign policy. These efforts by rank and file activists and progressive labor leaders are notable for their willingness to question past labor movement practices and for their fighting spirit. However, they remain sporadic and difficult to coordinate on more than just a local or regional basis. Moreover, they have not as yet found a political framework within which to unify their grassroots activities.

Activists in this wing of the labor movement disagree with the national AFL-CIO's political direction and also do not see increased labor/management cooperation as the answer to labor's problems. Members of the progressive wing of the labor movement, however, seem to have a better idea of what they are against than the principles that they ultimately stand for. Consequently, there are few indications at present that such rank and file activists will coalesce and form the basis for a new direction for the American labor movement.

As the 1990s approach, the American labor movement is faced with difficult choices. With 17% of the workforce organized, the labor movement in the U.S. is heading toward becoming a historical artifact. Organized labor still seems to be searching for a coherent response to the politics of stagnation. The national AFL-CIO leadership seems to believe that with minimal changes, its fortunes could still improve, if the politics of stagnation could be transformed into the politics of prosperity. However, there is no turning back the clock and the 1990s are unlikely to duplicate the long wave of economic growth that America experienced after World War II. In contrast to the national federation, progressives within the labor movement have called for a return to the militant spirit and tactics of a broader social unionism.

In the concluding section, we will examine labor's options and outline the historical possibilities open to it in the 1990s. As the 1980s come to a close, one thing is clear, the American labor movement is at a crossroads.

V. Conclusion

In the course of this chapter, we have reviewed the changing political fortunes, following World War II, of the American labor movement. The high point for organized labor's political influence actually came in the late 1930s, when the CIO was at its peak. After the Second World War, the labor movement did not increase its organizing efforts or its leverage in the political arena. Divided internally over its pledge to fight communism and its commitment to business unionism, the labor movement stumbled into the 1950s and lost its social movement character. With the percentage of the workforce organized in the early 1950s at approximately the same point as immediately after World War II, the American labor movement was at a standstill.

Since the mid-1950s, the American labor movement has experienced a dramatic decline in its ability to win new members and in its political clout. While the economy was booming, and the business/labor compact was in effect, labor was able to exert considerable influence over collective bargaining and retain some of its political leverage in the electoral arena. Even before the economy stagnated, the labor movement was fighting a holding action, trying to keep its membership intact as well as its political influence.

In the midst of the postwar economic boom, it was difficult to discern that the American labor movement was in trouble. The wave of economic growth which the United States experienced concealed organized labor's weaknesses. It was true that from the late 1940s, the labor movement had lost its ability to go on the offensive and was unable to shape the substance of the nation's larger political agenda. Yet, it was only in the 1980s that it became clear that organized labor had lost something more profound--its claim to represent the best interests of the majority of Americans. The principal reasons for joining labor unions, as well as what it meant to be a union member, had become incomprehensible to most workers.

As corporate elites expanded their sphere of influence in the 1980s, they successfully labeled the labor movement a "special interest group." Eight years of reign by one of the most politically conservative administrations in American history had taken its toll. By the late 1980s, the political atmosphere in the United States had become anti-liberal, anti-union, and decidedly pro-business.

By 1988, the social and economic effects of the Reagan administration's policies could no longer be submerged. Poverty was up, homelessness was up, racism and sexism were up, deficits were up and a two-tier society was fast becoming a reality. Despite continued reassurances that the economic recovery would continue, to many Americans it was becoming clear that the economy rested on a foundation of bad checks. Rumblings of discontent emerged in a number of communities and found expression in Jesse Jackson's efforts to forge a coalition of all those who were locked out of Reagan's America.

It is within this political context that we examine the options available to the American labor movement in the 1990s. If organized labor is indeed at a crossroads, how much political power will it wield by the year 2000? Below, we will examine two scenarios for the American labor movement and comment on the likelihood of their occurrence.

Clearly, other scenarios are plausible. These might include: a) a relatively unchanged labor movement which drifts towards the year 2000, b) a labor movement which continues to modernize its political and lobbying tactics without dramatically increasing the percentage of organized workers, c) a union movement which remains relatively unchanged but experiences organizing successes due to favorable demographic trends, d) a labor movement which combines political gains and organizing successes within the context of business unionism and regains the political power it lost in the 1970s and 1980s.

Of the possibilities outlined above, the last scenario clearly represents the most favorable outcome for the union movement. However, even if the labor movement should recapture its past position in the power structure it would be operating in a political system which places considerable restrictions on the scope of its political power. Moreover, political power often is directly related to economic power and the labor movement's economic leverage in the 1980s has been substantially reduced by the restructuring of the American economy.

In the remainder of the chapter we will examine two additional scenarios which involve more fundamental changes in the relationship between business and labor: 1) the American labor movement will experience an even further reduction in its size and political influence and, while it will still exist, it will never regain its previous status as a major league player in capitalism; 2) the labor movement will experience a resurgence, by embracing a 1990s version of social unionism and by participating in a broad coalition of progressive forces. These scenarios are on opposite ends of a continuum and can be boiled down to a single question. Will the American labor movement experience an even greater political decline in the future or will it experience a political revival which tests the boundaries of conventional American politics? By examining polar opposite scenarios we hope to shed light on a wider spectrum of political alternatives and the strategies necessary to accomplish them.

The first scenario, which in the late 1980s appears more likely, has the leadership of organized labor overseeing the downsizing of the labor movement and administering its decline as an independent political actor. In other words, the leadership of the AFL-CIO would continue to accept the groundrules given to it by corporate elites and their political allies and try to survive as best as it can in this environment. As has been the case in the 1980s, this would mean that the labor movement would adopt essentially a defensive posture, hoping that the economy would change for the better and in turn bring about a more benevolent corporate policy. As part of the process of creating a more favorable economic climate, labor would be called on to promote greater cooperation with business.

In political terms, this first scenario might result in either the planned obsolescence of labor as a political force or a new social compact between business and labor. Should such a new social compact develop, it is possible that organized labor would be given a larger voice if it permanently renounced adversarial tactics and became a complete team player. It goes without saying that the team in this case would be a corporate team, with management almost completely in control of the major decisions, and labor serving largely in an advisory capacity. (Parker and Slaughter, 1988)

Since World War II the leadership of the AFL-CIO has shown no inclination to fundamentally challenge the institutional structure of American society. Keeping in mind this political legacy and the fact that the time may have passed for labor to mount an effective challenge to business dominance, the first scenario gains greater plausibility. Labor's existence would depend on its continued usefulness to business in the workplace as a team player and in the polity as a necessary component of an ideological system which pays lip service to democratic institutions, while it solidifies corporate control.

The second scenario, which rests on a political resurgence of the labor movement based on social unionism and the participation of organized labor in a broader progressive coalition, would appear less likely. Several significant factors work against this possible outcome. These include: 1) the long-term trend toward depoliticization in American society, 2) the fragmentation and lack of common political framework among opponents of corporate domination, 3) the lack of a political party to bring together diverse opposition groups and the difficulty that third parties have experienced in American politics, 4) the highly organized business community which currently sets the limits on public policy, 5) the weight of labor's past history of political defeat, and 6) the hold of racism, sexism, and anti-communism on the American population.

Despite this long list of possible factors inhibiting a potential political resurgence by labor, it is important to remember that political climates can change overnight. Who would have predicted in the 1920s the upheaval of the 1930s? Or that the 1950s would be followed by the social movements of the 1960s? In these instances social movements such as the industrial union movement, civil rights movement, and anti-war movement were triggered by a series of events which galvanized popular support. It is difficult to pinpoint a crisis area which could trigger social movements in the 1990s but the "stability" of the Reagan years has depended on mortgaging the country's future and hoping that existing crises would disappear on their own.

While the 1980s have generally been bleak for organized labor, recently there have been several positive signs for the labor movement. Among these are: 1) that after a 20% plunge in union ranks since 1979, the worst is over and membership figures should improve; 2) workers' appeals for organizing help are the highest in years and workers appear more receptive to unionization than any time since 1979; 3) labor shortages in some markets have given workers increased leverage as the fear of job loss declines; 4) labor shortages may also reduce the number of two-tier contracts signed by labor organizations; 5) both minority and women workers are expected to enter the workforce at an increasing rate and both tend to be more favorable to unions than white males.

The demographic trends in the near future appear to be in favor of the labor movement. Labor shortages are more likely in the years ahead as the baby boom's effect is diminished. The workforce will expand much more slowly in the 1990s than in the 1970s and 1980s, and women and minorities will make up a larger part of it. While in recent years the union movement's membership has been dropping as a whole, the number of women union members has been increasing. Women and minority workers may well provide the spark which reignites the labor movement in the years to come. In light of the favorable demographic trends mentioned above, the question still remains, whether the labor movement will develop a broader more progressive political agenda or be satisfied with its traditional political role?

Ironically, the Reagan administration's policies have also unwittingly provided the social basis for a resurgent labor movement. The creation of a more polarized, two-tier society provides the social and material base for a broad coalition movement for social justice, in which the labor movement could play a crucial part.

While the American labor movement can no longer single-handedly organize such a movement, any coalition which develops must include the labor movement as a key element, simply because organized labor still represents a very large bloc of people. The labor movement, however, which joins a possible progressive coalition will have to be considerably different in its attitudes and practices from its present form.

It will have to be more vigorous in fighting sexism and racism inside and outside the workplace and it will have to acknowledge and learn from labor's left-wing. It will also have to come to the defense of unorganized workers in the United States and abroad and make them the focus of its efforts. In other words, the labor movement will have to develop in the future a much broader view of its goals and its mission. This chapter has argued that labor's best hope for escaping the political bind it has been in since the 1940s is to recapture its social movement roots and return to social unionism. Clearly, the labor movement could become stronger in the future even without embracing social unionism but in so doing, it would remain vulnerable to the same political and economic forces that have been responsible for its current decline.

If a new social unionism is what labor needs, we must first define it. The core components of modern social unionism have been outlined by trade union activist and writer, Kim Moody. They include: 1) the realization that the interests of worker and employer, labor and capital, are always opposed; 2) the notion that economic solidarity is the necessary starting point for the improvement of living standards but solidarity also requires social equality within unions. Unions must become a leading force in fighting sexism and racism; 3) union democracy-a union is its membership and a union derives its power from its ability to mobilize the rank and file; 4) organization of the unorganized-to do this requires bringing social concerns such as child care and comparable worth into the workplace; 5) strategic and tactical creativity-traditional methods have failed, therefore new approaches must be developed; 6) internationalism-increased efforts are necessary to build international labor solidarity; 7) active opposition to the current foreign policy line of the AFL-CIO, which has aided the export of U.S. capital by propping up corrupt dictatorships. (Moody, 1986)

The shape of a new direction for the American labor movement in the 1990s will undoubtedly include many of the items outlined by Moody. It is clear that to accomplish this task will not be easy. If labor is to become a social movement again and not just a lobbying group directed by the national AFL-CIO leadership, a major transformation is necessary. This transformation will require major changes by organized labor in its tactics, its goals, its relation to its rank and file, and its relation to other progressive social movements.

The odds are obviously against a political resurgence and a major role in a progressive coalition for the labor movement, especially if a galvanizing issue does not emerge. The labor movement, however, has been regarded before in American history as all but dead but has returned to fight for social justice.

Looking back over the post-World War II period in the United States, two master trends stand out--corporate power has grown enormously and there has been a long-term trend towards depoliticization of the American population. The fate of the American labor movement is implicated in both of these master trends. As the political power of the labor movement in the United States declined after the Second World War, corporate interests stepped in to fill the vacuum. Without the power of the labor movement to check the power of big business, American society became more of a democratic shell than a functioning democracy. More often than not, corporate interests called the tune on major policy questions.

In the absence of a militant labor movement committed to social unionism, Americans lacked an alternative political framework to challenge corporate initiatives. Over a period of decades, Americans grew tired of political debates which did not offer any clear alternatives or vision of a society committed to social justice. Politics and political discussions became passé by the 1980s and political activity became something which the bulk of working Americans did not consider an important part of their lives.

The critical point in this brief overview of post-World War II American politics is that corporate power rose in almost direct proportion to the decline in labor's political influence. Political debate was narrowed as business interests increasingly set the limits of political dialogue.

Historically, the relative strength of the labor movement in the United States has provided a good indicator of the vitality of American democratic institutions. This is also true of Western Europe where strong labor movements, such as in Sweden and Austria, yield broader political debates, extended citizenship rights, and expanded government social programs, compared to the United States. (Edsall, 1984:146-147) To date, the United States as a modern capitalist society is quite unusual in its restricted interpretation of citizenship rights, relatively narrow scope of government activity and planning, and meager social wage provided for its citizens.

We can only conclude that this is the result of an American labor movement which is very weak in comparison to Western European societies and which operates in a political economy dominated by business interests. This chapter has provided a framework to understand the American labor movement's relative weakness and its political decline.

Difficult decisions loom ahead for labor leaders and the rank and file, but the fate of more than just organized labor is at stake. If growing corporate power is not confronted by a substantially revitalized labor movement, there is little hope for achieving a society which maximizes social justice. Only a labor movement which rediscovers its social movement heritage and repudiates business unionism can meet future challenges at home and abroad. For the American labor movement, there is no turning back from the crossroads.

BIBLIOGRAPHY

1. Balliet, Lee, Survey of Labor Relations (Washington, D.C.: Bureau of National Affairs, 1987). An excellent overview of the history of American labor relations and the structure and function of trade unions.

2. Boyer, Richard O., and Herbert M. Morais, Labor's Untold Story (New York: United Electrical Workers, 1955). Recent American labor history from the perspective of rank-and-file workers and the left wing of the labor movement.

3. Cantor, David, and Juliet Schor, Tunnel Vision-Labor, The World Economy, and Central America (Boston: South End Press, 1987). A short book outlining the AFL-CIO's foreign policy errors in Central America.

4. Chomsky, Noam, On Power and Ideology (Boston: South End Press, 1987). Speeches by the noted critic of American government regarding the process by which social control over knowledge and public debate is maintained in the U.S.

5. Chomsky, Noam, Towards a New Cold War (New York: Vintage Books, 1979). An analysis of the Carter administration's restarting of the Cold War and its implications for world politics.

6. Clawson, Dan, and Mary Ann Clawson, "Reagan Or Business? Foundations of the New Conservatism," in Schwartz, Michael (ed.), The Structure of Power in America (New York: Holmes and Meier, 1987). The social, political, and economic roots of the new conservative agenda of American business in the 1970s. It shows that Reaganism existed well before Reagan took office.

7. Cohen, Joshua, and Joel Rogers, Rules of the Game-American Politics and the Central America Movement (Boston: South End Press, 1986). A brief outline of the main features of the American political system and its application to Central American policy issues.

8. Cohen, Joshua, and Joel Rogers, On Democracy (New York: Penguin Books, 1983). A broad sketch of the transformation of the political economy in the United States with special emphasis on growing corporate influence.

9. Collins, Sheila, The Rainbow Challenge (New York: Monthly Review Press, 1986). An insider's account of the 1984 Jackson campaign which is packed with insights about coalition building as well as the changing structure of American politics.

10. Davis, Mike, Prisoners of the American Dream (London: Verso, 1986). An incisive account of American labor's marriage to the Democratic party and the politics of post-World War II capitalist society.

11. Davis, Mike, Fred Pfeil, and Michael Sprinker, The Year Left-- An American Socialist Yearbook (London: Verso, 1985). Part I contains an enlightening discussion of politics in the U.S. since the 1984 election.

12. Eakins, David, "The Development of Corporate Liberal Policy Research in the U.S.," Ph.D. dissertation, University of Wisconsin, 1966. A comprehensive look at elite research and planning groups from the 1930s to the 1960s and their impact on public policy.

13. Edsall, Thomas, The New Politics of Inequality (New York: W.W. Norton, 1984). An excellent overview of the changing nature of American politics. Chapter 4 on labor unions and political power offers brilliant insights into the dilemmas faced by the American labor movement.

14. Fantasia, Rick, Cultures of Solidarity (Berkeley, University of California Press, 1987). An important criticism of survey research as applied to workers and unions. This book contains several interesting case studies of militant actions by rank and file workers.

15. Ferguson, Thomas, and Joel Rogers, Right Turn-The Decline of the Democrats and the Future of American Politics (New York: Hill and Wang, 1986). This volume challenges the notion that Americans have become considerably more conservative in the 1980s.

16. Ferguson, Thomas, and Joel Rogers, The Hidden Election (New York: Pantheon Books, 1981). The best book on the 1980

election. It is packed with insights concerning the political economy and its hidden effects on electoral politics.

17. Ford Foundation, Report of the Study Committee (New York: The Ford Foundation, 1948). The basic planning committee report which guided the foundation as it became a national entity in the 1950s.

18. Freeman, Richard B., and James L. Medoff, What Do Unions Do? (New York: Basic Books, 1984). An important study which updates our view of American unions and the larger system of industrial relations.

19. Gartman, David, Auto Slavery (New Brunswick, N.J., Rutgers University Press, 1986). One of the best books on the history of the American auto industry from the perspective of those who work on the line.

20. Ginger, Ann Fagan, and David Christiano, The Cold War Against Labor, Volumes 1 and 2 (Berkeley, CA: Meiklejohn Civil Liberties Institute, 1987). A comprehensive oral history of the repression of left-wing trade unions in the United States. Contains excerpts from trade unionists who bore the brunt of the McCarthy era witch hunts.

21. Gramsci, Antonio, Selections From the Prison Notebooks (New York: International Publishers, 1971) A definitive statement on ideological hegemony in capitalist society by the noted Italian social theorist. Written in the 1920s, it is still one of the finest treatments of this subject.

22. Green, James R., The World of the Worker (New York: Hill and Wang, 1980). A very well written history of American workers and unions in the twentieth century.

23. Jezer, Marty, The Dark Ages-Life in the U.S., 1945-1960 (Boston: South End Press, 1982). A penetrating critique of the view that little happened in the United States during the 1950s. An important social and cultural analysis of this period.

24. Lekachman, Robert, Visions and Nightmares-America After Reagan (New York: Macmillan Books, 1987). A devastating account of the Reagan era which outlines the limited options which Reagan's successor will have in dealing with larger issues.

25. Mann, Eric, Taking on General Motors (Los Angeles: UCLA Center for Labor Research and Education, 1988). The account of one UAW local which fought a possible plant closing through an organized campaign that mobilized the rank and file.

26. Miliband, Ralph, and Marcel Liebman, "Reflections on Anti-Communism," Monthly Review, July-August 1985, Vol. 37, Number 3. An important treatment of the use of anti-communism by elites to divide and conquer workers and their allies.

27. Mills, C. Wright, The Sociological Imagination (New York: Oxford University Press, 1959) The classic statement on the promise of sociology and the responsibility of social critics.

28. Mills, C. Wright, The New Men of Power (1948, reprinted Fairfield, N.J.: Augustus Kelley Publishers, 1969) A critical look at the changing role of American labor leaders in the 1940s.

29. Milton, David, The Politics of U.S. Labor--From the Depression to the New Deal (New York: Monthly Review Press, 1982). A general treatment of the changing politics of labor unions in America during this crucial period.

30. Moody, Kim, " A New Vision for a New Direction," Labor Notes, November 1986. This article provides a broad outline of the components of a new social unionism which will surely provoke discussion.

31. Oppenheimer, Martin, White Collar Politics (New York: Monthly Review Press, 1985). One of the best recent books on white collar workers, their contradictory class location and their resulting political attitudes.

32. Parenti, Michael, Inventing Reality--The Politics of the Mass Media (New York: St. Martin's Press, 1986). This book places the American mass media in its larger political and economic context and discusses how the media aids corporate interests in the U.S.

33. Parenti, Michael, Democracy for the Few (New York: St. Martin's Press, 1983) A basic critique of the workings of American democracy which shows how corporate elites dominate the political process.

34. Parker, Mike and Jane Slaughter, Choosing Sides: Unions and the Team Concept (Boston: South End Press, 1988). A penetrating study of efforts by unions and companies to develop cooperative labor relations. Its major contention is that the new system of labor relations is potentially more exploitative than earlier systems.

35. Parkin, Frank, Class Inequality and Political Order (New York: Praeger Publishers, 1971). A good overview of class dynamics in capitalist society and the contradictory consciousness it produces within the working class.

36. Piven, Frances Fox, and Richard E. Cloward, The New Class War (New York: Pantheon, 1982). A scathing critique of the Reagan administration's full-scale attack on the social wage.

37. Piven, Frances Fox, and Richard E. Cloward, Poor People's Movements (New York: Vintage Books, 1979). A moving account of social protests by poor people which covers the 1930s and the 1960s.

38. Schwartz, Michael (ed.), The Structure of Power in America- The Corporate Elite As A Ruling Class (New York: Holmes and Meier, 1987). A compilation of some of the best recent power structure research which provides important insights into the organization of big business in America.

39. Shoup, Laurence H. and William Minter, Imperial Brain Trust (New York: Monthly Review Press, 1977). A detailed account of the role of the Council on Foreign Relations in shaping American foreign policy since the 1940s.

40. Williams, Raymond, The Year 2000 (New York: Pantheon Books, 1983). A look into the future by an esteemed social and cultural critic which challenges conventional socialist ideas.

41. Yates, Michael, Labor Law Handbook (Boston: South End Press, 1987). A very well-organized and tightly written guide to

American labor law that places law in its political and economic context.

42. Zinn, Howard, <u>A People's History of the United States</u> (New York: Harper and Row, 1980). This book provides a fascinating account of American history from the perspective of non-elites. An important corrective to standard official histories.

CHAPTER 3

The Constraints of Public Policy: Legal Perspectives on the Decline of the Labor Movement Since World War II

Paul Rainsberger

I. INTRODUCTION

Discussion of legal perspectives on the declining membership and influence of the American labor movement since World War II must be undertaken in a context defined primarily in the 1930s. Specifically, the twelve year period between 1935 and 1947 represents an historical aberration in the development of labor law which radically altered the interrelationship and interdependence of the institutions of federal administrative law and the American labor movement.

The overwhelming legal tradition in the United States has been one of hostility toward organized labor, interrupted by a brief period of at least superficial legal support for the institutions and practices of trade unionism. From the days of the criminal conspiracy doctrine through the application of anti-trust legislation as a union busting device, neither federal courts nor legislators regarded organized labor as much more than an anti-competitive, external interruption to the wheels of the free enterprise system. With a dramatic disruption of popular values in the 1930s and a federal government which attempted to change the assumptions about the interrelationship between the public and private sectors, organized labor experienced a short period of governmental recognition at a level more substantial than token legitimitization. Beginning with the restructuring of federal judicial jurisdiction by the Norris-LaGuardia Act[1] and culminating with the twelve short years between 1935 and 1947, the labor movement succeeded in using the power of the law to advance but became increasingly dependent upon an administrative process which was soon to return to a traditional posture of hostility.

The modern era of American trade unionism is a dichotomy between the recognition of legal rights as the basis for organization and a union tradition of achieving greatest gains through the exercise of extralegal economic power. The modern labor movement has achieved a goal of legitimacy by sacrificing its autonomy and its independence from the legal structure of regulation. A strategy of expediency in using legal procedures to achieve the short term goals of organizing and bargaining collectively has been undertaken at the price of a growing dependency on a hostile regulatory environment.

A.   Relationship between Politics and the Law

Legal and political perspectives on the decline of the labor movement cannot be separated. Much of the political activity of organized labor since World War II has been directed at the goal of preserving legal recognition of labor's institutional goals. At this level, most of the political agenda has been negative, focusing on resistance to undesirable legislation rather than pressing for progressive change.

Since the regulatory mechanism of the National Labor Relations Act[2] was created in 1935, labor has undertaken a constant political and legal struggle to preserve a bureaucracy which is often hostile to the fundamental goals and tactics of the labor movement. Out of dependence upon the legal recognition of the right to organize and bargain and fear of continued erosion of the statutory framework for collective bargaining, organized labor has rarely pressed the assumptions of law. Rather, in both organizing and bargaining activity, unions have pursued a course of moderation and institutional stability. In contrast, the management community has applied pressure to limit the interpretation of worker and union rights under the law. In short, management has controlled the agenda for legal precedent.

With statutory recognition of the right to organize and bargain collectively, the primary focus of union activity has been the practice of collective bargaining with little effort dedicated to expanding the base of wages and working conditions through social legislation. In contrast to the labor movements of most other western industrial nations, organized labor in the United States has looked to collective bargaining as the mechanism for establishing job rights. In doing so, the labor movement has allowed the institutions of administrative law, most notably the National Labor Relations Board, to define the appropriate scope of economic activity. Labor has accepted administrative definition of the methods and goals of the collective bargaining process. The result has been relative success in the economics of collective bargaining through much of the modern era, but declining power for labor organizations in the political arena. As the technology of management and production advanced in response to the economic gains of unions, the net result became an extensive base of benefits for a declining number of organized workers. The labor movement has not been successful, either legally or politically, in expanding its scope of influence into the broad goals of the working class but has been reduced to an interest group acting on behalf of a narrow slice of relatively affluent workers. The gains of union members in the economics of a collective bargaining agreement have not been paralleled in the political and legislative arenas.

Erosion of the legal standing of unions over the past fifty years may be explained either as a cause or a symptom of the administrative structure of modern labor law. The relationship between the administrative system of law and the organized labor movement has been a dialectic interaction of mutual accommodation and hostility. Agencies have adopted the posture of regulators rather than supporters or opponents of organized labor. Union strategies and tactics have been developed in response to real and perceived rulings, precedents and regulatory trends.

B.   Liberal and Conservative Legal Theory

American labor law since the 1930s reflects an important tradition of liberal policy based upon acceptance of conservative premises concerning property rights, the role of the state, and the sanctity of contracts. Union leaders and members often assume that the objectives of Norris-LaGuardia, the Wagner Act and other pieces of New Deal legislation represented a fundamental recognition by the federal government of the rights of workers in the workplace and in the broader political economy. Such respect for the objectives of the legal and legislative process may be misplaced. What the 1930s represent in the development of law is a shift from conservative premises of nonintervention to the liberal theories of controlled regulation. The New Deal developed as a response to recognition that capital can make mistakes, not as a basic shift in public beliefs concerning the inherent rights of owners of property to control that property. The liberal premise for an active government is that the excesses of private ownership should be controlled, not that other sources of rights should be elevated.

Within this context, the central purposes of the Norris-LaGuardia and Wagner Acts are the regulation of abuses of private power, not the elevation of individual or collective rights of workers. The objective of the Wagner Act was to promote industrial peace, not to promote the practice of unionization and collective bargaining. Recognition of the rights of workers to organize and bargain collectively was the vehicle of regulation, not the ultimate purpose of law. Similarly, control of the injunctive power of the courts through Norris-LaGuardia was a statement that courts should not aid capital in exercising its power, not a statement that capital should not have the power to abuse.

Organized labor accepted the framework of liberal regulation of labor in the 1930s and 1940s. After 160 years of legal and legislative hostility, union leaders could be expected to do little else. In fact, the major gains made from 1935 to 1947 would indicate that acceptance of this regulatory compromise was an appropriate political strategy. Moreover, the rapid growth in membership during the same era reinforced the short term benefits of exclusive representation as the basis of organization while perhaps hiding the long term difficulties of expanding an economic and political base.

Organized labor's institutional acceptance of the validity of the liberal model of regulation is compounded by a societal acceptance of the myth of legal detachment.   Judges, adjudicative bodies and arbitrators tend to be regarded as objective, isolated decision makers immune from the pressures of economic reality and class bias. Critics of a particular board or court regard undesirable decisions or precedents as being the product of a subtle shift in political incumbency. However, the integrity of the process is respected as essentially sound and deserving of respect. Within this framework, it is difficult to envision a critical challenge to the premises of liberal regulatory law. Specifically, workers and unions who have become dependent on the regulatory environment of the National Labor Relations Act are reluctant to regard that environment as one which is fundamentally aligned with the interests of private property and against activity which impairs the rights of ownership.

The extent to which liberal legal theory has limited the interests of workers can be demonstrated by a wide range of developments under the National Labor Relations Act and its progeny. Under the detached theory of balancing the inherent rights of property ownership with the statutory rights of workers to organize, bargain and engage in other forms of concerted activity, the National Labor Relations Board and the federal court system have generated a body of precedent which increasingly limits the focus and form of worker collective action. While it is possible to construct a theoretical model of labor law which advances and expands the rights of workers to control their economic and political destinies, such a model would today seem alien to the tradition of dependence on regulatory protection. Respect for the preeminence of the rights of property ownership are too deeply ingrained in the mainstream of American social and legal tradition.

1.   *Myths and Assumptions about New Deal Labor Law*

The short era of rapid growth of organized labor within a system of federal labor law began with the very limited legislative agenda of the Norris-LaGuardia Anti-Injunction Act of 1932. Norris-LaGuardia represents the pinnacle of old (pre-New Deal) liberal legal theory under which Congress attempted to curb the most flagrant abuses of judicial alignment with the interests of capital. The labor injunction and yellow dog contracts had been major weapons of employers in their struggle against workers since the late 1800s, but it was not until 1932 that Congress exercised its jurisdictional power over the federal court system. The use of legal standing and judicial authority as an economic weapon had not escaped the attention of legal scholars and noted jurists,[3] but the judicial system repeatedly demonstrated its collective comfort with the position of property ownership.

Norris-LaGuardia created no new rights for workers or unions. Its sole objective was to restrict the jurisdiction of federal courts to intercede in labor disputes. Labor's enthusiastic acceptance of the act symbolizes the willingness of workers to accept even the most guarded concessions from adversarial institutions. While Norris-LaGuardia is most often cited for what it did, it may be equally significant for its limits. Federal courts retained their authority to enjoin union and worker behavior which transcended narrowly defined boundaries of proper strike and picket behavior. Only the polite primary strike with its symbolic, non-coercive picket line escaped the jurisdictional authority of the federal court system.

The National Labor Relations Act of 1935 (Wagner Act) continued the premises of liberal legal theory into the new arena of active regulation by the federal government. From a theoretical

perspective, the New Deal is significant for the active role of federal
administrative agencies in regulating economic activity. However, the
Wagner Act and other New Deal legislation did little to alter the
fundamental priority of property rights under both traditional
conservative and liberal legal theory. The basic premise of liberal
regulation of only the abuses of power of ownership continued.

As with Norris-LaGuardia, the Wagner Act was hailed as a
Magna Carta for organized labor. However, close scrutiny of the
underlying statement of public policy on which the regulatory
framework was built discloses a different objective. The justification
for the National Labor Relations Act was the Congressional
determination that recognition of the institutional legitimacy of one
model of collective bargaining was an important method for achieving
the primary objective of promoting industrial peace. The failure of
employers to engage in collective bargaining was condemned because it
led to strikes which interfered with the "instrumentalities of commerce,"
not because Congress recognized a basic right of workers to exercise
collective control of the means and methods of production. Moreover,
the principal social benefit articulated in the declaration of public policy
was the consistency of negotiated wage stability with the demand side
macroeconomic policies of the New Deal.[4]

The legal result of the Wagner Act was the institutionalization
of a model of collective bargaining based on the premise of exclusive
representation. A union establishes bargaining rights through its
demonstrated support of a majority of the workers in a bargaining unit.
While the principle of exclusive representation is consistent with the
organizational goal of stabilizing a base of membership, it may serve as
an impediment to expanding the agenda of unionism into broader class
conscious issues and activities. Out of a liberal model of legal
administration came endorsement of a conservative structure of business
unionism.

2.   *From the Wagner Act to Taft-Hartley*

After 160 years of judicial hostility, labor's support for the
New Deal endorsement of collective bargaining was not surprising.
However, it is significant that the popular perception of the law was
more important for the rapid expansion of the labor movement than the
legal theory or administrative rulings. Between 1935 and 1937,
organized labor began a period of ascendancy which has been
symbolized by the successful organization of the General Motors
Corporation by the young United Automobile Workers union. The
historic use of the sit-down strike by autoworkers in Flint and

elsewhere is an example of the gap between legal right and economic power as the basis for worker self-organization. The sit-down strikes occurred during the two year period in which the Constitutional status of the Wagner Act was uncertain. Unions and employers both functioned as though the law would be held unconstitutional, but workers continued to press for recognition in record numbers. The administrative procedures of the National Labor Relations Board were rarely a factor in the establishing of bargaining rights for hundreds of thousands of workers between 1935 and 1937. Moreover, there were serious doubts that the tactics employed by autoworkers as tools of organization would be sanctioned by the Board or courts. The sit-down strike is inconsistent with the priority of property rights under traditional legal theory. In fact, after the strike was used successfully by autoworkers and other unionists, the Supreme Court suggested that the sit-down was not a tactic which enjoyed the protection of the National Labor Relations Act.[5]

The rapid gains experienced by the organized labor movement between 1935 and the end of World War II went beyond the economic arena. Leaders of the AFL and CIO were able to translate economic gain into political influence through their support of the Roosevelt administration during the war years. Political and economic power led to institutionalization of the labor movement and a model of centralized collective bargaining. Political recognition also led to moderation as union leaders took their place in the center of the political spectrum. To preserve integrity in the arena of politics required moderation in economic activity. When confronted with militancy on the shop floor, leadership of the labor movement chose to preserve political respect. Those who pressured for a more militant political and economic presence for workers lost their rooms in the houses of labor.

The political strategy of moderation was unsuccessful. Public opinion continued to shift to the right, and anti-union forces lobbied successfully for major revision of the National Labor Relations Act. The role of the government in labor relations would again be redefined as Congress enacted the Labor Management Relations Act of 1947,[6] commonly known as Taft-Hartley.

The policy of Taft-Hartley represents a major shift from the liberal endorsement of collective bargaining underlying the Wagner Act. While the Wagner Act recognized unionization and collective bargaining as important processes in the assurance of industrial peace and stability, Taft-Hartley was based on a perceived need to curb the power of unions. The role of government shifted from the general encouragement of collective bargaining as a beneficial process to a position of regulating the distribution of power in bargaining relationships.

The substance of the Taft-Hartley amendments was conservative while the structure of regulation continued the liberal model of administrative distribution of power. Under Taft-Hartley, the right of unions to exercise economic power was made subordinate to the individual rights of workers. Legal recognition of class solidarity was displaced by Congressional recognition of the right of individual workers to abandon collective goals. Within the framework of a model of collective bargaining based on exclusive representation, this constituted a significant shift of power to employers. Similarly, the Congressional recognition of the right of states to restrict negotiated union security agreements effectively redistributed bargaining power.

Taft-Hartley represents institutionalization of the perception of unions as a third force in the workforce. Restrictions imposed on union activity are a modern version of the criminal conspiracy doctrine under which associations of workers were prevented from interfering with the sanctity of the individual contract of employment between workers and their employers. Since the enactment of Taft-Hartley, evaluation of the legality of union activity is undertaken with an assumption that the rights of the employer and the individual worker must be accommodated first. Management's right to control the processes of work and the individual worker's right to abandon the union take precedence over the right of unionized workers to bargain collectively and to engage in other concerted activity for mutual aid and protection. Unions are reduced to the standing of a third party intervenor in the employment relationship.

3.   *From Taft-Hartley to the Present*

Taft-Hartley epitomizes both the legal causes and effects of labor's decline since World War II. The dramatic shift in the public policy of labor law parallels the shift from a pattern of union growth to one of decline. The legal standing, membership base and political influence of organized labor entered a prolonged era of decline in 1947. The nature of legislation enacted since 1947 demonstrates the inability of organized labor to reassert its institutional goals.

The most significant legislation concerning labor relations enacted since Taft-Hartley is the Labor Management Reporting and Disclosure Act of 1959,[7] popularly known as Landrum-Griffin. While Landrum-Griffin made some revisions to the regulatory structure of Taft-Hartley, it is the shift in legal recognition of the standing of unions for which the law is most significant.

Landrum-Griffin changed the legal status of labor organizations. Prior to 1959, unions were regarded as private membership organizations and generally exempt from regulation of internal affairs. Two significant developments changed that status. With Taft-Hartley, federal court jurisdiction over collective bargaining agreements and the right of unions to sue and be sued in their own right were codified. That jurisdiction was expanded to include the substance of the law of collective bargaining agreements in the 1957 Supreme Court decision in Textile Workers Union v. Lincoln Mills.[8] The second development was the intensified public and membership concern with corrupt and undemocratic practices which were prevalent within some unions.

Major unions were concerned with the practices of unions with a reputation of corruption. The inability of the American Federation of Labor to control internal practices of its affiliates was one important incentive behind the merger with the Congress of Industrial Organizations in 1955. However, internal efforts to control corruption were ineffective and Congressional inquiry into the scope and nature of such corruption was initiated. The Senate Select Committee on Improper Activities in the Labor or Management Fields, also known as the McClellan Committee, launched extensive public hearings on the presence of corrupt and undemocratic practices in a few important unions. Pressures for reform made clear that the price of political legitimacy for unions included public disclosure and regulation of organizational activities. Congressional debate leading to the enactment of Landrum-Griffin demonstrated diverse pressures for public regulation of internal union practices. Among advocates of various forms of union regulation were rank and file unionists, progressive civil libertarians and anti-union advocates of the business community.

The regulatory framework resulting from Landrum-Griffin is one of the most complex compromises ever enacted. Advocates of democracy within the labor movement were successful in pressuring for minimal safeguards of the rights of members enforced both by individual legal action and regulatory control by the United States Department of Labor. Those who demonstrated a concern for regulation of corrupt practices were successful in including legislation provisions which require financial disclosure of union activities. Other advocates of reform were able to restrict the use of effective concerted activity in labor disputes by tightening the Taft-Hartley limitations on the use of secondary pressure. The least successful political force in fashioning Landrum-Griffin was the AFL-CIO which was unable to convince Congress that labor could maintain order in its own house.

Landrum-Griffin represents the weakened political position of organized labor when faced with direct institutional challenges by the legislative and regulatory community. Unions have had little success in pursuing legislative reform of any basic areas of labor relations law. When revisions of bargaining law have occurred, the developments have been reactive. Postal workers struck the United States Postal Service in 1969 and Congress enacted the Postal Reorganization Act[9] which included stronger jurisdictional controls over activities of postal unions. Postal workers were placed under the jurisdiction of the National Labor Relations Act but only with the clear assurance that there was no right to strike and no right to negotiate union security agreements. Health care workers began to organize in increasing numbers in the early 1970s, and Congress extended coverage of the National Labor Relations Act to non-profit proprietary hospitals. Coverage included rigid controls over the right to strike and picket a health care facility.[10]

In the public sector, the same pattern emerged. In states with a strong base of organized public sector workers, legislative controls were enacted to restrict the forms of collective action. Where public sector unionization was weak, there was little incentive for states to extend recognition of workers' right to organize and bargain. In all but a few states, the one clear pattern is prohibition of strikes by public sector workers. In 1981, a strike by air traffic controllers led to Presidential use of the power of the federal government to terminate strikers. The mass firings of controllers symbolize a new era in which it is politically acceptable for employers to fight collective action by workers with all available legal and economic weapons.

Organized labor made legislative gains through the 1960s and 1970s. However, it is significant that the gains made were in areas of general worker rights, not the institutional interests of unions. Also, gains which were achieved were rarely initiated by unions but represented the collective interests of broad based coalitions of activist organizations. Fair employment practices, occupational health and safety and pension reform were topics of federal legislation. However, unions were only one force for reform and were often slow in committing their support to class-wide legislative regulation of employment practices. When labor pursued legislative reforms which were perceived as limited to the self-interest of unions, as with the labor law reform movement of the 1970s, it was unsuccessful.

The legislative and administrative record of organized labor since 1947 is one which is characterized by an increasing dependence by unions on a hostile regulatory structure. The dilemma facing unions is that basic organizing and bargaining activity is constrained by a legal structure. Unions have allowed the National Labor Relations Board and the federal judiciary to define the acceptable limits of organizing, bargaining and strike behaviors. While unions accept the imposed limitations, the business community aggressively presses for tightening those same limits. Thus, a cycle of increasingly rigid constraints on collective action continues. The environment is hostile to the interests of organized labor, but labor has lost the ability to establish its standing without legal or administrative intervention.

C.   Conceptual Framework--Distribution of Power

In basic areas of labor management conflict, the law is most significant as a reactive force, sanctioning or condemning specific forms of behavior and through this process distributing power between employers and unions. Historically, unions have established power extralegally and have lost power within the legal and administrative process. The legal system can distribute power in labor disputes by defining the acceptable range of behavior. How the definitions are written determines whether employers or unions are placed in a favorable position to exercise power without fear of legal condemnation.

Respect for the law is often more important in the distribution of power than is legal reasoning. For example, in organizing drives, unions have accepted the constraints imposed by the Board. The result is an organizing model that becomes ritualistic. The union develops organizing strategies which reflect NLRB representation case procedures and rulings concerning the balancing of employer property rights with the right of workers to organize. It becomes irrelevant whether or not this is the most effective method of organizing. Strategy is determined not by what is in the interest of the union and workers but by what has been blessed by the Board as acceptable behavior in organizing. Unions pursue a safe, non-controversial course of action designed exclusively for the objective of demonstrating worker support to the satisfaction of the Board. In contrast, management, particularly since the mid-1970s, has been much more willing to press the limits of the law, seeking administrative approval of new and innovative tactics of union avoidance. As in collective bargaining, the party which controls the agenda for change is in a position of power within the administrative process. Management has moved away from the position of legal detachment and has learned to use the regulatory process as a distributor of power. Unions continue to act as though the Board is a neutral and objective arbiter of disputes rather than as a broker of power.

D.   Five Areas of Analysis

Examples of the influence of legal reasoning in the decline of organized labor since World War II can be drawn from five major areas of labor relations law. These are: (1) regulatory involvement in the organizing process, (2) the structure of collective bargaining and enforcement of bargaining obligations, (3) judicial involvement in the resolution of rights disputes and the enforcement of collective bargaining agreements, (4) administrative and judicial intervention in the use of economic power during labor disputes, and (5) the administrative practice and procedures of the National Labor Relations Board. Federal law is significant beyond these five areas of analysis. However, these topics reflect the most direct examples of federal regulation of the collective bargaining process.

II. DISTRIBUTION OF POWER IN ORGANIZING

A.   The Doctrine of Exclusive Representation

In the regulation of organizing activity, the National Labor Relations Board is actively involved in determining procedural and tactical issues. While the National Labor Relations Act leaves open the possibility of minority union representation, the procedural mechanisms for intervention in organizing disputes is centered on the principle of exclusive representation. If a union is certified or recognized as the exclusive representative of workers in an appropriate bargaining unit, the employer may not negotiate with other representatives of the workers. In the absence of a majority representative, the law allows but does not require multilateral negotiations.

After fifty years of regulatory history, the doctrine of exclusive representation has become institutionalized. There is no method available for unions to apply pressure for pluralistic recognition in partially organized plants. As a result, organizing law has become an all-or-nothing process. If the union establishes majority support to the satisfaction of the Board it has bargaining rights and a base of potential members. If it cannot establish such majority support, the union is out and the employer is free to operate on a purely non-union basis.

While the doctrine of exclusive representation allows for the concentration of union bargaining power in organized workplaces, it is a detriment to expanding the membership base of the labor movement. Union-oriented workers are denied participation in labor organizations simply because a majority of their co-workers are not of a similar ideology or have been intimidated into withholding support for unionization. From a historical perspective, the relative ease of establishing majority support for unionization from 1935 through 1947 contributed to the rapid growth of union membership and power. Since Taft-Hartley, the regulatory control of organizing tactics has become more extensive and employers have become more sophisticated in using the law as a delaying tactic to impede union strategy.

The corollary to union certification as an exclusive representation is the ability of workers to use the regulatory process to reject union bargaining rights. Through administrative decertification procedures, the Board may use its election procedures to revoke exclusive bargaining rights of a union. While it is technically illegal for an employer to initiate a decertification process, employers have considerable latitude to indirectly assist anti-union movements in organized shops. Even when a union establishes majority status as a bargaining agent, its continued presence in a growing number of shops is kept under pressure because of the decertification threat.

Statistically, the regulatory barriers to organizing are well documented. In the 1970s and 1980s, the percentage of representation elections which result in certification of an exclusive representation has been in decline, while the number of decertification elections has grown exponentially.[11] A major factor in this trend is the sophistication which employers and labor relations consultants bring into the arena of organizing law.

B. The Pressure for Precedent

Through their attitudes and practices in organizing drives, unions and employers (particularly those employing the services of a management consulting firm) demonstrate radically different perspectives on the goals of representation elections. Unions tend to enter organizing drives with the single, quantifiable objective of winning the votes of a majority of the workers within the bargaining unit. Anti-union employers certainly enter an election campaign with a goal of defeating the union, but employers are also more willing to press the limits of legal precedent to establish the future right to engage in new levels of union avoidance. Legal precedent develops in response to pressure. If unions pursue a safe course of action within established limits of behavior, they are not in a position to expand the list of acceptable organizing tactics. Since the 1940s, union organizing campaigns have been characterized by restraint.

In contrast, employers have little to lose by aggressively implementing new, potentially coercive methods of defeating union organization. Even if the Board or a court determines subsequently that a particular employer tactic is improper, time functions as a strategic tool of the employer. If a union loses a representation election because the employer exceeds acceptable limits of conduct, the standard remedy of the Board is to set aside the election and hold a new one. By the time a second election can be held, the effect of the objectionable tactic has already been felt, and more often than not, the momentum generated by the union in the original organizing drive has been lost due to the passage of time.

The election procedures of the National Labor Relations Board allow considerable room for delaying elections but little means for expediting the process. Delay in organizing under the constraints of Board representation case procedures inevitably works to the advantage of the employer. Thus, the procedures implemented for the purpose of determining whether a union should be certified as a bargaining agent have become a powerful weapon in preventing unions from establishing exclusive bargaining rights.

C.   Preeminence of Property Rights

As in all areas of federal labor law, the Board and courts have frequent occasion to balance the statutory right of workers to organize with the common law right of ownership to control private property. With rare exceptions, the balance of justice inevitably leads to a preferential recognition of property rights. Employer control of the workplace has led to significant restrictions on the right of workers to organize.

The heart of the National Labor Relations Act is section 7 which recognizes the basic rights of workers to organize, bargain collectively through representatives of their own choosing, and to engage in other concerted activity for purposes of mutual aid or protection. Since Taft-Hartley, section 7 also recognizes the right of individual workers to refrain from most forms of union activity. Enforcement of the section 7 rights of workers is accomplished theoretically through the unfair labor practices of section 8. Of particular significance is section 8(a) which states that it is an unfair labor practice for an employer to interfere with, restrain or coerce employees in the exercise of their section 7 rights.

The status of employer property rights in resistance to worker self-organization arises in defenses to unfair labor practice charges alleging employer interference with the section 7 rights of workers. The National Labor Relations Board, with the approval of the Supreme Court, allows employers to defend against many forms of unfair labor practice charges if the employer can claim a legitimate business justification (i.e., property rights) for the coercive action.[12] The list of approved forms of employer interference with worker rights is extensive. In organizing drives, the ability of the employer to restrict employee and organizer solicitation of support for the union and the ability to restrict the distribution of union literature on company property are significant examples of the preeminence of the employer's property rights.

The right of workers to discuss unionization on the job is generally recognized. However, the employer may restrict even this fundamental exercise of self-organization if the restriction is limited in a non-discriminatory manner to actual working times and places.[13] Virtually any concrete step beyond simple oral solicitation of support for unionization is subject to more extensive employer control. Non-employee organizers can generally be prevented from entering the private property of the employer[14] and employers can restrict employee distribution of literature in working areas as long as the employer claims some legitimate justification for the restriction (e.g., the desire to keep the plant free of litter).[15] Discussion of the need to balance property and organizing rights always begins with the premise than owners should be able to do with their property as they see fit even though workers have a direct and substantial reason for being on that property.

The right of workers to control their own labor is not extended the same recognition as the right of the employer to control its property. If workers respond to the property constraints of organizing at the workplace by removing their labor from the control of the employer, the National Labor Relations Act forces the workers to accept the burdensome representation election procedures as the sole means of enforcing their right to organize. If workers strike for recognition, the Board is available to assist employers in controlling the timing of representation elections and the effects of the strike. Under Section 8(b)(7), it is an unfair labor practice for a union to picket for recognition unless the picketing is confined to a relatively short period of time or unless the union promptly petitions for a representation election. The Board is required to seek an injunction against such picketing if the restrictions are not satisfied.[16] The Board can therefore do for the employer that which the employer cannot do directly by obtaining an injunction against peaceful picketing. Such an injunction would otherwise be prohibited by the provisions of the Norris-LaGuardia Act.

D. Legalistic Definition of Rights

In addition to narrowing the rights of workers to organize through recognition of employer's property right defenses to unfair labor practices, the precedents of the National Labor Relations Board have reduced basic rights of workers to legalistic exercises and have expanded the right of employers to exert extensive power over individual workers with little fear of legal sanction. Several important examples illustrate the impact of restrictive Board interpretations of workers' rights in the organizing process.

Among the amendments added to the National Labor Relations Act by Taft-Hartley is the "free speech" provision of Section 8(c). That section states that the expression of any views, arguments or opinions shall not constitute or be evidence of an unfair labor practice if the expression contains no threat of reprisal or promise of benefit. On its face, this amendment represents a neutral recognition of the right to speak freely if such speech is non-coercive. However, as it has been interpreted, the free speech provision is a powerful weapon in the arsenal of anti-union employers. First of all, it must be emphasized that the free speech provision does not apply to employers and workers equally. Section 8(c) does not prevent employers from disciplining workers for disloyal or other non-coercive forms of employee speech.[17] While workers and unions cannot challenge many forms of employer communications because of section 8(c), employers are free to restrict the speech of workers under the general right of management to control the workplace.

The most significant problem with section 8(c) in organizing drives is its interpretation by the National Labor Relations Board. Theoretically, the coercive nature of speech can be evaluated either from the perspective of the sender of the message or the receiver of that message. Despite repeated assertion by the courts and the Board that the coercive nature of speech cannot be determined by a simple dissection of the words selected, the clear pattern in free speech cases is to evaluate speech from the perspective of the message sent by management, not the impact of the message received by workers.[18] If an employer chooses its words carefully it is protected in delivering a message which would be received by a reasonable listener as a threat or promise. Thus, management can predict that dire consequences may result from a decision of workers to unionize, as long as those consequences are not within the direct control of the employer. The fine line distinction between a threatening statement of what the employer will do and a prediction of the general economic impact of a decision to organize is one which may meet a test of logical symmetry, but it is not an effective means of evaluating the coercive impact of speech.

An important right of workers which has been reduced to a legalistic exercise is the right of a worker to refuse to face the accusatory questions of the employer alone. In an important recognition of the rights of workers, the Supreme Court in 1975 decided that a worker who was the subject of an investigatory interview by the employer had the right to request the presence of a union representative.[19] The Supreme Court based its decision on an interpretation of the section 7 right of workers to engage in mutual aid or protection and the section 8(a)(1) restriction on employer interference with the section 7 rights of workers. The history of the Weingarten rights is a classic example of the reduction of worker rights to a vacuum. The first administrative assault on the right to representation was the removal of any effective remedy for employer violations. For a short period the National Labor Relations Board applied an exclusionary rule to violations of the Weingarten rights.[20] If an employer violated the rights, no evidence gathered during the investigatory interview could be used to justify any disciplinary action. By the 1980s, the remedy was reduced to a simple "cease and desist order" unless a worker was disciplined specifically because he or she exercised the right to request representation.[21]

In organizing, restriction of the Weingarten rights was even more dramatic. Although the Supreme Court based its decision on the provisions of Section 8(a)(1), the National Labor Relations Board determined in 1985 that the proper interpretation should have been under the general duty of employers to bargain with exclusive representatives.[22] As a result, the right to the presence of a coworker during investigatory interviews was removed for the non-union workers most in need of the protection. While the right to refuse to face the accusations of one's employer alone would seem to be a fundamental example of worker mutual aid or protection, the Board has reinterpreted the right to be an extension of the bargaining process.

The remedial powers of the Board are a significant cause of employer abuse of representation case procedures. Consistent with the myth of legal detachment, the remedial policies of the Board are considered to be corrective and not punitive. Even if an employer commits wholesale violations of the rights of workers, such behavior is tolerated as long as the employer is willing at some future point to pay a portion of the financial costs of the violations. If an employer fires a substantial number of union advocates immediately before a representation election, the election will in all likelihood result in a defeat for the union. The fact that the employer may subsequently have to reinstate the discharged workers and pay a portion of their lost wages will not enable the union to win a new election. It also will not help the discharged workers pay rent and buy food while they await a Board order of reinstatement. Since the Board remedies are reactive, the employer is free to profit from flagrant violations until a final order is issued.

In cases of flagrant violations designed to affect the outcome of a representation election, the Board has the authority to order the employer to bargain with the union even though the union lost the representation election.[23] Such bargaining orders are issued as remedies for flagrant unfair labor practices which destroy the majority support of the union and make it impossible for the Board to conduct a fair election. Under current Board interpretations, such bargaining orders will be issued only if the union can demonstrate that at some point it had the support of a majority of the workers in the appropriate unit. Although the Supreme Court indicated that it was feasible to envision a situation in which a bargaining order might be appropriate as a remedy for flagrant violations which prevented a union from establishing majority support, the Board is unwilling to extend its remedial power to such cases.[24]

Bargaining order cases are significant because of the gap between theoretical remedies and the realities of collective bargaining. If the employer's flagrant unfair labor practices have destroyed the majority support for a union, the ability of the union to use its bargaining rights are meaningless. Union bargaining power is not based on the presence or absence of a piece of paper recognizing bargaining rights. Bargaining power is based on the support of workers. If the real effect of employer violations is destruction of that support, no remedial order will restore the status quo.

E.   Encouragement of Competitive Unionism

The principle of exclusive representation and the representation procedures of the National Labor Relations Board encourage competitive unionism which is a contributing factor in the decline of union power. Since the certification of exclusive representatives is based on a winner-take-all election process, it is very common for more than one union to seek representation of the same workers. In addition to creating a direct competition between the unions involved, this process allows the employer to whipsaw the unions. A union may assist the employer's anti-union campaign by denigrating the other organizations involved in the campaign. Organizing is a process of competition for the loyalty of workers. From the perspective of the employer, it is irrelevant whether the loyalty of workers for an organization is destroyed by the employer or by another union.

In all organizing campaigns, an employer is free to express opinions about either unionism in general or about the specific unions involved in an organizing campaign. Since the free speech provisions of Section 8(c) extend to substantial misrepresentations of fact, the employer is free to lie about the record or reputation of the unions involved. The effect of this is to give the employer two sources of adverse publicity in anti-union campaigns.

An alternative model of election procedures can be proposed to illustrate the extent to which the representation procedures encourage competitive unionism and factual misrepresentations. If representation election ballots asked simply whether workers wanted representation for purposes of collective bargaining rather than representation by a named union, the incentive for competitive unionism and misrepresentations about a given union would be substantially removed from at least one round of Board election procedures. Hypothetically, the question of which union or unions obtained bargaining rights could be determined in subsequent procedures if there was a jurisdictional dispute. A basic problem with this model is that American unions have a tradition of competition. Such an alternative model of organizing would require unions to elevate the shared goal of expanding the base of the labor movement above the individual organizational goal of obtaining dues paying members. Unions might have to commit organizing resources to a campaign that eventually led to certification of a different organization.

III. COLLECTIVE BARGAINING

The regulation of collective bargaining under the National Labor Relations Act has followed a pattern consistent with the policy of promotion of industrial peace and stability articulated in the act. Collective bargaining, as defined by Taft-Hartley, is the "performance of the mutual obligation of the employer and exclusive bargaining agent to meet at reasonable times, confer in good faith with respect to wages, hours and other terms and conditions of employment."[25] Legal regulation of the practice of collective bargaining is limited, but regulation of the substance of bargaining is a major example of the use of legal precedent to redistribute economic power.

Under Sections 8(a)(5) and 8(b)(3), the National Labor Relations Board regulates collective bargaining through its unfair labor practice procedures. It is an unfair labor practice for either an employer or union with exclusive bargaining rights to fail or refuse to bargain in good faith. Violations may result either from a failure to meet required procedural obligations of bargaining or from a determination that a party has not entered negotiations with a good faith intent to reach agreement.

For the most part, Board regulation of the practice of collective bargaining is consistent with the economic model of bargaining which emerged out of organized labor's position of power in World War II. Labor, not the National Labor Relations Board, developed a model of centralized bargaining in which most issues are reduced to an extension of the economic wage agreement. Labor, management (particularly of basic industries) and the War Labor Board developed the predominant model of the fixed term collective bargaining agreement with a bureaucratic enforcement procedure, binding no-strike and lockout pledges, and institutional union security and management rights clauses.[26] Following World War II, National Labor Relations Board precedent enforcing the duty to bargain generally endorsed this bargaining model of business unionism.

A.   The Subject Matter of Bargaining

In its regulation of collective bargaining, the principal contribution of the National Labor Relations Board to the decline of organized labor has been a result of its ability to classify the subject matter of bargaining. In assessing whether a party has fulfilled the procedural requirements of collective bargaining, an important criterion is whether a proposed subject is considered a mandatory, permissive or illegal subject of bargaining. How the Board classifies a particular subject determines not only the legality of bargaining strategy relating to that subject but also the legality of strikes or other forms of economic pressure applied to obtain acceptance of the proposal.

If a subject of bargaining is classified by the Board as a mandatory subject, negotiation about that subject is required if either side makes a proposal. Because of the statutory proviso that neither party can be forced to agree to any proposal or make any concession, a party may force negotiations to a point of impasse to obtain its position on a proposal concerning mandatory subjects of bargaining. Strikes or lockouts to obtain acceptance of a mandatory subject are also presumed to be legal.

In contrast, efforts to include illegal subjects of bargaining are *per se* unlawful. Neither side may initiate proposals, negotiate to a point of impasse, or strike or lockout to obtain illegal subjects. Subjects which are considered neither mandatory nor illegal are classified as permissive or voluntary subjects. In this amorphous category, power is distributed to the party which controls the status quo. For the vast majority of proposals, this is management. Either party may initiate proposals over permissive subjects, but the other side is within its rights if it refuses to negotiate. Neither side may insist to the point of impasse on inclusion of a permissive subject in a final agreement, and strikes or lockouts to obtain permissive subjects are unlawful.

1.   *Mandatory Subjects and Management's Agenda*

The Board's use of its ability to classify the subject matter of bargaining is significant in the distribution of power for several reasons. In its determination of subjects over which negotiations are mandatory, the Board has included a long list of concerns of workers and union bargaining representatives. However, management rights and zipper clauses are among the most significant of the list of mandatory subjects. Management enters negotiations with a prior position of power, having control over workplace and the means and methods of production. Unions are placed in a posture of attempting to negotiate restrictions on the exercise of that control. With management rights and zipper clauses classified as mandatory subjects of bargaining, management is placed in the enviable bargaining position of being able to insist on only two proposals to preserve its position of power.

The management rights clause reserves to management all rights not eliminated by concessions to the union during the formalities of negotiations, and the zipper clause forecloses union efforts to expand the scope of negotiating during the life of the contract. Without deviating from the legally sanctioned parameters of collective bargaining, management can literally enter negotiations with proposals to preserve the status quo and to include in the executed agreement a management rights and zipper clause. Management can then reject all proposed changes in the status quo offered by the union, await impasse, and if the union strikes, hire permanent replacement workers, implement changes no better than those offered to the union and await decertification.[27] Since the mid-1970s, this has become an increasingly common bargaining scenario for employers in their pursuit of a union-free environment. It is one which can now be pursued without deviation from the established precedent of the National Labor Relations Board.

The forced strike scenario is a clear example of the manipulation of the classification of subjects of bargaining and the effects of such classification. Labor law is a dynamic process under which one set of Board rules triggers a different effect of distributing power. As an abstraction, each set of rulings leading to the legality of this course of action can be justified on the basis of accepted legal precedent. However, the cumulative effect of the separate issues is a concentration of immense power in the hands of management.

2.   *Illegal Subjects and Labor's Agenda*

Illegal subjects are potential issues which have been removed from the bargaining table by Congressional action or judicial or administrative condemnation. While many illegal subjects properly deserve such classification (e.g., invidious discrimination), others represent clear statutory efforts to limit the institutional stability and economic power of unions. Two examples are the restriction on negotiated union security agreements included in the National Labor Relations Act by the Taft-Hartley amendments in 1947 and the prohibition of negotiated hot cargo agreements added by the Landrum-Griffin amendments of 1959.

Secondary pressure is often an effective method of exerting economic power in labor disputes. A producer of goods or services is subject to three distinct forms of economic pressure. A union may attempt to curtail the primary production process by striking the employer with whom the dispute exists. However, the union may accomplish the same goal through secondary pressure applied to suppliers or customers of the product or services of the targeted employer.

Under the auspices of the policy of industrial peace, Taft-Hartley attempted to outlaw most forms of coercive secondary pressure.[28] However, an opening existed in the amended law for negotiated agreements under which unions could obtain the right to refuse to handle struck or non-union goods. Many employers in the strategic transportation and distribution industries could not reject such hot cargo agreements at the bargaining table so the business community turned to Congress for help. The result was section 8(e) of the National Labor Relations Act which prohibited the negotiation of voluntary agreements allowing union members to refuse to handle hot cargo.[29] By removing hot cargo agreements from the agenda, Congress effectively redistributed power in bargaining relationships. The scope of prohibited agreements was extensive, reaching to many forms of picket line clauses and union signatory restrictions on subcontracting as well as the pure hot cargo agreement.

A similar use of legislation to restrict the scope of bargaining occurred with the addition of significant limitations on negotiated union security agreements by Taft-Hartley. The 1947 amendments outlawed the closed shop, placed restrictions on union shop agreements and allowed states to outlaw additional forms of union security agreements. From a theoretical perspective, the addition of Section 14(b) is most significant.[30] Section 14(b) gives to the states the authority to enforce so-called "right to work" laws which prohibit enforcement of many forms of union security agreements. This section is an exception to the general policy of federal preemption in labor relations law under the National Labor Relations Act. The preemption doctrine is an important legal principle for organized labor. If states are permitted to make and enforce radically different laws concerning the bargaining relationship, unions will constantly face a downward pressure on bargaining power. Employers are able to use the most favorable legal climate as a weapon in negotiations. Although Section 14(b) extends only to union security agreements, there is some indication that it does contribute to a redistribution of bargaining power. Most of the twenty states which have enacted right-to-work clauses do have much lower levels of unionization and wages than states without such laws.[31]

The erosion of negotiated union security agreements began with Taft-Hartley but has spread extensively in recent years through a number of Board and court decisions. Unions are severely restricted in the extent to which they can require membership obligations under a union security agreement. Membership has been reduced to a financial transaction with non-payment of dues and initiation fees the only obligation that can be required as a condition of employment.[32] The ability to enforce membership obligations concerning work standards and picket line recognition have also been curtailed through court elevation of the right of a member to resign from full membership at will.[33]   These restrictions on enforcement of union membership obligations are illustrative of the dialectic relationship between legal precedent and union dependency on that precedent. Restrictive legal controls of union security are significant primarily if a union relies on obligated membership. Such restrictions are less important if unions base their power on shop floor solidarity.

3.   *Permissive Subjects and Workers' Agenda*

It is within the broad category of topics which are neither mandatory nor illegal subjects of bargaining that the legal process has been most significant in restricting union bargaining goals. If a subject is classified as permissive, the parties may negotiate but neither party may insist to the point of impasse that the other side accept a proposal. Strikes to obtain permissive subjects are unlawful. The classification of subjects as permissive allows management to refuse all negotiations over those subjects.[34]

The concept of a range of permissive subjects is rational. If a subject is too far removed from the labor-management relationship or deals only abstractly with wages, hours and other terms and conditions of employment, it may be a subject that is appropriately excluded from the range of mandatory negotiations. However, many subjects which are closely tied to the fundamental objectives of organized labor in the bargaining process have been placed by the Board in the classification of permissive topics. By refusing to classify such subjects as mandatory subjects of bargaining, the Board has enforced a narrow model of collective bargaining which leaves management unfettered in its control of basic decisions affecting the stability of work.

There are four major reasons why a subject may be classified as a permissive subject of bargaining: (1) the subject has only a remote connection to wages, hours and other terms and conditions of workers in the represented bargaining unit, (2) the subject is of unilateral interest to either the company or the union, (3) the subject is one which is relevant only to workers who are not part of the bargaining unit, and (4) the subject deals with a procedural prerequisite to bargaining rather than the substance of negotiations. While each of these stated reasons appears to be a rational limitation of the scope of bargaining, when the reasons are applied to actual topics, the result is often significant.

The result of Board authority to determine whether a subject is sufficiently connected to the scope of mandatory bargaining has been a circumscribed definition of conditions of work. The stability of work, the ability of the employer to meet wage demands, the conditions under which work is performed are all related to such basic decisions as price, product design, process technology, and the location of work, but for the most part, the Board has refused to compel management negotiations over such topics, claiming either that the union has no legitimate interest in such negotiations or that the right of management to control its capital without union intervention overrides any interest workers may have in such decisions. Particularly compared to the scope of influence of unions in other advanced industrial democracies, the impact of these decisions has been a narrow scope for union influence in the economics of business.

Many permissive subjects are directly tied to the ability of unions to achieve fundamental objectives in collective bargaining. For example, in negotiations of pension benefits, the Supreme Court has distinguished between benefits for workers currently retired and future benefits for active workers.[35] The unwillingness to compel negotiations over pension benefits for current retirees is justified on the basis that retirees are no longer part of the bargaining unit. This may be a decision that meets an abstract test of statutory interpretation, but it contradicts the history and objectives of pension negotiations. Similarly, the ability of a union to negotiate a strike settlement agreement is directly and substantially connected to the ability of the union to negotiate mandatory subjects during an economic dispute. However, the Board has refused to recognize the connection between the strike for a contract and the contract itself.[36] The strike and its settlement are considered in the same light as the arrangement of chairs around the bargaining table. By reducing strike settlement agreements to procedural prerequisites for negotiations, the Board has exercised significant control over the effective use of power during economic crises.

4.   *Implementation of Unilateral Changes*

The influence of the Board in the subject matter of negotiations is intensified by Board recognition of management's right to control the *status quo.* Under its theory of the right of ownership to exercise broad control over the workplace, the Board has minimized the influence of the union even over those matters classified as mandatory subjects of bargaining. Management is not required to reach agreement with the union as a condition for implementing basic changes in working conditions unless the collective bargaining agreement restricts the specific change proposed. In the absence of such contractual limitations, management may propose changes, negotiate with the union to the point of impasse and then implement the changes unilaterally.[37] During the life of most collective bargaining agreements (with their binding no-strike agreements), this process often leaves the union powerless to resist proposed changes.

As with most Board precedent, the recognition of management's right to control the status quo is logically consistent with its respect for the rights of property. With equal rationality, a more progressive legal tradition could have led to a theory which required agreement with the union as a condition for implementing change. When two interpretations are possible, the Board consistently follows that which elevates property rights and diminishes the bargaining rights of the union.

In recent years, this tradition has been extended dramatically to managerial control over basic capital decisions. The ultimate test of the adequacy of the collective bargaining process is its operation when the issue in dispute is the continued existence of the work. The National Labor Relations Board and the Supreme Court have extended the control of management to the final termination of bargaining unit work with no more than a token obligation to the bargaining process.

B.   Capital Decisions and Their Effects

Since the 1960s, substantial questions concerning the obligation of employers to negotiate over basic capital decisions and the effects of those decisions have reached the National Labor Relations Board and the federal judiciary. Since the important Supreme Court Fibreboard decision in 1964,[38] two distinct theories of the management obligation to negotiate over basic capital decisions developed. Under one theory, management was permitted to implement basic capital decisions unilaterally, subject only to negotiations with the union over the effects of the decision on bargaining unit workers.[39] Under a more liberal theory, the Board occasionally ruled that the termination of bargaining unit work was a mandatory subject over which the employer was required to bargain prior to implementing the proposed changes.[40]

The Supreme Court considered the opposing theories of management's obligation to bargain in the 1981 case of First National Maintenance Corp. v. NLRB.[41] In First National Maintenance, the Court ruled that the employer was permitted to terminate a part of its business without negotiations with the union over the decision to terminate the work. The only obligation of the employer was to negotiate the effects of the decision on the bargaining unit.

Although the Supreme Court emphasized in First National
Maintenance that the factors leading to the decision to terminate the
work were beyond the economic control of the employer, the Board has
since taken a much broader view of management's rights. The Board
requires bargaining over only the effects of capital decisions unless the
union can prove that the decision is motivated specifically by a desire of
the employer to take advantage of lower labor costs elsewhere. As long
as the employer can claim that the decision is based on the general
scope, direction or nature of the business,[42] the union has no right to
negotiate over the decision. In a related set of cases, the Board has ruled
that an existing collective bargaining agreement can be used to restrict
management termination of bargaining unit work only if the contract
contains explicit work preservation language.[43]

These decisions are significant beyond their institutionalization
of the preeminent legal status of management's rights. Leaving unions
with only the *post hoc* right to negotiate the effects of capital decisions
reinforces an insurance policy model of unionization. Union
performance is measured by the adequacies of a severance agreement, not
whether the union can prevent worker dislocation. Management is
given control over both the *status quo* and the instruments of change.
Workers and their bargaining representatives are rendered powerless to
exercise control over the means and methods of work.

IV. CONCERTED ACTIVITY

The fundamental source of power of workers to control wages
and working conditions is the power to withhold their labor. While the
right to strike has long been regarded by workers as a basic right, the
legal system has been very narrow in its recognition of the use of
economic power in labor disputes. The success of a strike is primarily
a function of power, not of legal right. However, the law is significant
in strikes because it distributes power by sanctioning or condemning
specific tactics.

Despite statutory recognition of the right of workers to strike,
the National Labor Relations Act contains extensive restrictions on the
use of economic power in labor disputes. As labor law has developed
under Taft-Hartley, an ends/means test is applied to determine the
legality of specific strikes and tactics. Strikes or picketing may be

condemned as unlawful either if the goal of the activity is improper or if the tactics used exceed standards accepted by the Board and courts.

The framework for any analysis of the legal regulation of economic power is the policy of industrial peace. Use of the strike as an economic weapon is in conflict with the policy of promotion of industrial peace and stability. For a strike to be effective, there must be a disruption of the flow of goods in commerce. When confronted with a dispute between management's right to operate its business and a union's right to strike, the Board and courts have consistently expanded the rights of management through limitations on effective economic pressure.

A.   Policy of Industrial Peace

Enforcement of the policy of industrial peace reduces legal strikes to symbolic protests. Despite the broad assertion of Section 13 of the National Labor Relations Act that "nothing in this Act, except as specifically provided for herein, shall be construed so as either to interfere with or impede or diminish in any way the right to strike, or to affect the limitations or qualifications on that right,"[44] the National Labor Relations Board has an active role in restricting the right to strike. Substantial portions of the 1947, 1959 and 1974 amendments to the Act have outlawed broad categories of strike objectives and tactics.

The principal mechanism for restricting effective strike tactics has been Section 8(b)(4), added by Taft-Hartley, which attempted to prohibit secondary strikes and picketing. Under the stated objective of preserving industrial peace, Congress and the Board have attempted to outlaw any strike which has a substantial impact on any employer other than the primary target of the dispute. From an economic perspective, outlawing secondary strikes and picketing eliminates two of the three methods of applying significant pressure on an employer. Strikes directed at either the suppliers to or customers of a primary employer may be effective economic weapons, but they are considered beyond the protection of the law. Token recognition of the right to strike is extended only to primary strikes.

1.   *Primary and Secondary Activity*

The distinction between primary and secondary activity is most dramatic in picketing cases. Complex tests have been developed by the National Labor Relations Board to confine the effects of picketing to the primary employer. Most insidious are the rules of common situs picketing and reserved gates which restrict both primary and secondary picketing on work sites at which more than one employer are engaged in regular business activities. In the modern economic world, common situs problems are routine, as few employers confine their business activity to remote and isolated locations.

The rules of the National Labor Relations Board concerning common situs picketing demonstrate the restrictive limitations imposed on activity which disrupts commercial activity. Under its Moore Dry Dock decision,[45] the Board outlaws union primary picketing at a secondary site unless four specific conditions are met: (1) the picketing must be confined to times when the situs of the dispute is located on the secondary employer's property, (2) the primary employer must be engaged in its normal business activity on the secondary site, (3) the picketing must be kept reasonably close to the work of the primary employer, and (4) the pickets must clearly disclose the identity of the targeted employer. Even if a union is able to meet these conditions, the picketing is subject to challenge as signal picketing if any zealous picket communicates to workers a desire to instigate more than a symbolic primary effect.

Even at the primary site of the struck employer, a union is restricted from picketing if the employer takes steps to isolate entrances for secondary work. An employer is free to continue business activities, even at the struck work location, as long as it establishes and maintains separate entrances for secondary contractors to use during the strike. Only activities which are directly related to the nature of the labor dispute are excluded from the ability of the employer to continue secondary relations on the primary site.[46]

2.   *Sympathy Strikes*

To exercise the right to honor a picket line, a worker confronting a picket is expected to make instantaneous determinations of the legality and status of that picket. The rules defining the distinction between legal and illegal picketing are among the most complex ever developed under an administrative agency. However, in enforcing those rules, the Board has adopted a convenient and simple formula. If a worker honors an illegal picket line, the worker is engaged in unprotected activity and is subject to disciplinary action by the employer, despite the Section 8(a)(3) prohibition against discrimination to encourage or discourage union activity. A worker is subject to disciplinary action, without recourse to the unfair labor practice procedures of the National Labor Relations Board if it is determined, *post facto,* that the picket line honored did not meet the legalistic tests of the Board.[47] Honoring a picket line may be an act of conscience, but it is measured by the restrictive Board tests of picket line legality.

The right to honor a picket line is compounded by the distinction between honoring a primary picket line at the primary work location and honoring a stranger picket line. The Board has allowed employers to discipline workers who honor legal primary pickets at other locations if the employer establishes some justification for the action.[48] In an important reversal of previous rulings, the Board now considers the right to honor any picket line to be waived by a general no-strike clause.[49]

B.   Preeminence of Property Rights

Board regulation of strikes and picketing is consistent with its overriding policy of protecting the property rights of the employer. Even when workers confine strike activity to the rigid rules of the Board, the employer is protected in its right to continue normal business operations during the course of the strike. The right to continue operations extends even to the ability of the employer to hire replacement workers.[50]

Strikes are classified by the Board as either economic or unfair labor practice strikes depending on the cause of the walkout. If a strike is caused or prolonged by the serious unfair labor practices of the employer, it may be considered an unfair labor practice strike. Otherwise, it will be considered economic. In either case, the employer is free to continue operations and hire replacement workers. However, if the strike is considered economic, replacements may be hired on a permanent basis. While it is an unfair labor practice for an employer to discharge a worker because the worker has engaged in a legal strike, this is a somewhat meaningless protection of the right to strike. For the worker, the distinction between termination and permanent replacement may escape recognition.

Under the law, strikes, pickets and other forms of union economic pressure have been reduced to symbolic acts. If effective pressure is applied by a union during a labor dispute, the opportunity of the employer to obtain Board or injunctive relief against the union activity is substantial. If a union confines its pressure to the limits imposed by the National Labor Relations Board and state and federal courts, the union will be left to the polite strike scenario. With the onset of a strike, token pickets will be established at the primary gates of the employer at the primary work site of the striking workers. No more than three pickets will be maintained at any given gate and no effort will be made to convince anyone to refuse to cross the picket line. At the end of the strike, the workers will take their place at the end of a reinstatement list that will allow them to return to their jobs only as openings arise. They will refrain from even token intimidation of strikebreakers either during the strike or after returning to work, if that ever happens. The law condemns the fundamental right of workers to engage in collective action in solidarity with other members of the working class.

V. ENFORCEMENT OF CONTRACTS

The legal status of collective bargaining agreements and methods of enforcing those agreements is generally consistent with union bargaining goals since World War II. In fact, the federal judiciary has developed a substantive law of collective bargaining agreements which epitomizes the tradition of liberal theory which has predominated labor law since the 1930's. For mainstream unions, that theory is consistent with the practice of collective bargaining since World War II. While such a liberal tradition may contribute to a decline of the labor movement, in this area of law the effect has been endorsed enthusiastically by most unions.

The emergence of a federal law of collective bargaining agreements began with a conflict between the practice of collective bargaining and the common law status of arbitration as a method of dispute resolution. From World War II to the present, a primary method for the enforcement of collective bargaining agreements has been the use of voluntary rights arbitration. However, in most states, agreements to arbitrate were viewed with disdain under the common law. As a result, it was difficult for unions to enforce their arbitration clauses. By 1957, questions concerning the legal status of negotiated arbitration agreements reached the Supreme Court.

A. Grievance Arbitration and the Policy of Peace

The Supreme Court decision in the landmark case of <u>Textile Workers Union v. Lincoln Mills</u>[51] was based on an interpretation of Section 301 of Taft-Hartley. While most scholars had regarded Section

301 as primarily a procedural section establishing federal jurisdiction over collective bargaining agreements, the Court used that section, the declaration of public policy of the Act and assertions in Section 201 and 202 to frame a substantive body of federal law concerning the enforcement of collective bargaining agreements. The Lincoln Mills case involved a grievance dispute in which the employer relied on state common law to reject unilaterally a general agreement to arbitrate. On review, the Supreme Court endorsed the legal theory of arbitration advanced by the union involved.

The Lincoln Mills decision is a classic example of liberal judicial activism. The critical issue before the Court was whether federal courts should enforce a negotiated arbitration clause which would not be enforced under the appropriate state law. In ruling in the affirmative, the Court held that Section 301 should be regarded as the source of a body of substantive federal law concerning collective bargaining agreements. A major premise of that new law was the general policy of Taft-Hartley of promoting industrial peace and stability. The basis for a uniform set of standards of federal law was the need for consistent advancement of the preference for peaceful means of resolving labor disputes. The court recognized that an agreement to arbitrate was negotiated as a *quid pro quo* for the union's concession of a binding no-strike agreement. Since federal law prefers peaceful means of resolving labor disputes, federal courts should give meaning and effect to no-strike agreements by specifically enforcing negotiated arbitration agreements.

Lincoln Mills and its progeny are clearly decisions which advance arbitration as the preferred means of peaceful dispute resolution. Lincoln Mills was followed in 1960 by the Steelworkers Trilogy,[52] three cases which further clarified the legal status of arbitration by removing virtually all questions from the court other than whether a collective bargaining agreement included an arbitration agreement that arguably covered the dispute. Courts were directed to avoid any determination of the merits of the dispute and awards issued by arbitrators were extended a broad presumption of legitimacy.

The extent to which the federal judiciary has endorsed arbitration as the preferred method of dispute resolution is illustrated by two additional Supreme Court decisions which followed Lincoln Mills and the Steelworkers Trilogy. In Teamsters Local 174 v. Lucas Flour Co.,[53] the Court ruled that a no-strike agreement may be implied from a collective bargaining agreement which contains a binding arbitration clause. Under this decision, a union could lose its right to strike in the courts even if the right was preserved in negotiations. The extent to which the policy of peace has been advanced is demonstrated by the absence of a corollary to Lucas Flour. While the courts are free to imply an agreement not to strike from the presence of an arbitration clause, they are not free to imply an agreement to arbitrate from the existence of the no-strike clause.

Following Lucas Flour, the Supreme Court advanced the policy of preference for peaceful dispute resolution to its logical and controversial conclusion. In Boys Market Inc. v. Retail Clerks Local 770,[54] the Supreme Court crafted an exception to the anti-injunction provisions of the Norris-LaGuardia Act. Although Norris-LaGuardia prohibits federal courts from enjoining peaceful strikes, the Supreme Court gave to the courts a conditional exception to Norris-LaGuardia in wildcat strike cases. Under Boys Market, a strike in violation of a negotiated no-strike agreement may be enjoined despite the provisions of Norris-LaGuardia if the underlying dispute is subject to binding arbitration. Employers may obtain injunctions against wildcat strikes as long as the employer is willing to submit the dispute to arbitration.

B.   Impact of Section 301 Law on Union Solidarity

While the federal law of collective bargaining agreements which has developed under Section 301 is generally consistent with modern union objectives in collective bargaining, that law may be a factor in the decline of union power in recent years. The model of collective bargaining which is preferred under negotiated agreements and in the courts is a model which replaces bureaucratic, impersonal grievance procedures for shop floor solidarity as the basis for enforcement of the union position.

Negotiated grievance procedures with binding arbitration are a major source of industrial peace and stability, but little analysis of the cost of that stability for workers and unions has been undertaken. The attitude of labor organizations concerning the nature of disputes has undergone a subtle transformation during the post-World War II era. Disputes are now regarded as rational protests to be resolved peacefully on the relative merits of the parties rather than as fundamental conflicts between management and labor concerning the exercise of power on the shop floor. Solidarity is minimized as disputes are removed from the point of production and resolved instead in conference rooms with closed doors. As union power peaks at the point of production, the grievance procedure has an automatic bias in favor of the management position.

Union power is also undermined in negotiated grievance procedures because of the traditional precedents of contract law in the United States. Any party to a contract is free to breach an agreement if that party is willing at some uncertain future date to compensate the damaged party for the loss suffered. Grievances are reduced to financial transactions rather than matters of principle. Management is free to violate the collective bargaining agreement, capitalize on that violation, create an appearance of union ineptitude because of the inability to prevent the violation, and then after the emotional turmoil of the violation has subsided, compensate the union for the past iniquities.

IV. ADMINISTRATIVE PROCESS

While the judicial law of collective bargaining agreements has been generally consistent with union strategies, the administrative enforcement of the National Labor Relations Act has not. While unions operate on the myth of legal detachment, regarding the institution of the National Labor Relations Board as a structurally neutral entity, management has developed extensive sophistication in using administrative law as a political weapon. As a result, the structure, procedures and precedents of the Board have all become important factors in the distribution of power in labor disputes.

A.   Structural Neutrality or Administrative Activism

As with most agencies emerging from the liberal model of a regulatory government, the National Labor Relations Board is structured to appear as a neutral arbiter of disputes concerning the enabling legislation. Board membership consists of individuals appointed by the President for substantial fixed terms of office to assure agency immunity from the volatilities of politics. Since Taft-Hartley, the structural neutrality has been reinforced by the separation of quasi-judicial and quasi-prosecutorial functions. Taft-Hartley created the office of the General Counsel to prosecute unfair labor practice cases, leaving to the Board *per se* the obligation to resolve contested disputes.

From the 1940s through the early 1970s, the Board operated in a manner consistent with this general model of structural neutrality. Most appointments to the Board and General Counsel positions were professional neutrals, often career bureaucrats employed within the

Board structure. While there were clear political distinctions between some "Republican" Boards and some "Democrat" Boards reflecting the occupancy of the White House, the major difference in the Boards tended to be moderate shifts in policy from relatively liberal to relatively conservative precedent.

The 1980s represent a major shift in the ideology of the Board. Management has become willing to shed the veil of administrative neutrality by engaging in clear efforts to stack the Board membership with advocates of its positions. Career neutrals of both partisan persuasions have been replaced with corporate management attorneys and avowed advocates of management's agenda at the Board. Labor, in contrast, has not pursued this course of activism in the appointment process. Labor responds to appointments with either concern or praise. Union leaders have not been as active as the business community in advancing candidates for appointment.

B.   Administrative Law as a Political Weapon

The procedures of the National Labor Relations Board are as much a source of political power as is the membership of the Board. In organizing and unfair labor practice cases, the procedures of the Board may be as significant in the distribution of power as its most extreme decisions.

In organizing, the ease with which the representation and unfair labor practice procedures may be used to delay certification of union representatives is a major problem for unions. As discussed, above, organizing has been reduced in most cases to a procedural reiteration of Board election requirements. However, the ease with which pre- and post-election procedures may be used to delay the finality of Board action often renders union victories meaningless. Certification has value only if the union is left with sufficient support to exercise its right to bargain.

Union resistance strategies of employers and management consultants are designed to maximize and take advantage of the procedural delays that are inevitable in administrative process. In organizing drives, union power tends to peak at the time the union petitions for a Board representation election. All effort prior to that time is directed at generating substantial support within the bargaining unit. From the time of the petition to the time of the election, the union is placed in a defensive posture, attempting to resist erosion of its support resulting from management tactics. The extent of the shift in power from the petition to the election is extensive, with one study indicating that a union with 62.5% support of a bargaining unit at the time of a petition has a 50% chance of winning the election.[55] The longer management can delay the election, the greater the impact on the organizing drive.

The pro-management bias of representation case procedures is intensified when management is willing to commit unfair labor practices to defeat the union. Unfair labor practices add additional delays to the process, and the inadequate remedies for even the most flagrant violations assure that the destructive impact of violations will never be reversed. Wholesale violations of the law become a calculated cost of resisting the union.

C.   The Deferral Doctrine

In unfair labor practices arising during the life of a collective bargaining agreement, a different procedural problem weakens the ability of unions to enforce statutory rights. Since the 1950s, the Board has developed and enforced a controversial set of deferral doctrines under which the Board privatizes the resolution of many alleged unfair labor practice charges.

1.   Spielberg and Dubo Deferral

The deferral doctrines began in the 1955 Spielberg decision of the Board.[56] That case presented a question concerning the appropriate relationship between Board unfair labor practice procedures and an award of an arbitrator under the collective bargaining agreement. Under the principle of stare decisis, the Board decided that it would accept the arbitrator's award as determinative of the unfair labor practice issue if four conditions were met: (1) the parties must have agreed to be bound by the determination of the arbitrator, (2) the proceedings in arbitration must have appeared to be fair and regular, (3) the decision of the arbitrator must not have been "clearly repugnant" to the purposes and policies of the Act, and (4) the arbitrator must have considered and decided the unfair labor practice issue.

In a related case, the Board expanded the deferral doctrine in 1963 to cases which have not reached arbitration. Under Dubo Manufacturing,[57] if a grievance and unfair labor practice have both been filed, but the grievance has not reached arbitration, the Board will withhold action on the unfair labor practice until the grievance procedure is exhausted. If the grievance procedure results in an arbitration award, the Spielberg criteria will then be applied.

Deferral under Spielberg attempts to merge issues which are fundamentally different. The role of arbitrators is to enforce negotiated collective bargaining agreements, while the role of the Board in unfair labor practice cases is to enforce statutory rights. While there may be consistent principles and facts involved, the issue and authority of the tribunal in the two procedures are inherently different. Among the most vocal critics of Spielberg deferral are arbitrators who do not want to be placed in the position of interpreting and enforcing the unfair labor practice provisions. Because of the reluctance of many arbitrators to consider and decide unfair labor practices, the Board has expanded deferral by accepting awards as long as the same factual conditions led to both the unfair labor practice charge and the grievance.[58] The arbitrator is no longer required to consider and decide the statutory issue directly.

2.   *Collyer Deferral*

The most controversial of the Board deferral doctrines is deferral under the Collyer Insulated Wire precedent established in 1967.[59] Under Collyer, the Board defers to the existence of a grievance procedure rather than to an existent or expected arbitration award. A union is expected to use its grievance procedure to resolve the unfair labor practice issues which are related to a grievance. The Collyer doctrine has been severely criticized as an abandonment of the Board's administrative obligation to enforce the law. While the Dubo and Spielberg doctrines allow deferral, a union seeking to pursue its potential remedies through the Board is not prevented from doing so. Under Collyer, any discretion of the union to shut down the grievance procedure in order to initiate the Board hearing procedures is eliminated. The union is required to exhaust its contractual procedure.

The impact of Collyer is most dramatic when distressed grievance procedures are involved. While the Board does not defer in cases alleging unfair labor practices which are related to breakdowns of the bargaining process, many grievance procedures are overloaded as an indirect result of management assaults on the integrity of the process. In these cases, a union is left with an ineffective grievance procedure to remedy unfair labor practices.

Collyer deferral was established with the Board borrowing the logic of the Supreme Court in Lincoln Mills and the Steelworkers Trilogy. However, the judicial determination that voluntary arbitration is preferable to litigation in resolving contract disputes is based on substantially different conditions than the Board determination that it should give preference to negotiated grievance procedures in the determination of unfair labor practice cases. The issue before a court in a Section 301 suit is identical to the issue presented in arbitration. Each tribunal is charged with the determination of whether the employer violated a collective bargaining agreement. For the court to defer to the expertise of an arbitrator is consistent with the collective bargaining agreement as long as that agreement includes an arbitration clause. However, the issues underlying a grievance and an unfair labor practice charge in Collyer deferral cases are different. The grievance is an allegation that the employer violated contractual obligations while the unfair labor practice charge is an allegation that the employer violated the National Labor Relations Act. Even if the underlying facts are identical, the issue itself is different. An arbitrator is not competent to resolve the legal issue, and the Board is not empowered to enforce the collective bargaining agreement.

From a pragmatic perspective, Board deferral also differs from judicial deferral. While a union might prefer arbitration as a less costly and less time-consuming alternative to litigation, the same logic does not extend to Board deferral. It is significant that the deferral policies of the National Labor Relations Board have been rejected by other federal agencies confronted with overlapping contractual and statutory issues. While other agencies may give considerable weight to an arbitration award, none have become bound to accept private remedies as determinative of public rights.[60]

VII. CONCLUSIONS

The legal system cannot cause organized labor to grow or decline. However, the operation of law can create more or less favorable conditions for the expansion or erosion of unionization. Since the 1930s, both the rapid growth and the gradual decline of the labor movement have paralleled the relative degree of legal sympathy or hostility toward organized labor. From 1935 until 1947, the structure of labor relations law was more favorable for unions than at any time before or after that period of rapid expansion. As the legal system moderated its institutional support of the labor movement, unions entered a prolonged period of decline.

The institutions of labor law in the United States have become a paradigm of liberal regulatory law. Whether the legal system appears at any point in time to be relatively more or less sympathetic to organized labor is an issue subordinate to the clear and consistent policy of promoting industrial peace and stability. For unions to establish and maintain credibility within the legal system of the United States, they must accept the preeminent position afforded to the rights of property within the regulatory state. That is the ultimate paradox for workers in the development of modern labor law. The system which regulates the rights to organize, to bargain collectively and to apply economic pressure in labor disputes is a system which is fundamentally hostile to the goals and tactics of autonomous worker control over the methods of production.

Unionization is tolerated within the legal and political framework of the United States only so long as unions confine their activity to restrictive standards of conduct determined externally. If a collection of workers attempts to exercise autonomous power outside the narrow parameters of administrative, legislative and judicial definition of rights and powers, that effort will be condemned through the combined efforts of management, government and even those unions which have struggled vainly for political legitimacy.

The restrictive model of job-conscious unionism, conceding to ownership the right to control the workplace and reducing labor disputes to formal and symbolic economic transactions, is a model which has a favored place within the regulatory climate of the National Labor Relations Act. That model served a small percentage of the working class well during the prosperous years of the 1950s and 1960s. However, the system is not one which enhances the ability of workers to expand the base of unionization in the United States. Organizing is reduced to a ritualistic set of administrative procedures and collective bargaining is constrained to a financial transaction. The liberal regulatory system works efficiently only if both management and labor enter the arena of conflict in good faith. As management intensified its resistance to even the most conservative forms of trade unionism during the 1970s and 1980s, the regulatory system demonstrated its inability to restore a *status quo* of mutual toleration. For organized labor to reverse the legal implications of decline since World War II, it will be necessary for unions to reassess their support of and dependency on the liberal model of public regulation.

NOTES

1 Anti-Injunction Act of 1932, 47 Stat. 70 (1932), 29 USC Section 101 et seq.

2 49 Stat. 449 (1935), 29 USC Section 151 et seq.

3 F. Frankfurter and N. Greene, The Labor Injunction (New York, 1930).

4 29 USC Section 151.

5 NLRB v. Fansteel Metallurgical Corp., 306 U.S. 249 (1939).

6 61 Stat. 136 (1947), 29 USC Section 141 et seq.

7 73 Stat. 519 (1959), 29 USC Section 401 et seq.

8 355 U.S. 448 (1957).

9 84 Stat. 719 (1970).

10 88 Stat. 395 (1974).

11 For example, in 1968, a total of 7931 certification elections and 239 decertification elections were conducted, with unions winning 57% of the total elections. Thirty-Third Annual Report of the National Labor Relations Board (1968). Fifteen years later, only 3483 certification elections were conducted but the number of decertification elections had grown to 922. The rate of union victories in all elections had dropped to 43%. Forty-Eighth Annual Report of the National Labor Relations Board (1983).

12 See, e.g., NLRB v. Babcock & Wilcox Co., 351 U.S. 105 (1956).

13 See, e.g., Our Way, Inc., 268 NLRB 934 (1983).

14 NLRB v. Babcock & Wilcox Co., supra at note 12.

15 Stoddard-Quirk Mfg. Co., 138 NLRB 615 (1962).

16 29 USC Section 160(1).

17 NLRB v. International Brotherhood of Electrical Workers Local 1229 [Jefferson Standard Broadcasting Co.], 346 U.S. 464 (1953).

18 See, e.g., NLRB v. Gissel Packing Co., 395 U.S. 595 (1969), NLRB v. Herman Wilson Lumber Co., 355 F.2d 426 (8th Cir. 1966), Dal-Tex Optical Co., Inc., 137 NLRB 1782 (1962).

19 NLRB v. J. Weingarten, Inc., 420 U.S. 251 (1975).

20 Kraft Foods, Inc., 251 NLRB 598 (1980).

21 Taracorp, 273 NLRB 221 (1984).

22 Sears, Roebuck and Co., 274 NLRB 230 (1985).

23 NLRB v. Gissel Packing Co., 305 U.S. 575 (1969).

24 Gourmet Foods, 270 NLRB 578 (1984).

25 29 USC Section 158(d).

26 See, J. Gross, The Reshaping of the National Labor Relations Board: National Labor Policy in Transition (Albany, New York, 1981), and R. Chapman, Contours of Public Policy, 1939-1945 (New York, 1981).

27 K. Gagala, Union Organizing and Staying Organized (Reston, Virginia, 1983).

28 E.g., 73 Stat. 542 (1959).

29 73 Stat. 542 (1959).

30 61 Stat. 151 (1947).

31 Of course, it is difficult to ascertain whether a state has low levels of wages and unionization because it is a right-to-work state or whether it is a right to work state because of its low level of unionization.

32 29 USC Section 158(a)(3). NLRB v. General Motors Corp., 373 U.S. 734 (1963).

33 Pattern Makers League v. NLRB, 473 U.S. 95 (1985).

34 NLRB v. Wooster Div. of Borg-Warner Corp., 356 U.S. 342 (1958).

35 Allied Chemical and Alkali Workers Local 1 vs Pittsburgh Plate Glass Co., 404 U.S. 157 (1971).

36 See, e.g., American Optical Co., 138 NLRB 681 (1962).

37 NLRB v. Katz, 369 U.S. 736 (1962).

38 Fibreboard Paper Products, Inc. v. NLRB, 379 U.S. 203 (1964).

39 E.g., General Motors Corp., 191 NLRB 951 (1971).

40 For an excellent discussion of the different theories concerning the duty to bargain over basic capital decisions which followed the Fibreboard decision, see, S. Gacek, "The Employer's Duty to Bargain on Termination of Bargaining Unit Work," Labor Law Journal, October 1981, at 659-678, and November 1981, at 699-724.

41 452 U.S. 666 (1981).

42 Otis Elevator Co., 269 NLRB 891 (1984).

43 Milwaukee Springs Div., Illinois Coil Spring Co. (Milwaukee Springs II), 288 NLRB 601 (1984), superseding, 265 NLRB 206 (1982). The reversal of the Board's position between the two Milwaukee Springs cases is an excellent example of the political realities of Board precedent. In the first decision, the Board ruled

that the presence of a zipper clause and recognition clause allowed the union to refuse to discuss mid-term concessions and prevented the employer from unilaterally moving bargaining unit work. With a change in the composition of the Board by 1984, the case was reconsidered and the new Board ruled that the absence of a work preservation clause prevented the union from stopping the relocation of the work.

44 29 USC Section 163.

45 Sailors Union of the Pacific and Moore Dry Dock Co., 92 NLRB 547 (1950).

46 International Union of Electrical, Radio and Machine Workers Local 761 v. NLRB [General Electric Co.], 366 U.S. 667 (1961).

47 American Telephone & Telegraph Co., 231 NLRB 556 (1977).

48 Business Services Inc., 272 NLRB 827 (1984).

49 Indianapolis Power & Light Co., 273 NLRB 1715 (1985).

50 NLRB v. Mackay Radio and Telegraph Co., 304 U.S. 333 (1938). The date of this decision is an interesting commentary concerning popular perception of the ideology of the original Wagner Act. Immediately after upholding the Constitutionality of the Wagner Act in NLRB v. Jones & Laughlin Steel Corp., 301 U.S. 1 (1937), the Court followed with the Mackay Radio decision reaffirming the preeminence of property rights.

51 353 U.S. 448 (1957).

52 United Steelworkers v. American Mfg. Co., 363 U.S. 564 (1960), United Steelworkers v. Warrior & Gulf Navigation Co., 363 U.S.574 (1960), United Steelworkers v. Enterprise Wheel & Car Corp., 363 U.S. 593 (1960).

53 369 U.S. 95 (1962).

54 398 U.S. 235 (1970).

55 L. Cooper, "Authorization Cards and Union Representation Election Outcome: An Empirical Assessment of the Assumptions Underlying the Supreme Court's Gissel Decision," 79 NW.U.L.Rev. 87 (1984).

56 Spielberg Mfg. Co., 112 NLRB 1080 (1955).

57 Dubo Mfg. Co., 142 NLRB 812 (1963).

58 Olin Corp., 268 NLRB 563 (1984).

59 Collyer Insulated Wire, 192 NLRB 837 (1967).

60 E.g., Alexander v. Gardner-Denver Co., 415 U.S. 36 (1974).

Further Readings

Atleson, James B., <u>Values and Assumptions in American Labor Law</u> (University of Massachusetts Press, Boston, 1983). This is one of the leading contributions to the development of a new critical theory of labor law. Atleson has analyzed the major ideological assumptions of federal administrative and judicial labor law from a sociological and economic perspective.

Aaron, Benjamin, and R. Blanpain <u>Comparative Labor Law and Industrial Relations</u> (Kluwer Law and Taxation Publishers, Norwell, Mass., 1987). This volume is recommended for an international comparative look at labor law and industrial relations policy. It is a summary version for class use of some of the information included in the comprehensive international encyclopedia of labor policy, listed below.

Blanpain, R., editor, <u>International Encyclopedia for Labor Law and Industrial Relations</u> (Kluwer Law and Taxation Publishers, Norwell, Mass., 1989). For detailed international comparisons in labor policy, this multi-volume compilation of national reports, legislation and regional labor policies is a valuable reference.

Chapman, Richard N., <u>Contours of Public Policy, 1939-1945</u> (Garland Publishing, New York, 1981). Much of the explanation for the restructuring of labor policy following World War II can be explained best through the pressures for change which existed during the war years. This book analyzes those conditions which set the stage for Taft-Hartley.

Editorial Staff, <u>Labor Relations Reference Manual</u> (Bureau of National Affairs, Washington, D.C., 1989). Of the various reporters and references services, this is the recommended source for Board and Court decisions in labor law. The Reference Manual and its companion volume, <u>Labor Relations Expeditor</u>, include an excellent classification system and digest which can learned with minimal effort.

<u>The Failure of Labor Law--A Betrayal of American Workers: Report of the Subcommittee on Labor-Management Relations of the Committee on Education and Labor, U.S. House of Representatives</u>

(Government Printing Office, Washington, D.C., 1984). Over the years, there have been many Congressional inquiries into various aspects of labor law and its administrative enforcement mechanisms. This particular report is an interesting critique of the performance of the National Labor Relations Board during one of its most politically charged eras, the early years of the Reagan administration.

Gross, James A., The Making of the National Labor Relations Board: A Study in Economics, Politics and the Law (State University of New York Press, Albany, 1974). In this book and its companion volume, The Transformation of the National Labor Relations Board, Gross has presented a thorough institutional history of the evolution of the National Labor Relations Board from its creation in 1935 through the restructuring of the Board by Taft-Hartley in 1947. The first volume covers the formative years of the Board from 1933 through 1937.

Gross, James A., The Reshaping of the National Labor Relations Board: National Labor Policy in Transition (State University of New York Press, Albany, 1981). This is the second part of the important institutional history of the National Labor Relations Board in which Gross analyzes the impact of Board membership on the shaping of labor policy. This volume covers the period from 1937 through 1947.

Harris, Howell J., The Right to Manage: Industrial Relations Policies of American Business in the 1940s (University of Wisconsin Press, Madison, 1982). While most works on the development of labor law focus on the ideology and interest of unions or the National Labor Relations Board, Harris has filled an important gap with this evaluation of business strategy for the preservation of managerial prerogatives in the 1940s. The discussion of the interrelationship between the National War Labor Board and the NLRB is very useful.

Kairys, David, Editor, The Politics of Law: A Progressive Critique (Pantheon Books, New York, 1982). Kairys has compiled a valuable collection of essays proposing the framework for development of modern Marxist legal theory. Of particular significance to this chapter is Klare, Karl E., "Critical Theory and Labor Relations Law," which uses the *Boys Market* injunction as an appropriate example of the premises of liberal labor law theory.

Lee, R. Alton, Truman and Taft-Hartley: A Question of Mandate (University of Kentucky Press, Lexington, 1966). The impact of the various pressures for revision of labor law after World War II on the Truman administration and the response of Truman is the theme of Lee's work. This volume, with those of Chapman, Gross, Harris, and Lichtenstein, provides a comprehensive view of post-War labor policy formation.

Lichtenstein, Nelson, Labor's War at Home: The CIO in World War II (Cambridge University Press, New York, 1987). After its early years of turbulent growth, the CIO attempted to move into the mainstream of American labor relations during the 1940s. Its successes and failures in the legal, economic and political realities of labor policy are analyzed in this volume.

Millis, Harry A. and Emily Clark Brown, From the Wagner Act to Taft-Hartley: A Study of National Labor Relations Policy and Labor Relations (University of Chicago Press, Chicago, 1950). Harry Millis was chairman of the National Labor Relations Board from 1940 through 1945, an important period during which the Board faced significant pressures from labor, the business community and the National War Labor Board. Millis has presented his analysis of the role of the NLRB in the shaping of federal labor policy and a significant institutional critique of the pressures for reform which culminated with the enactment of Taft-Hartley.

National Lawyers Guild, Employee and Union Member Guide to Labor Law (Clark Boardman, Ltd., New York, 1988). The National Labor Committee of the Lawyers Guild has prepared this two volume practical guide for union activists and attorneys. The materials are updated periodically and present good basic information on the major substantive and procedural issues of labor law.

Ross, Philip, The Government as a Source of Union Power: The Role of Public Policy in Collective Bargaining (Brown University Press, Providence, 1965). While most of the volumes listed here analyze the negative impact on union strategy of post-War labor policy, Ross argues that unions owe much of their success to compulsory bargaining obligations imposed on employers. However, he also suggests that Taft-Hartley made only minor changes to the Wagner Act.

Schlossberg, Stephen and Judith A. Scott, <u>Organizing and the Law</u> (Bureau of National Affairs, Washington, D.C., 1983). Since the release of its first edition in 1967, this book has become a standard reference on the law of organizing. While it is limited in scope, it is of substantial value to anyone actively engaged in organizing activity.

Tomlins, Christopher, <u>The State and The Unions: Labor Relations, Law and the Organized Labor Movement in America, 1880-1960</u> (Cambridge University Press, New York, 1985). Tomlins has prepared an excellent historical analysis of the underlying assumptions of New Deal collective bargaining policy. Although the book covers the evolution of law from the nineteenth century, its emphasis is on the legalistic role of the National Labor Relations Board in defining the constraints of labor-management policy from 1935 through the 1950s.

Yates, Michael, <u>Labor Law Handbook</u> (South End Press, Boston, 1987). Yates has written a simple, straight-forward guide to the most common questions workers raise concerning the operation of the law. The book is able to answer these basic questions while providing significant discussion of the political realities of the operation of the law from the perspective of the rank and file worker.

CHAPTER 4

The Historical Context
of Postwar Industrial Relations

Ronald L. Filippelli

In 1948, George W. Taylor, ex-chairman of the War Labor
Board and one of the leading industrial relations academics and
practitioners in America, wrote that careful analysis of the "labor
problem" in the United States led one to the conclusion that collective
bargaining had to be preserved and strengthened as the "bulwark of
industrial relations in a democracy." Taylor was sanguine about the
prospects for collective bargaining, knowing as he did that by the end of
World War II, practically the whole of America's basic manufacturing
and transportation sectors were unionized. He was pleased that "a rare
unanimity of opinion" existed among industrial relations specialists
that collective bargaining was the most appropriate means for
establishing conditions of employment.[1] Nearly twenty years later
another dean of industrial relations academics, John Dunlop, declared
that the "collective bargaining system must be classed as one of the
more successful distinctive American institutions. . ." According to
Dunlop, the industrial working class had been assimilated into the
mainstream of the community, and had altered the values and directions
of society, "without disruptive conflict and alienation and with a
stimulus to economic efficiency."[2] What Taylor and Dunlop were so
enthusiastic about was what had come to be called the industrial
relations "accord"--a pluralist system based on "free collective
bargaining" between labor and management with government as

impartial regulator. Until recently this reigning paradigm in industrial relations has gone largely unchallenged in spite of overwhelming historical evidence that its core assumption, that management and labor have roughly equal power in the workplace and in the political arena, has never been true. As Katherine Stone has argued, the model is a false description--a set of prism glasses that distorts rather than clarifies the industrial world.[3] Indeed there has never been a time in American history when labor has held anywhere near the power or been accorded anywhere near the legitimacy by society in general or by management in particular that would permit a system such as the pluralist industrial relations model to function. American labor history has been marked by conflict--not primarily over contract issues but over the labor movement's right to exist. Periods of relative success and security for labor have been rare and brief. According to David Montgomery, the history of American workers is neither one of progressive rise from oppression to securely established rights, nor one of irreversible decline from "a moment of democratic process," but of constant struggle. Unions in America have always been fragile institutions trying to survive in an inherently hostile and unstable situation. The fundamental factors that contributed to this hostile environment remain as operative today as at anytime in American history. From this perspective, labor's current agony is merely the latest in a long series of crises.[4]

There is much discussion these days concerning the "decline" of the American labor movement. Surely there can be no question that the past two decades have witnessed the steady retreat of organized labor in the face of punishing defeats on the economic and political fronts. Any reasonably alert observer of labor relations can recite the litany of problems: declining membership, failed strikes, concession bargaining, rising decertifications, organizing paralysis, and growing political impotence. Yet for an historian, this decline, real though it is, reflects a short-term standard of comparison that has the potential to mask the fundamental, and long term, condition of organized labor in the United States. That is to say, what appears to be a dramatic decline when measured against the sudden rise of labor's fortunes from the New Deal through the World War II, looks less exceptional if one places the events of the past thirty years in the context of the entire sweep of the history of industrial America.

I am indebted to Melvyn Dubofsky for analyzing the historical statistics on union membership in the United States.[5] Dubofsky identified five major periods of growth or decline in union membership: (1) 1873-1897, (2) 1898-1920, (3) 1921-1932, (4) 1933-1946, (5) 1947-1970. When one measures the rise and fall of union membership and strike activity using this chronology, it becomes clear that labor's fortunes do not correspond directly to economic cycles. Period two, during which unions experienced considerable growth, was largely marked by economic growth and prosperity. However the third period, one of general prosperity and capitalist expansion, saw a sharp decline in union membership. On the other hand, the years from 1933 to 1939, marked by the deepest depression on record, witnessed remarkable union growth. In other words, the upswings and downswings of union membership cut across periods of economic expansion and contraction.[6]

Prior to the 1930s, Labor's greatest expansion came during Dubofsky's second period, 1898-1920. Indeed union membership rose from 500,000 at the beginning of the period to approximately 5,000,000 by 1920. This amounted to 18.9% of the civilian non-agricultural labor force.[7] Alert readers will note immediately that this figure represents a higher proportion of organized workers than exists in 1989. When one considers that practically all of these workers were in the private sector, there having been no significant unionization among public employees, it becomes clear that current private sector unionization as measured by union density is substantially below what it was in 1920. Taken over the entire period, and using the end of the great depression of the 1890s as a starting point, labor's gains were impressive. Yet a closer look indicates that the membership growth was concentrated in two bursts at the beginning and end of the period. Between 1897 and 1904, total union membership grew fourfold, from 4,440,000 to 2,067,000. Another spurt of growth occurred between 1916 and 1920, which nearly doubled the number of union members.[8] According to David Montgomery, these two periods were also marked by a major upsurge in strike activity over the issues of workplace control.[9] In the intervening years management regained the initiative through a variety of union prevention methods. These were the years of the open shop movement and the surge of injunctions under the Sherman Anti-Trust Act. Both periods of growth were marked by special circumstances. The first corresponded with the prosperity associated with the Spanish-American War, and the second with World War I. In both periods labor benefitted from economic expansion, much of it war related, and in the second period, part of which was during America's involvement in the First World War, government agencies regulated industrial relations to the relative benefit of organized labor. The merchant marine offers an example of this. With American merchant shipping under the control of the Shipping Board during World War I, the membership of the International Seamen's Union nearly tripled.[10]

The gains of the war, as we know, were short-lived. Arising as they did out of special circumstances, they were swept away in the tide of anti-unionism and anti-radicalism that marked the twenties. Between 1921 and 1933 union membership declined to 2,973,000 workers, or by approximately 41%.[11] Most of that decline occurred between 1921 and 1923 as the result of a combination of management anti-unionism, the "Red Scare" campaign against the radicals, the end of the Progressive Era and its replacement by a conservative Republican regime, and a business recession. Forced to tolerate collective bargaining by the federal government because of the Wilson administration's desire for industrial harmony during the war, American management struck back with a vengeance when wartime controls were lifted. By the end of the decade membership was back at about the level of 1914, a year when the American unionization rate was about 20% less than those of European nations with similar income levels.[12] In other words, America's current retrograde position with regard to unionization levels in other advanced market economies is nothing new. American rates approached those of advanced European nations, for example, only under what appear to be historically extraordinary circumstances.

Of course, everyone knows what happened next. Despite the fact that the Great Depression occupied more than half of the period, union membership soared to 13,263,000 workers between 1933 and 1946. Once again the growth was not evenly distributed across the period. Two periods, 1936-1939 and 1941-1944, accounted for 62% of the 10,290,000 new union members.[13] One need not be a historian to recognize that both were marked by exceptional circumstances. The first saw the passage of the Wagner Act and the forging of the New Deal coalition, and the second was shaped by American participation in World War II. Although no one can gainsay the gains made during the 1930s and 1940s, it is well to remember in retrospect that the density levels achieved by the end of the War under the most favorable circumstances in history--approximately 30% of the non-agricultural labor force in unions--were improved upon only slightly shortly thereafter and then quickly began to recede.

This takes us to the fifth period which roughly corresponds to the first two thirds of the period under analysis in this book. Union membership remained stagnant for several years after 1946, then grew between 1950 and 1953 to peak at approximately 32% of the non-agricultural labor force. These were, of course, the years of the Korean War. Once again note the importance of wartime production and government intervention during periods of organized labor's growth. It appears that the combination of these factors, not economic cycles, explains the relatively few surges of union success during the twentieth century. This seems to have been true even during the recent period of declining membership. Although from 1953 to 1986 the decline has been continuous in terms of proportion of the labor force unionized, the one significant growth spurt in absolute members that did occur during those years took place between 1962 and 1970 when membership grew by almost 18%.[14] These years, of course, corresponded with America's involvement in Vietnam and the "guns and butter" policies of the Johnson administration.

Looked at in this fashion, Dubofsky's data are enlightening. While it obviously does not provide explanations for American labor's historically weak position over the past century, it does, it seems to me, put forth a tentative hypotheses to account for labor's relatively few periods of success. Four of the five largest surges in union membership (and strike activity)--1898-1903, 1916-1919, 1941-1945, and 1951-1953--corresponded, at least in part, with wars. Dubofsky suggests that the impact of war and its aftermath--economic, social, and political--is the factor (perhaps even the independent variable) most closely correlated with rises in union membership, strike rates, and all forms of worker militancy.[15] The one growth period that does not fit this mold, 1933-1939, was characterized by an extraordinary domestic crisis which led, for the first time since the Civil War, to the reshaping of the nation's political alignment in a direction favorable, for the first time in history, to organized labor. Dubofsky's data support similar tentative hypotheses of union growth put forward by John Dunlop and Irving Bernstein. Both identified war or economic crisis as the major variables in explaining periods of union growth in American history.[16]

What this suggests is that organized labor's current inability to affect the environmental factors shaping its destiny is nothing new. It makes little sense to blame American labor leadership for this. In spite of all of the charges of sell outs, cooptation, or lack of vision, the United States has had more than its share of dedicated, visionary, and militant labor leaders. But throughout most of its history American labor was, as David Brody has characterized it, essentially a passive agent in relation to its economic setting--lacking the capacity, or even the intention, of influencing the technological, political, or economic changes that were determining its strength.[17] In the earlier, "classical" period of union history which ended in 1933, the small labor movement made up of skilled and highly paid workers was effectively unable to interfere with the structure and functions of an environment of classical capitalism. Its fortunes followed the ups and downs of the economy. After 1933, a much stronger labor movement, at the core rather than the periphery of the economy, partially escaped the constraints of classical markets because of the adoption of Keynesian economic policies by the state. But in the process, because its strength depended in large measure on the continuation of intervention by the government in the economy, it remained largely dependent on external factors, particularly political support, to determine its destiny.[18] As we have seen in recent years, this dependency made labor extremely vulnerable to changes in the structure of the economy, the demographics of the labor force, and changing political alignments.

There is no paucity of explanations for American organized labor's relative weakness--its tendency to operate within, rather than against, the macro tendencies of the American social, economic, and political environment: the absence of a feudal tradition, the early installation of universal white male suffrage, high rates of social mobility, the ethnic, religious, and geographic heterogeneity of the labor force, the pressure valve of the frontier, the high value placed on individualism and independence, and more.[19] The debate among historians as to the relative importance of these factors continues, but its focus is generally limited to their effects on the decision of workers to support unions or to the choices labor made about organizational structure and goals--craft vs. industrial unionism, reform or revolutionary unionism vs. pure and simple unionism, etc. There is a truncated quality about this debate because it generally undervalues the impact of these environmental factors on the other half of the industrial relations equation--management. In other words workers, and unions, are treated as the independent variables. Most of the evidence points to the fact that workers, and their organizations, were more often the acted upon rather than the actors in the unfolding drama. Perhaps some understanding of how that has happened will help us to understand why it continues to function today. In other words, while it is important to acknowledge that in many ways an "exceptional" model of unionism emerged in the American environment, it is equally as important to recognize that American management was and is extraordinarily hostile to unions and has been remarkably successful in preventing collective action on the part of its workers.

The same values that hindered collective action strengthened the legitimacy of management and mobilized public opinion against unions. With few exceptions in American history--the Great Depression being the most notable--employers have easily held the high ground as defenders of American values. One need only think of the ideological underpinnings of the "American Plan" and the open shop campaigns, including the current "right to work" movement. This management hegemony, as much the result of the "exceptional" nature of the American employment relationship as of the unique characteristics of the American working class, forced American labor to cast itself in organizational and ideological terms which brought it into synch with the value system. Thus, "pure and simple" unionism emerged as a solution to survival in a hostile environment.

According to Sanford Jacoby in a recent study, the salient characteristic of the American employment relationship, and a constant which runs from the earliest days of the industrial revolution in America to today, was the extreme hostility of American management for trade unionism. Lloyd Ulman has also suggested that national variations in union density can best be explained not in terms of worker propensities to join unions but as a result of varying national levels of employer hostility to unionism.[20] Instead of concentrating on what made American workers different from workers abroad, one might more profitably examine exceptionalism as it applies to American employers and managers.

While pointing out that in no nation did employers welcome unionization, Jacoby argues that an exceptionally high degree of employer hostility to unions in the United States has led to a number of serious consequences for organized labor, including the highest level of industrial violence in the world, the low density of union membership and the spasmodic character of union growth.

Although labor exceptionalists often attribute the failure of the left to the hostility of American workers for utopian or radical alternatives, Jacoby argues that equal weight should be given to the systematic destruction of radical union movements in the United States by American business with the forces of law and order as willing allies. While repression proved a major hindrance to organized labor as a whole, it was especially destructive to the most radical elements of the labor movement.[21] The effective elimination of a radical alternative to pure and simple unionism removed any incentive for American managers to buy off American workers in order to forestall the coming to power of more radical, even revolutionary alternatives. Jacoby contrasts this to the situation of European managers who often confronted powerful socialist union movements that posed serious threats to the economic order. Employers in countries such as Germany, the Netherlands, and Sweden, countered these threats by buying off workers with collective bargaining and state welfare benefits. In others, such as France and Italy, the challenge was met in the political arena in the framework of class-based politics, not on the shop floor.[22]

In the United States the situation has always been reversed. For a variety of reasons, not the least of which has been business and government repression, the American labor movement has renounced socialism, thus largely rejecting a global solution as a means to reforming the economic and political orders. Even much milder forms of political action have always been carefully circumscribed. This resulted in a truncated syndicalist focus over job control issues such as wages, dismissals, layoffs, job classifications, and production standards. Challenges to management prerogatives in these areas gave American employers strong economic incentives to resist unionization, especially where, in a system characterized by low union density and decentralized bargaining, the cost of being unionized can be substantial. Jacoby contends that this combination, the fear of losing management prerogatives and the higher relative labor costs associated with unionization, has always given American managers very strong incentives to resist unionization drives and to try to rid themselves of unions where they exist.[23]

American managers have not only had powerful incentives to resist unionization, they have also enjoyed a unique set of circumstances which have provided them, with few exceptions, with the means to relegate unions to the margin of American life. Jacoby points out that American managerial ideology came to maturity in the context of a unique pattern of economic development. Prior to the New Deal, the United States had the weakest government in the Western World. It was relatively small, lacked cohesion as a result of the federal system, and exercised little or no directive power over the nation's economic and social development. Indeed, that government should not exercise such power was both an article of faith in the anti-statist creed of American business and a bedrock component of the individualistic American ethic, as well as a precept of pure and simple unionism. Although business enterprise is by nature the fundamental institution in any society built on an advanced market economy, for most of the history of American capitalism the large business corporation in the United States has enjoyed a level of political and institutional power, and legitimacy, unmatched anywhere else in the world.[24] American employers and their management agents never had to share power with other groups--such as a landed gentry, an established church, a military class, or an aristocracy--to achieve their goals, nor did they have to share economic power with the government as did many of their European counterparts. American business confronted no effective economic or political competitors to its expansion or prestige. In this environment of largely unchecked power, union attempts to infringe on management rights through collective bargaining were met with particular vehemence.[25]

The fortuitous circumstances in which American managers have operated have allowed them relatively free reign for their innate anti-unionism. Not only did the state not put forth a coherent industrial relations policy before the New Deal, it willingly supported management's struggle against organized labor. Jacoby points out that, in contrast with the political centralization that characterizes Europe, the decentralized political landscape in the United States has also always played into the hands of employer anti-unionism. Each city, county and state has its own police force and politicians. On the rare occasions when federal courts were not amenable to management pressure, state and local courts were always available. In the American system of collective bargaining, labor disputes are most often local disputes, subject to pressure from local politicians, local newspapers, and local opinion.[26] The advantages that our system of multiple political jurisdictions confer upon management remain significant today. States, counties, and cities vie bitterly with one another to persuade the managers of private capital to locate production in their territories. One of the most common weapons in these battles is the lack of unionization of which a political unit can boast.

The local nature of most labor-management confrontation in the United States was, and is, the perfect setting in which to bring to bear the considerable advantages historically enjoyed by American management. One of these advantages has always been the size of American industry. Jacoby and David Brody both point to the fact that on Average American firms have been larger and more geographically dispersed than most of their counterparts abroad. Size flowed naturally from the early development of mass production in the United States and the great size of the American market. Size also led to the refinement of bureaucracy. Workers in these giant firms suffered from a new imbalance of power. The traditional job control mechanisms of the craft unions were no longer sufficient to confront the professionalized bureaucracy. Events generally supported Max Weber's dictum that bureaucracy was superior to every form of collective action, establishing as it did a form of power relation which was practically unshatterable.[27] The great size of American capitalist enterprises also provided enormous financial resources to battle unions. American firms could often call upon private armies and arsenals beyond the comprehension of a typical firm in Europe where the centralized state monopolized the means of repression.[28]

Had employer repression been based on naked force alone, it might have given rise to a counter force among the working class. That did not happen, not the least because the values that employers called upon to justify their use of extreme methods in defense of property--achievement, individualism, opportunity, and equality--were, and are, shared widely by the American working class. In his classic study, Work and Authority in Industry, Reinhard Bendix showed how management control is facilitated by promoting a set of logically consistent ideas which justify the existing distribution of authority in companies. Bendix started from the premise that domination is easier if those subordinated can be rendered willing to accept the relationship as, in some sense, right and proper.[29] While this was obviously not the case at all times in American history, nor for all workers at any time, it was and is a powerful factor in American history. In 1935 Robert and Helen Lynd, authors of the classic 1920s sociological study, Middletown, returned to Muncie, Indiana, the scene of the study. There, in the midst of the depression, they found a working class caught up in consumerism, not protest--a working class more concerned with holding on to that symbol of the American dream, the automobile, than with unionization.[30] Indeed, polls continue to show that a sizeable portion of the American population continues to espouse the values of entrepreneurial achievement and independence.[31] Not surprisingly, the American managerial class internalizes these values at a high level. They are, according to several studies, at the extreme end of the scale, both nationally and internationally, when traits such as individualism and the importance of personal achievement are measured. This has been true throughout the period of American industrialization. Jacoby has suggested that these deep beliefs of American managers made them particularly hostile to collective bargaining and other goals of unionism. This hostility is complemented by the negative attitudes of a majority of the American people towards unions as demonstrated in public opinion polls over the years.[32]

Management hegemony reached its zenith during the prosperity decade of the 1920s, Dubofsky's third period which was marked by precipitous union decline. Frequently contemporary observers of labor's current agony will point to the similarity of the decline of the 1920s. Although comparisons of historical periods should be undertaken only with the greatest caution, a study of the twenties does illuminate certain of labor's current problems. Factors evident in the period--a conservative, aggressively pro-business government, a weak labor movement, the reorganization of work, the intensive application of new technology, and the "human relations" emphasis of personnel management--are familiar themes to observers of the United States in the last third of the twentieth century.

By the 1920s what Professors Gordon, Edwards and Reich describe as the "homogenization" of labor had reached its climax. From the late nineteenth century on, employers had responded to productivity problems, including the power of craft unions in many enterprises, with mechanization, increased supervision, and less reliance on skilled workers. What emerged came to be known as the "drive system." Its characteristics were an increased capital-labor ratio, an increase in the proportion of operatives, intensified supervision, a decrease in skill differentials, and an expanded labor supply fueled by massive immigration. But homogenization had a contradiction. These innovations produced spreading labor unrest characterized by bursts of strike activity and high labor turnover. In order to counter these by products of the drive system, management introduced a series of reforms that have come to be lumped under the rubric of welfare capitalism.[33]

It should be noted that the bulk of these reforms were instituted after the growth of the labor movement during World War I. The wartime experience of relative cooperation between labor, management, and government had given AFL president Samuel Gompers hope that cooperative labor-management relations were at hand. But although the AFL and the Railroad Brotherhoods were brought in as junior partners in the war effort, strikes and labor unrest increased, not decreased during the war. Just as in the period after World War II, management's basic orientation toward unions was not changed by the experience of increased unionization through government pressure. Employers were determined to quickly restore the pre-war balance of power in industrial relations. In response to Woodrow Wilson's attempt in 1919 to foster union-management cooperation to reduce the level of conflict, managers representing the country's greatest corporations advocated instead a campaign to "extirpate unionism, root and branch, from the United States."[34] The cruder methods used to accomplish this were familiar: industrial espionage, blacklisting of union supporters, red baiting, strike breaking, and the use of private police. That kind of vicious repression did not characterize the period after World War II, nor does it play a major role in the crisis of the labor movement today. But there was a great deal more to the twenties than repression. Then as now, management's goal was to ensure its control of the work place, and then as now, its tools were the reorganization of work and the application of industrial psychology so as to integrate the worker into the "family" of the firm.[35]

This "industrial efficiency" movement took place under propitious circumstances. The magnitude of wartime production transformed a number of industries. Electricity and chemistry led to technological breakthroughs that resulted in more efficient machinery. Technological innovations and the increase in size and complexity of industry accelerated the process of workforce homogenization. The new machinery led to simplified, standardized operations. By war's end, the most numerous group of workers in the major metal working industries were specialized, semiskilled machine operators. Between 1915 and 1920 this category increased by 40% a year in the automobile industry. A 1923 survey of the industry found only 9% in the skilled trades and less than that performing common labor.[36] In the twenties big corporations grew, on the average, three times as fast as smaller ones. The faster they grew, the greater became their problems of management. In 1911, Frederick Taylor, the father of scientific management had written: "No great man can (with the old system of personal management) hope to compete with a number of ordinary men who have been properly organized so as to efficiently cooperate.[37] In this setting scientific management blended economic incentives and industrial engineering techniques to produce the "one best way" for organizing work. By tying the individual worker's wages to output, it was assumed that the worker's interest in higher earnings and the firm's interest in productivity could be made compatible. Management's function was to design the jobs, supervise, and compensate the work force so as to eliminate any potential conflict of interest between workers and employers. Industrial engineering principles, such as time and motion studies and piece rates, were the means to these ends.[38] The point of scientific management, of course, was to bring the shopfloor organization of work within complete control of management. It was the system, par excellence by which Edwards' and Reich's homogenization of the labor force was carried out. Scientific management demonstrated the possibility of breaking many jobs into bundles of specific tasks that could be carefully monitored and measured. The adoption of the assembly line just before World War I added the possibility of pacing the fragmented tasks by machine, reducing worker autonomy even further. Although rarely adopted in its entirety, important aspects of scientific management found disciples in many of America's large companies and remains difficult to dislodge even today.[39]

Of course, scientific management left no room for collective bargaining. Management hostility to trade unionism remained constant. The advocates of scientific management believed that appropriate task design and wage systems would do away with conflict as an inherent part of the employment relationship. Workers needed no outside representation to protect their interests. The effects on craft unionism in the large-scale industrial enterprises were devastating. It made nonstrike weapons such as control of apprenticeship training much less effective by reducing the need for "intuitive" working knowledge. It also made the strike a much less effective weapon. The days when a single craft union could shut down a large manufacturing firm were over.[40]

Along with scientific management came "welfare capitalism." There is no question that welfare capitalism sustained a power system that granted management full authority over the terms of employment, or that its advocates measured its success by the prevention of class consciousness and unionization. But David Brody has also argued persuasively that the rise of welfare work in the large consolidated companies that emerged from the first two great merger movements of the twentieth century had a rationale unconnected to both anti-unionism and productivity. In the words of Elbert Gary, management's trusteeship of its workers was "a simple duty that industry owes to labor,"--an obligation of the "big, broad employers of labor."[41] Discussing U.S. Steel's expenditure of over ten million dollars a year on welfare capitalism in the early 1920s, Judge Gary assured the stockholders that it was necessary "because it is the way men ought to be treated, and secondly because it pays to treat men that way."[42] The movement had its roots in the business consolidation movement of the early years of the century. The larger scale of the major firms increased the resources available for welfare policies. These policies were concentrated in large corporations in industries such as oil, agricultural implements, electrical equipment, automobiles, rubber, meatpacking, and to a lesser extent textiles and steel.[43] While it is true that welfare capitalism was always a minority phenomenon, one survey of large employers found that over 90% of the companies surveyed operated safety programs; 70% had group insurance; and 60% had mutual aid associations. One in five provided formal pension plans, stock purchase opportunities, or savings and loan facilities.[44]

Although the results of welfare capitalism fell far short of the rhetoric of its champions, it is foolish to dismiss it as a failed policy. As Brody pointed out, as an idea that management accepted an obligation for the well-being of its employees, it was a more vital phenomenon than it has seemed from the modern perspective. A significant number of prominent businessmen did seriously attempt to minimize the human problems created by industrialization. Corporate Liberals like Owen Young of General Electric, Walter Teagle of Standard of New Jersey, and Edward Filene of Filene's Department Store in Boston and others instituted employee representation plans on their own, with no pressure from their employees or from unions.[45] Yet no matter the degree of good will and good intentions in welfare capitalism, the measures of its effectiveness were a cooperative labor force and an absence of interest in unionization.

Although the various components of welfare capitalism smoothed the sharp edges of the drive system, it was employee representation that had as its primary function the avoidance of collective bargaining. The motivation and justification for the ERPs should be familiar to observers of the current employee involvement movement.

Although the origins of employee representation, or a systematic and formalized means of communication between owners and workers, can be traced to the early years of the century, the employee representation plan developed by John D. Rockefeller at the Colorado Fuel and Iron Company in 1915, after the horrors of the Ludlow Massacre, was particularly influential in its further development.[46] The movement really took off during World War I when the government, through the War Labor Board, ordered the establishment of shop committees. The Board's purpose was to reduce strikes and labor conflict during the war by encouraging collective bargaining as a normal process in industry.[47] A number of employers also voluntarily adopted plans after 1918, including such well-known concerns as American Telephone and Telegraph, Eastman Kodak, National Cash Register Company, and the Consolidation Coal Company. Following the post World War I strike wave, 317 more companies instituted plans whereby their workers could elect spokesmen from among their ranks.[48] For enlightened industry supporters such as Gerard Swope of General Electric, the plans provided a means through which workers could air their grievances and ideas, and in turn receive an understanding of the policies of their employer. "The men," according to Swope, "must be dealt with as thinking men."[49] But the well-known industrial relations scholar Sumner Slichter understood that for the most part the policies were aimed at preventing workers from becoming class conscious and from organizing trade unions."[50] The advantages to management were clearly put in a report by the National Industrial Conference Board. Executives found plant morale improved by employee representation. Workers were more willing to be flexible, offering suggestions and short cuts that saved money for the company. Grievances could be heard and resolved peacefully. But most important of all, employee representation served to weld management and workers together into a single, cohesive unit, into the "family" of the firm.[51] According to its advocates the advantages of the ERPs over unionization were clear. Unions preached enmity and antagonism, while employee representation offered the rule of reason rather than recourse to the law of the jungle.

Employee representation had nothing to do with scientific management. Taylor and the engineers who followed him did not believe that participation in decision making had much to do with productivity. They believed that under the various incentive systems workers would be well compensated and therefore satisfied. By 1920 a competing model of the social engineering of workplace systems had emerged, one that stressed the social significance of work and work groups. The proponents of the human relations school believed that happy workers would be productive workers. For the advocates of the human relations school, the ERPs provided an ideal channel to give workers a sense of participation and security. This view was given considerable substance in the early thirties by the famous Hawthorne experiments at Western Electric.[52] The scientific management and human relations schools shared a common goal, however. Both believed their approaches would eliminate the adversarial relationship between managers and workers, thus making unions unnecessary.[53] The growth of the human relations school led to the professionalization of the personnel function in a relatively few, highly influential firms. Many of the functions formerly controlled by the foremen--hiring, firing, discipline, promotion, and compensation policies--were now carried out from standardized and centralized personnel departments. Also controlled and managed by these new professionals were the employee representation plans and the anti-union open shop movement that flourished side by side during the 1920s. Thus, what we now know as "union avoidance" was a fundamental part of the professionalized personnel function from the beginning.

Neither employee representation nor the professionalization of the personnel function spread much beyond a handful of large companies during the 1920s. The mailed fist rather than the velvet glove remained the most effective strategy for management to use to maintain its power in the employment relationship. There was no real incentive for most companies to leave this tried and true path. During the twenties management's status had rarely been higher, its power less threatened by the labor movement or the political left, its dominance of a pro-business government more secure. One survey found industrial relations departments in only 6.5% of companies employing under 500 men, in approximately 30% of companies employing between 500 and 2,000 men, and 50% of those over 2,000. The same could be said of employee representation. At the end of the decade ERPs covered 1.5 million workers. Eight out of ten worked for companies with more than 5,000 employees. Yet numbers are not the full measure of the significance of the policies tried by many of America's largest companies in the twenties. If they did not spread far beyond the core industries and the large consolidated firms, they were experiments that would bear fruit several decades hence after the social, economic, and political factors that management had enjoyed for the first third of the century had changed dramatically.

Considering the thrashing that organized labor took during the twenties, indeed for most of its history, how was it able to achieve the enormous membership increases that came during the period from 1933 to 1945? I believe that the answer lies in the confluence of four significant factors: first, the homogenization process had reached its climax by the time that the depression hit. The large class of industrial operatives that had been created could only be expected to accept the drive system without protest so long as prosperity provided the promised trade off of material rewards and security.[54] Second, as the depression deepened, employers could no longer maintain welfare capitalism policies. This meant the scrapping of many of the employee representation plans and other welfare policies that had considerably softened the sharp edge of the drive system. Workers felt betrayed and turned their anger toward the employer. This provided the opportunity for the "conscious minority" of militant activists to exploit the anger and sense of betrayal among industrial workers and to lead the mass strikes in 1933 and 1934 that touched off the industrial union movement.[55] It is not surprising that the great surge of industrial unionism took place in those industries in which both the drive system and welfare capitalism were most developed.[56] Third, and perhaps most important, this crisis of management control took place in the midst of a massive transformation of the nation's political alignment. This political sea change led to the creation of the New Deal Democratic Party, a realignment that took place before the rise of the CIO; this led to the passage of federal legislation, first the NIRA and then, most significantly, the Wagner Act which sanctioned collective bargaining. Fourth, these fortuitous circumstances, in terms of organized labor's interests, were followed by another, the advent of a war that replaced the Depression with prosperity and brought the nation together. The combined effect of these changes was to temporarily increase the ideological, political, and economic resources available to employers, while at the same time reducing those of organized labor.

When trying to understand the postwar fortunes of organized labor, it is important to remember that two of the fundamental environmental factors that assisted labor, the Great Depression and World War II, were extraordinary and temporary phenomena. Had neither of them occurred, it is likely that union density in 1945 would have been much lower, perhaps as low as it was in 1929.

This is an important point to recognize in a study of labor's "decline" after World War II. It points up the perils of focusing on the exception rather than the rule. There has been, it seems to me, a good deal of this in the writing of labor history. It is not surprising that labor's heroic age has drawn so much scholarly interest. It falls, I believe, into two categories. First, there are the liberal historians for whom the triumph of the CIO was the culmination of an evolution, one might say maturation, of labor's institutional development, especially its leadership, and of the inevitable spread of collective bargaining. In this approach the great events of history, such as the depression, the New Deal, and the War, serve as backdrops for labor's arrival, after years of trial and error, at its rightful place of power and legitimacy.[57] In opposition to this is the work of the radical historians for whom the rise of industrial unionism resulted mainly from the self-mobilization of class conscious workers as the result of the contradiction in the drive system, the creation of a class conscious proletariat. For these historians, the real story of the thirties is the dampening of this militancy by conservative labor leaders and government.[58]

I think it is clear that what emerged from the industrial union drive of the thirties was old wine in new bottles. In all but structure it was essentially an extension of the existing labor movement, still focusing on the pragmatic issues of job control, the limited use of the strike, and collective bargaining. But was this a result of government cooptation, or of a leadership sellout, or did it truly reflect the temperament of a cautious, if not conservative workforce? In other words, just how extensive was the labor militancy of the thirties? While no one can ignore the great upsurge of militancy that marked the period, one should remember that the vast majority of workers were neither unemployed nor on strike. In 1934, the year of the San Francisco maritime strike, the Toledo Auto Lite Strike, and the Minneapolis Teamster strike, among others, only seven tenths of the country's workers were on strike. A similar percentage held for the peak strike year of the decade, 1937. In gauging the temper of the working class as much attention should be paid to the other 93%.[59] David Brody has argued that the brief upsurge of the early NRA period marked the highwater mark for mass involvement and rank and file militancy. Thereafter rank and file activism, while it existed in all the mass-production industries, was restricted to small groups of workers. Even the great strikes in Akron and Flint in 1936 and 1937 involved only a minority of workers.[60] There is also the incontrovertible fact that the main objective of all of the CIO drives was a contract. The most militant actions were focused on limited, job related goals. Even the bold seizure of Chevy 4 in Flint resulted from the frustration with General Motors' unwillingness to negotiate with the union. According to Bob Travis, the key man in the sit-down strike, the union was prepared to "cooperate fully toward the efficient functioning of the industry."[61] In the drive to organize the steelworkers the apathy of a large part of the workforce was a serious problem. As late as 1940, although the Steel Workers Organizing Committee claimed a membership of 500,000, only half were actually regular dues payers.[62] John Bodnar's work on Slavic steelworkers points up their wait and see attitude, their "realism" in weighing the pros and cons of unionization. Most joined the union when they believed that it would win, not before.[63] Bodnar's findings are supported by Philip Murray's top aide, David J. McDonald, who claimed that the steelworkers did not rush to sign SWOC cards. What the organizers hoped would be a torrent, turned out to be a trickle. McDonald attributed this to fear, the open shop tradition, and the fact that "some workers were as apprehensive about dictatorship by an international union as they were of arm twisting by the company.[64] According to Frederick Harbison, in his chapter on Steel in Harry Millis' How Collective Bargaining Works, the steelworkers had neither the leadership nor the rank-and-file enthusiasm to organize spontaneously.[65]

In fact, the degree of militancy varied a great deal from industry to industry, depending in large measure on the dominant social and cultural influences of the mine, mill and factory towns. The auto workers are generally credited with having been in the vanguard of militancy. Yet even in the auto industry circumstances differed. In one study of the building of unionization at an auto parts plant in Detroit, the evidence seems to indicate that only after three years, when the union had demonstrated staying power in the face of company resistance, did the majority of workers sign union cards.[66]

And in Flint on the eve of the sit-down, only a small minority of the workers belonged to the UAW.[67] In the steel industry two generations of steelworkers, sons and grandsons, made up the workforce. They were fundamentally conservative and security conscious.[68] This continuity also probably explains the relative strength of the employee representation plans in steel and the decision of Little Steel to fight at a time when the CIO tide seemed unstoppable. The failure of the Little Steel Strike can also be attributed, in part, to the loyalty of workers to the company unions, a major factor, no doubt, in the success of the "back-to-work" movements in the company towns.

In the absence of any sustained mass militancy on the part of industrial workers, one must look for explanations for the growth of the labor movement in other places. The most fruitful is the area of government intervention. It seems clear that the passage of the labor provision of the NIRA and the Wagner Act came about, not because of the power of the labor movement, because it was tiny at the time, but rather because of the presence in the Roosevelt coalition of many pro-labor liberals and progressives and the new industrial working class. In large measure, the New Deal and the CIO had the same constituencies, but they were Roosevelt's constituency *first.* The Wagner Act was by far the most important factor in the surge of growth between 1936 and 1939. Although it must have seemed revolutionary to labor and management at the time, it did not constitute a completely new or untried way for resolving labor-management disputes. It is clear that the bill endorsed the pure and simple unionism of the AFL tradition. While it guaranteed unions some security during the duration of the contract, management's right to make strategic business decisions was left untouched. There was no quarrel with this from the labor side. No one in leadership positions in the AFL or the CIO believed that unions should share responsibility for directing the enterprise. Nor did the arrival of established rules for collective bargaining alter in any way the organization of work. The principles of scientific management and industrial engineering were deeply imbedded. Collective bargaining merely codified the existing work systems within the contract, made them enforceable through the grievance procedure, and strengthened the role of seniority as a means for allocating scare job opportunities in internal labor markets.[69] What emerged was job control unionism. The system met the needs of both management and labor. Labor checked the arbitrary power of management and gained a say in a constricted, but important sphere of the firm's activity. Management avoided disaster and achieved work force stability and predictability. Government achieved its goal of fostering industrial peace by replacing violent conflicts with orderly election and certification procedures and by giving certified unions a degree of permanence and security.[70] Given the potential for trouble for management in the depression and the New Deal, employers should have been happy with the rather mild requirements of the NLRA and the conservative course that organized labor followed. That was hardly the case. The Wagner act was not passed without bitter opposition from employer groups, and it was not until it was ruled constitutional by the Supreme Court in the <u>Jones and Laughlin</u> case that significant numbers of employers reluctantly adjusted their managerial practices to the reality of collective bargaining.[71]

One such adjustment was the rapid growth in the number of firms creating personnel departments. Indeed, this explosion actually started before the Wagner Act. It dates particularly from the years following the passage of the NIRA and the first upsurge of strike activity after 1933. Between 1933 and 1935, the percentage of firms with personnel departments increased dramatically. Centralized hiring increased by half, while the percentage of large firms applying formal rating systems for internal promotion grew by nearly three quarters.[72] It is important to note that this rapid spread of new personnel policies did not only occur in those firms that were directly experiencing unionization. But it was the fear of unionization that prompted widespread employer exploration with new organizational approaches to industrial relations. One study of employer reaction to the NIRA in early 1934 found employers obsessed with a fear of unionization.[73] In 1935, the Lynds found the Muncie, Indiana, business community more determined than ever to stay open shop.[74] At the same time, according to Jacoby, management believed that they could turn the tide if they instituted more enlightened personnel policies. One such response was a new surge of employee representation plans. Another was the institution of seniority systems in many non-union firms. Companies that used these policies successfully to ward off unionization were credited with having good personnel administration.[75]

The second great government intervention that solidified collective bargaining occurred during the war. By 1939 the CIO drive was flagging. The early triumphs at U.S. Steel and General Motors had not been repeated. Little Steel had defeated the Steel Workers Organizing Committee, and Ford remained determined to maintain the open shop. A number of other large firms, such as DuPont, and most small ones, had managed to stay union free, as it turned out, for good. At this precarious moment the salvation of organized labor appeared in the guise of the War Labor Board. Roosevelt demanded that labor and management avoid both strikes and inflation. He created the War Labor Board in 1942 to oversee industrial relations. Although its recommendations could not be enforced except with the implicit threat of even stronger legislation, the Board had an enormous impact. From 1942 to 1945 it helped to settle over 20,000 labor-management disputes. In fashioning these settlements, the Board was largely responsible for institutionalizing grievance procedures, union security arrangements, the dues checkoff, and for expanding the range of subjects covered by bargaining to include vacations, sick leave, and holiday pay.[76] This assistance from government coupled with the enormous growth in the labor force during the War brought the labor movement by 1945 to a level of power and prestige unknown in American history.

After the War labor pressed to expand upon the range of subjects appropriate for bargaining. Management felt most threatened in the area of traditional prerogatives. Nowhere was the challenge felt more than on the shop floor where rank and file discontent had simmered throughout the war and where, in some shops, union stewards were threatening to take control of production away from first line supervisors.[77] While union bargaining successes were greatest in personnel matters such as seniority, layoff, transfer, and rehire, they also made inroads into areas such as job content, operation rates, and other production issues. No wonder then that many managers feared the loss of their ability to direct the enterprise.[78] Management's fears, which no doubt seemed real enough in 1945 and 1946, were largely uncalled for. American corporations emerged from World War II with more power than ever. The status and influence that they had lost as a result of the economic collapse of the thirties had been restored by their seeming invincibility in marshalling the war production effort. As part of the only great industrial economy spared by the war, American companies soon monopolized world markets. Their size, dominance in product markets, and planning capacity had grown enormously as a result of the war.[79]

Labor's brief parity of political influence had already begun to erode during the war. While managers and "dollar a year" men on loan from business ran industry and the wartime agencies, labor's stock fell as a result of wildcat strikes and the enormously controversial walkout of the miners in 1943. Public opinion began to shift away from support for labor after the war, returning in a sense to its normal state. In response to the massive postwar strike wave in 1945 and 1946, President Truman seized a number of industries under his war powers and proposed legislation to draft strikers into the army. The culmination of this counterattack by management came with the passage of the Taft-Hartley Act in 1947. The act, largely the creature of the National Association of Manufacturers, dramatically curbed the power of the labor movement. In addition to weakening union security guarantees, it banned the tactics that labor had used successfully during its organizing upsurge in the thirties such as secondary boycotts, mass picketing, and sympathy strikes. And it removed first line supervisors from protection under the nation's labor law. The Cold War also worked to management's advantage, just as had the red scare after World War I. The communist issue split the labor movement as the CIO expelled ten of its most important affiliates because of their alleged communist control.[80] Finally, and perhaps most important of all, there was the conservative postwar electoral trend that both weakened the New Deal ideology and reduced labor's influence in the Democratic Party. The decline of labor's fortunes could be seen most clearly in the almost total failure of the CIO's much-heralded "Operation Dixie" to organize the largely non-union South. In spite of the so-called protections of the Wagner Act, southern employers and northern employers with operations in the South fought the unions with sophisticated anti-union policies that ranged from a revival of welfare capitalism to race baiting and violence.

In this environment the bargaining challenges that management feared did not materialize. The 1946 and 1948 bargaining rounds between the UAW and GM set the pattern for collective bargaining across American industry. GM refused to discuss its prices, would not open its books to prove that it could not raise wages without raising prices, and refused to submit any impasse to arbitration. So determined was the company to contain the scope of collective bargaining in 1946 that it took a 113-day strike, suffered massive losses of money and potential markets, and brazenly and successfully defied the Truman administration. But there was no attempt to break the union. That was not possible. That much had changed from the twenties.[81] Instead, the union was given security, and a reasonably generous compensation package. This was no problem for the company. It, as many of the other large unionized mass-production firms, operated in oligopolistic markets in which administered prices, not market forces, determined profit margins.

This then is what the heralded postwar "accord" amounted to. As a result of the New Deal and the war, labor's strength rested in the great mass-production industries at the core of the American economy. In that setting unions and managers negotiated over a wide range of job-related issues. Management remained firmly in control of the strategic decision making process. Where union density was much lower, in the South and much of the West, in small and medium-sized companies on the periphery of the core, and in the growing service sector such as financial services and retailing, they were largely kept out.[82] Taft-Hartley made it much easier for employers to do this without resorting to the old tactics of intimidation and terror. The success of this strategy in the private sector was masked by the surge of labor growth in the public sector after the 1962 presidential special order which permitted collective bargaining in the federal service. This led to a spate of state laws permitting bargaining. Once again, government action was the key to union growth.

Just as they had in the early twentieth century, employers in the postwar years in search of profits and control of production once more shaped the labor process to their advantage. Although not necessarily its main rationale, one of the by products of the process was a severe weakening of the labor movement. Just as homogenization had eroded the old AFL's main constituency in the skilled trades, so segmentation isolated and chipped away at the blue collar core constituency of the industrial unions. According to the analysis of Gordon, Edwards and Reich, large corporations initiated a period of segmentation of the labor force after the war. This process involved the growing divergence between primary and secondary jobs and primary and secondary labor markets. In the primary sector, generally corresponding to the mass production industries where union density was highest, jobs involving relatively more "independent" work became increasingly differentiated from jobs involving relatively more "subordinate" work. Throughout the postwar period the latter jobs, which are most heavily unionized, have been losing relative weight within the occupational structure. In contrast, the largely non-union occupational categories in the firm in which management holds greater power, the more "independent" categories which offer opportunities for skills development, relatively autonomous job control, and some combination of security and opportunities for advancement, have increased their relative importance since World War II. In addition, the secondary sector of the economy, characterized by low-skill jobs in which minority workers and women predominate, is also growing. In this market as well management enjoys greater power because of the many handicaps that these disadvantaged workers face in dealing with their employers, not the least of which is a low level of unionization.[83]

The impact of this transformation of the structure of work and labor markets on the labor movement has only recently become apparent. This is true, I believe, because, although *as an institution* organized labor fell into relative decline, its members generally benefitted from the industrial relations system that emerged from the War. Between 1947 and 1967 the average weekly wages of workers in the heavily unionized core industries increased substantially, rising by more than 3% per year. Average unemployment rates among adult male workers fell to below 2% at the height of the mid-sixties boom, and many workers began to take for granted their employment security under collective bargaining. Working conditions also improved. The index of accidents in manufacturing declined steadily after World War II, falling by 40% from 1946 to 1963. In these circumstances, labor peace spread. Workdays lost to strikes declined fairly steadily through the mid-1960s and unions paid little attention to organizing.[84] Labor militancy also increased in the 1960s during the prosperity stimulated by tax cuts and the "guns and butter" policy pursued by the Johnson administration. The resulting tight labor markets and the mood of protest that characterized the period led to an increase in strikes and contract rejections by a more militant rank and file.[85] In spite of increasing foreign competition, union workers' wages continued to grow more rapidly throughout the 1970s than did non-union wages, thereby expanding the union labor cost differential and further eroding employment in unionized firms and industries. In three settlements under the Experimental Negotiating Agreement between the United Steelworkers and the steel industry, for example, the wages of steelworkers grew from 120 percent of the average wage in manufacturing in 1970 to 160 percent of the 1979 average. A similar increase took place in the auto industry.[86]

These conditions masked, for a time, the effects of the segmentation process and the emerging industrial relations strategy of management. Throughout the 1940s the large unionized firms strengthened and professionalized their industrial relations and personnel departments. Part of the reason for this was the need to stabilize labor-management relations, and it was this professionalization that academic observers and practitioners focused on when they spoke of the "accord" between labor and management that had emerged from the New Deal and the War Labor Board. These professionals had a vested interest in viewing the industrial relations system as pluralistic, with employers accepting unions as a legitimate pressure group engaged in joint rule making on behalf of workers with government and business. But much less attention was afforded to other management actions which signalled their weak commitment to collective bargaining. As early as the late 1940s, aggressive anti-union tactics were commonplace. At best management viewed labor-management relations in unionized firms as an armed truce. The personnel department's responsibility was to contain union inroads into management prerogatives and erode loyalty to the union wherever possible. But there was also the revival of sophisticated personnel policies to weaken the appeal of unions. Southern firms countered the CIO's "Operation Dixie" by adopting a variety of progressive policies such as seniority which unions had won elsewhere in collective bargaining. A 1950 study of the spread of seniority noted that a great many non-union firms were aware that the mishandling of their personnel procedures could lead to unionization. In addition, many companies, including giants such as General Electric and DuPont began to relocate operations in the South to avoid unionization.[87] By the late 1950s most managers, including those within the heavily unionized core industries, had a negative view of unions.[88]

Many of the anti-union strategies had been developed by companies which had remained non-union during the thirties and the war years. These included sophisticated communications and survey techniques based on behavioral science, an explosion of corporate recreation programs, and employee involvement programs.[89] Although the use of legally questionable tactics to skirt the NLRA continued, most of the approaches were descended from the human relations school. These tactics received a boost from pro-business NLRB decisions on free speech and company unions near the end of the war and became commonplace with Taft-Hartley's "free speech provision" which gave wide latitude for aggressive anti-union campaigns by employers. The labor movement learned again the painful lesson that

Samuel Gompers had taught, what the government gives, the government can take away.

We now know how damaging these anti-union personnel policies, both legal and illegal, have been to the labor movement since the war. Corporations have turned increasingly to private management consultants who specialize in union prevention. Union decertification elections, another Taft-Hartley provision, have soared. Unionized workers, even in the midst of the most prolonged economic recovery since the war, have frequently been forced to take concessions. Management's political power in the new Republican ascendency has enabled it to easily turn back the politically weakened labor movement's attempt at mild labor law reform. So low has labor's stock in the Democratic Party dropped, that endorsement of Democratic candidates by organized labor is seen by some professional politicians to be a detriment rather than an advantage.

The rout of the labor movement that has resulted from this strategy has all but returned the relations between workers and employers to the conditions of the 1920s, the golden age of management hegemony in American society. The ratio of supervisory to non-supervisory personnel has been rising steadily, with few exceptions, since immediately after the war. Disinvestment by large corporations of their facilities in traditional unionized regions such as the northeast and midwest and relocation to regions with low union density rates or abroad were common features of the 1970s and 1980s. New methods of production as a result of technological innovations, such as robotization and the microchip revolution, have profound implications for the relative power of managers and workers. So does the current explosion of interest in quality circles and other worker participation programs. Although usually justified in terms of "competitiveness" with foreign competitors, some observers believe that the employee participation plans are merely the modern manifestation of the employee representation plans of the twenties and early thirties, and that their primary purpose, now as then, is to wed the worker to the "family" of the firm and prevent unionization. Finally, just as they did following the merger waves of the 1890s and 1920s, rapid transformations in the size and structure of corporations have greatly enhanced their power vis a vis workers. Conglomerate firms, often with multinational dimensions, have far outpaced the industry and trade based jurisdictional structure of the labor movement. Just as the craft structure of the old AFL was ill suited to the new mass production industries in the first two decades of the century, so too is industrial unionism ill suited to the diversified corporate giants of the present day.

Of course, things looked even darker at the end of the twenties, but the following decade and one half was the greatest era in the history of the labor movement. Is that possible again? Who is to say? Who knows what another economic collapse might bring? But short of that kind of catastrophic event, a dramatic reversal of labor's fortunes seems unlikely. Non-union firms have widely adopted many of the innovations that were first introduced by collective bargaining. But if union density declines to the point where unionization is no longer a threat, will management discard these reforms and return to its old hard-line employment practices? That is possible, of course, and depends in part, as it did at the end of the twenties, on management's economic ability to keep the innovations going. But even if management regresses, there is a great deal more government employment protection in place now than was true in 1933. The web of government rules and supports has grown immensely since then. Affirmative action, minimum wages, ERISA, OSHA, the judicial erosion of employment at will, all provide protections that were available only through collective bargaining not so long ago. That is not likely to change, no matter the fortunes of trade unions.

In order to hold its own, labor will have to be innovative, to find ways, as it has in the past, to ensure institutional survival within the context of the changed American employment system. In particular, it will have to penetrate the secondary labor market where workers are exploited and the government's employment protections have little meaning. That will obviously be an extremely difficult task and may require, as in the thirties, a radical restructuring of the labor movement.

There is nothing new about labor's dilemma. The success that the movement enjoyed from 1933 to 1953 should not be looked upon as the culmination of labor's long, steady progress to legitimacy and power. Rather it was a brief window of opportunity presented by a combination of extraordinary circumstances. Unhappily, the painful descent from the heights which has taken place since 1953 is much more in keeping with the long-run historical tendencies of organized labor in American history.

Notes

1 George W. Taylor, Government Regulation of Industrial Relations, New York: Prentice-Hall, 1948, p. 1

2 John Dunlop, "The Social Utility of Collective Bargaining," in Challenges to Collective Bargaining, Lloyd Ulman, ed., Englewood Cliffs, NJ: Prentice-Hall, 1967, pp. 168-180.

3 Christopher Tomlins, "Of the Old Time Entombed: The Resurrection of the American Working Class and the Emerging Critique of American Industrial Relations," Industrial Relations Law Journal, 10 (1988), 444; Katherine Stone, "The Post-War Paradigm in American Labor Law," Yale Law Journal, 90 (1981), 1509-1580; See also Raymond Hogler, "Critical Labor Law, Working Class History, and the New Industrial Relations," Industrial Relations Law Journal, 10 (1988), 116-143, and Christopher Tomlins, "The New Deal, Collective Bargaining, and the Triumph of Industrial Relations," Industrial and Labor Relations Review, 39 (1985), 19-34.

4 Charles Heckscher, The New Unionism: Employee Involvement in the Changing Corporation, New York: Basic Books, 1988, p. 16; David Montgomery, The Fall of the House of Labor: The Workplace, The State, and American Labor Activism, Cambridge: Cambridge University Press, 1987, Introduction.

5 Melvyn Dubofsky, "Workers' Movements in North America, 1873-1970: A Preliminary Analysis," in Labor in the World Social Structure, Immanuel Wallerstein, ed., Beverly Hills: Sage Publications, 1983, pp. 22-43.

6 Ibid., 24

7 Ibid.; the figures cited from Dubofsky are taken from those compiled by the staff of the National Bureau of Economic Research which are generally slightly lower than those reported in the Bureau of Labor Statistics data.

8 Ibid.

9 David Montgomery, Workers' Control in America, New York: Cambridge University Press, 1979, pp. 97-101.

10 Joseph P. Goldberg, The Maritime Story: A Study in Labor-Management Relations, Cambridge, MA: Harvard University Press, 1957.

11 Dubofsky, "Workers' Movements in North America," 24, 28

12 Sanford Jacoby, "American Exceptionalism Revisited: The Importance of Management," unpublished paper to appear in American Employers: Historical Perspectives, New York: Columbia University Press, 1989, p. 1.

13 Dubofsky, "Workers' Movements in North America, " 28.

14 Ibid.

15 Ibid., 38.

16 John T. Dunlop, "The Development of Labor Organization," in Insights into Labor Issues, Richard Lester and Joseph Shister, eds., New York: Macmillan 1948, pp. 163-193; Irving Bernstein, "The Growth of American Unions," American Economic Review, 44 (June, 1954), pp. 305-318.

17 David Brody, "The Expansion of the American Labor Movement: Institutional Sources of Stimulus and restraint," in David Brody, ed. The American Labor Movement, New York: Harper & Row, 1971, pp. 122-123.

18 For an interesting presentation of the situation of the early craft unions in a classically capitalist economy see Goetz A. Briefs, Unionism Reappraised, Washington: American Enterprise Association, 1960.

19 The best compilation of the voluminous scholarship on this question can be found in Laslett, John H.M. and Seymour M. Lipset, Failure of a Dream: Essays in the History of American Socialism, Garden City, NY: Anchor Press, 1974.

20 Lloyd Ulman, "Who Wanted Collective Bargaining in the First Place?", Proceedings, Thirty-Ninth Annual Meeting of the Industrial Relations Research Association, Madison, 1987, pp. 1-13.

21 Jacoby, "American Exceptionalism," 24; Robert J. Goldstein, Political Repression in Modern America, Cambridge, MA: Schenckman Publishing Co., 1978, p. 550.

22 Jacoby, "American Exceptionalism," 25-27.

23 Ibid.

24 Ibid., 5; David Vogel, "Why Businessmen Distrust Their State: The Political Consciousness of American Corporate Executives," British Journal of Political Science, 8 (January 1978), p. 63.

25 Rowland Berthoff, "The'Freedom to control' in American Business History," in David Pinkney and Theodore Ropp, eds. A Festschrift for Frederick B. Artz, Durham, NC: Duke University Press, 1964, cited in Jacoby, "American Exceptionalism," 6.

26 Jacoby, "American Exceptionalism," 14; see also James Weinstein, The Corporate Ideal in the Liberal State, Boston: Beacon Press, 1968.

27 H.H. Gerth, and C. Wright Mills, eds., From Max Weber: Essays in Sociology, New York: Oxford University Press, 1946, p. 228.

28 Jacoby, "American Exceptionalism," 9; Howard Gitelman, "Perspectives on American industrial Violence," Business History Review, 47 (Spring 1973), pp. 1-23.

29 Reinhard Bendix, Work and Authority in Industry, New York: Wiley, 1959, p. 2; Richard Weiss, Managerial Ideology and the Social Control of Deviance in Organizations, New York: Praeger, 1986, p. 41.

30 Robert S., and Helen Lynd, Middletown In Transition, New York: Harcourt, Brace, & World, 1937, cited in Melvyn Dubofsky, "Not So 'Turbulent Years': Another Look at the American 1930's," America-studien(American Studies), 24 (1979), p. 14.

31 Ely Chinoy, Automobile Workers and the American Dream, Garden City: Doubleday, 1955; Richard Sennett and Jonathan Cobb, The Hidden Injuries of Class, New York: Alfred A. Knopf, 1972).

32 Jacoby, "American Exceptionalism," 4; Seymour Martin Lipset, "Labor Unions in the Public Mind," in Lipset, ed., Unions in Transition: Entering the Second Century, San Francisco: ICS Press, 1986, pp. 287-322. See also Geert Hofstede, Culture's Consequences: International Differences in Work-Related Values, Beverly Hills: Sage, 1984, Hofstede, "Nationality and Espoused Values of Managers," Journal of Applied Psychology, 61 (April 1976): 148-155, George England, The Manager and His Values: An International Perspective, Cambridge: Ballinger Pub. Co., 1975, Francis X. Sutton, Seymour Harris, Carl Kaysen, and James Tobin, The American Business Creed, Cambridge: Harvard University Press, 1956, and Bendix, Work and Authority in Industry.

33 David M. Gordon, Richard Edwards, and Michael Reich, Segmented Work, Divided Workers, Cambridge: Cambridge University Press, 1982, pp. 12-14, 121, 153-154; See also Richard Edwards, Contested Terrain: The Transformation of the Workplace in the Twentieth Century, New York: Basic Books, 1979.

34 Haggai Hurvitz, "Ideology and Industrial Conflict: President Wilson's First Industrial Conference," Labor History 18 (1977), pp. 509-524; Gordon, et al., p. 154.

35 David Brody, Workers in Industrial America, New York: Oxford University Press, 1980, p. 53.

36 Thomas C. Cochrane and William Miller, The Age of Enterprise: A Social History of Industrial America, New York: Harper, 1961, pp. 303-307; Ronald Filippelli, Labor in the USA: A History, New York: Alfred A. Knopf, 1984, p. 141.

37 Frederick Taylor, Principles of Scientific Management, New York: Harper & Brothers, 1911, pp. 6-7; Thomas Cochrane and William Miller, p. 307.

38 Thomas Kochan and Harry C. Katz, Collective Bargaining and Industrial Relations, 2nd ed., Homewood, IL: Irwin, 1988, pp. 32-33.

39 Heckscher, p. 21.

40 Ibid.

41 Brody, Workers in Industrial America, pp. 50-57.

42 "Minutes," United States Steel Corporation Stockholders Meeting, April 16, 1923, p. 9, cited in Ibid. 55.

43 Brody, Workers in Industrial America, pp. 49-50; Gordon, et al., p. 181.

44 National Industrial Conference Board, Effect of Depression on Industrial Relations Programs, New York, 1934, pp. 4-10; Brody, Workers in Industrial America, 59.

45 Brody, Workers in Industrial America, 49, 61; Kim McQuaide, "Corporate Liberalism in the American Business Community, 1920-1940," Business History Review, 52 (Autumn 1978), p. 345.

46 Raymond Hogler, "Employee Participation and Employer Anti-Unionism: Representation Plans in the Steel Industry, 1918-1937." Unpublished Paper; In 1913, during a recognition strike by the United Mine Workers against John D. Rockefeller's Colorado Fuel and Iron Company, the miners and their families established tent colonies at various locations, the largest of which was Ludlow. When the Colorado militia attacked the Ludlow colony, eleven children and two women were burned to death. The negative publicity resulting from the affair led Rockefeller to commission Canadian industrial relations expert McKenzie King to develop an employee representation plan. The workers subsequently voted to accept King's ERP by an overwhelming margin.

47 Ibid., p. 8.

48 Ernest Burton, Employee Representation, Baltimore: Williams and Wilkins Co., 1926, p. 30; National Industrial Conference Board Collective Bargaining Through Employee Representation, New York, 1933, pp. 12-13; Brody, Workers in Industrial America, 55.

49 Irving Bernstein, The Lean Years: A History of the American Worker, 1920-1933, Boston: Houghton Mifflin, 1960, p. 170; Brody, Workers in Industrial America, 58-59.

50 Sumner Slichter, "The Current Labor Polices of American Industries," Quarterly Journal of Economics, vol. 42 (1929), p. 432.

51 Brody, Workers in Industrial America, p. 56.

52 In an experiment carried out at the Hawthorne plant of the Western Electric Company in Chicago, researchers learned that the physical conditions of work had little to do with output changes. Instead, what seemed to be related to productivity were the psychological conditions of work, including good communications, worker involvement in decision making, and the development of an organized social group with an effective relationship with supervisors.

53 McQuaide, pp. 342-368.

54 Gordon, et al, pp. 175-184.

55 David Brody, "The CIO After 50 Years: A Historical Reckoning," Dissent (Fall 1985), pp. 457-472; See also Joshua Freeman, "Catholics, Communists, and Republicans: Irish Workers and the Organization of the Transport Workers Union," in Michael H. Frisch and Daniel J. Walkowitz, eds., Working-Class America, Urbana, IL: University of Illinois Press, 1983, Gary Gerstle, "The Mobilization of the Working Class Community: The Independent Textile Union in Woonsocket, 1931-1946," Radical History Review, 17 (Spring 1978), pp. 161-167, Bruce Nelson, "'Pentecost' on the Pacific: Maritime Workers and the Working-Class Consciousness in the 1930s," in Maurice Zeitlin, ed., Political Power and Social Theory: A Research Annual, 4 (1984), pp. 141-182, and Ronald Schatz, "Union Pioneers: The Founders of Local Unions at General Electric and Westinghouse, 1933-1937," Journal of American History, 66 (December 1979), pp. 586-602.

56 Brody, Workers in Industrial America, 77-78: Sanford Jacoby, Employing Bureaucracy, New York: Columbia University Press, 1985, p. 221.

57 For the best examples of the liberal school, see Irving Bernstein, The Turbulent Years: A History of American Workers, 1933-1941,

Boston: Houghton Mifflin, 1969, Robert R. Brooks, <u>As Steel Goes: Unionism in A Basic Industry</u>, New Haven, Conn.: Yale University Press, 1940, and Walter Galenson, <u>The CIO Challenge to the AFL: A History of the American Labor Movement, 1935-1941</u>, Cambridge, Mass.: Harvard University Press, 1960.

58 David Brody, "The CIO After 50 Years," 457-472. See also Stanley Aronowitz, <u>False Promises: The Shaping of American Working Class Consciousness</u>, New York: McGraw-Hill, 1973, Alice and Staughton Lynd, <u>Rank and File: Personal Histories of Working Class Organizers</u>, Boston: Beacon Press, 1973, Jeremy Brecher, <u>Strike</u>, Boston: South End Press, 1977, and James R. Green, ed., <u>Workers' Struggles, Past and Present: A "Radical America" Reader</u>, Philadelphia: Temple University Press, 1983.

59 Dubofsky, "Not so 'Turbulent Years,'" pp. 12-13.

60 Brody, <u>Workers in Industrial America</u>, pp. 134-135.

61 J.S. Auerbach, <u>American Labor: The Twentieth Century</u>, Indianapolis: Bobbs-Merrill, 1969, pp. 328-331.

62 Galenson, p. 113; Brooks, p. 162.

63 John Bodnar, "Immigration, Kinship, and the Rise of Working-Class Realism in Industrial America," <u>Journal of Social History</u>, 14 (Fall 1980), pp. 45-59.

64 David J. McDonald, <u>Union Man</u>, New York: Dutton, 1969, p. 93.

65 Frederick Harbison, "Steel," in <u>How Collective Bargaining Works</u>, New York: Twentieth Century Fund, 1942, pp. 517, 527.

66 Peter Friedlander, <u>The Emergence of a UAW Local, 1936-1939</u>, Pittsburgh: University of Pittsburgh Press, 1975.

67 Sidney Fine, <u>Sit-Down: The General Motors Strike of 1936-1937</u>, Ann Arbor: University of Michigan Press, 1969, p. 117.

68 Clinton S. Golden and Harold Ruttenberg, <u>The Dynamics of Industrial Democracy</u>, New York: Harper, 1942, pp. 110-118; John Bodnar, <u>Immigration and Industrialization: Ethnicity in an American Mill Town, 1870-1940</u>, Pittsburgh: University of Pittsburgh Press, 1977.

69 Sanford Jacoby, <u>Employing Bureaucracy</u>, 243-253.

70 Kochan, pp. 35-36.

71 Ibid.

72 Jacoby, <u>Employing Bureaucracy</u>, Chapter 7; Gordon, et al., p.176.

73 Bernstein, p. 804, no. 2.

74 Dubofsky, "Not so 'Turbulent Years,'" p. 14.

75 Jacoby, <u>Employing Bureaucracy</u>, p. 225.

76 Kochan, p. 37.

77 Brody, Workers in Industrial America, pp. 180-181.

78 Neil W. Chamberlain, The Union Challenge to Management, New York: Harper, 1948, chapter 4; E. Wight Bakke, ed., Unions, Management and the Public, New York: Harcourt, Brace, 1960, p. 216.

79 Gordon, et al., p. 185.

80 Ibid.

81 Brody, Workers in Industrial America , 183-184, 183-187.

82 Only 10% of American department store employees were unionized in 1955. Sanford M. Jacoby, "Employee Attitude Testing at Sears Roebuck, 1938-1960," Business History Review, 60 (Winter 1986), p. 603.

83 Gordon, et al., chapter 5.

84 Ibid., 217.

85 William E. Simkin, "Refusal to Ratify Contracts," in Trade Union Government and Administration, Joel Seidman, ed., New York: Praeger Publishers, 1970, pp. 107-148.

86 Harry C. Katz, Shifting Gears, Cambridge, Mass: MIT Press, 1985, pp. 13-48.

87 "Operation Dixie," Modern Industry (August 15, 1946), p. 51; Jacoby, Employing Bureaucracy, 245.

88 Jacoby, "American Exceptionalism," 31; Douglass V. Brown and Charles A. Myers, "The Changing Industrial Relations Philosophy of American Management," Proceedings, Ninth Annual Meeting of the Industrial Relations Research Association, Madison, 1957, pp. 84-89.

89 A recent New York Stock Exchange study found that attitude surveys were being used by 67% of large firms by 1982. New York Stock Exchange, A Report to Corporate America, New York, 1982, p. 44; After World War II, corporate recreation programs boomed as part of a widespread revival of welfare capitalism, particularly in non-union firms such as IBM and Eastman Kodak. Several companies attributed their defeat of union organizing drives to the presence of effective employee-run recreation programs. Elizabeth Fones-Wolfe, "Industrial Recreation, the Second World War, and the Revival of Welfare Capitalism, 1934-1960," Business History Review, 60 (Summer 1986), pp. 232-257.

Further Reading

The best examples of the liberal school, and the best narrative labor histories of the twenties and thirties, are Irving Bernstein's two volumes, The Lean Years (Boston: Houghton Mifflin, 1960), and The Turbulent Years (Boston: Houghton Mifflin, 1970). Another classic of this approach is Walter Galenson, The CIO Challenge to the AFL: A History of the American Labor Movement, 1935-1941 (Cambridge: Harvard University Press, 1960). Readers can find well-articulated critiques of this school from the left in James Green, ed., Workers' Struggles Past and Present: A "Radical America" Reader (Philadelphia: Temple University Press, 1983). Green's history of the twentieth century labor movement, World of the Worker (New York, 1980) is the best survey history from a left perspective. Works questioning the militancy of industrial workers during the thirties are Robert Zieger, "The Limits of Militancy: Organizing Paper Workers, 1933-1935." Journal of American History, 63 (December 1976), pp. 638-57, and Melvyn Dubofsky, "Not so 'Turbulent Years': Another Look at the American 1930s," Amerika-studien, 24 (1979), pp. 5-20. David Brody's provocative volume of essays on labor in the twentieth century, Workers in Industrial America (New York: Oxford, 1980) manages to raise the essential questions about modern labor history while at the same time providing judicious critiques of both the liberal school and its new left critics. Brody's slim volume is indispensable. For outstanding studies of the impact of the consolidation of industry and the transformation of work, see David Brody, Steelworkers in the Non-Union Era (Cambridge: Harvard University Press, 1960), and David Montgomery, Workers' Control in America (Cambridge: Cambridge

University Press, 1979) and The Fall of the House of Labor (Cambridge: Cambridge University Press, 1987). The best single study of the history of this process on the management side is Sanford Jacoby, Employing Bureaucracy: Managers, Unions, and the Transformation of Work in American Industry, 1900-1945 (New York: Columbia University Press, 1985). Essential theoretical studies are, David Gordon, Richard Edwards, and Michael Reich, Segmented Work, Divided Workers (Cambridge: Cambridge University Press, 1982), and Richard Edwards, Contested Terrain: The Transformation of the Workplace in the Twentieth Century (New York: Basic Books, 1979). Christopher Tomlin's The State and the Unions: Labor Relations, Law, and the Organized Labor Movement in America, 1880-1960 (Cambridge: Cambridge University Press, 1985) offers the best presentation of the critical legal theory school's argument that labor law, rather than having assisted the trade union movement, has been fashioned to contain labor's influence. For an understanding of the critical World War II years see Nelson Lichtenstein, Labor's War at Home: The CIO During World War II (Cambridge: Cambridge University Press, 1982). Readers seeking an illumination of the modern period through biography can do no better than to read Melvyn Dubofsky and Warren Van Tine, John L. Lewis: A Biography (New York: Quadrangle, 1977).

CHAPTER 5

A POST-WORLD WAR II "SOCIAL ACCORD?"

Bruce Nissen

In the 1970s and 1980s, a number of writers, academics, and interested observers have spoken of a "social accord" (or "social contract," "social compact," "peace treaty," etc.) between organized labor and the corporate community which is claimed to have existed in the decades following World War II. This accord is said to encompass a somewhat stable set of trade-offs and mutual expectations which emerged between the two sides in key sectors of the economy during that period.

The issue of a social accord has been raised in interesting ways, but discussion of the topic to date has been relatively unsystematic. Very little discussion or debate has occurred. Yet, there are issues which are crucial to our understanding of the period buried within the concept of a labor-capital social accord. For this reason alone, it is worth exploring in a more analytic fashion.

Most of the writers asserting a social accord state its terms rather briefly. They do not all agree about its terms, either. In fact, the imprecision in the use of the term is in some cases very great. Therefore, we need to sort out some of the various uses of the term as a prelude to a serious consideration of the major claims of its more thoughtful proponents.

In the remainder of this chapter I intend to (1) review some of the uses to which the concept has been put; (2) reject several of those uses as either overly broad and vacuous or lacking in historical accuracy; (3) examine the main features of the post-World War II

173

industrial system; and (4) examine the adequacy of the "social accord" notion in explaining that system. I will conclude that the basic features of the system are accurately captured in some of the "social accord" analyses, although significant qualifications must be added. Furthermore, these features are probably explained in a less confusing language if we avoid the terms "social accord" or "social contract" entirely. Finally, any such accord has been destroyed by the events of the 1980s, so it is no longer operative for the vast majority of unionized workers.

I. USES OF THE CONCEPT

The following review is in no way meant to be comprehensive. It does not document all attempts within the literature to employ the notion of an accord or contract to characterize the implied and recognized parameters to union and management behavior in the post-war period. Instead, it is intended to survey a representative sample, to give a sense of the ways in which industrial relations researchers and others have used the terms "social compact," "social contract," "social accord," "labor-capital truce," and the like.

First, it is important to clearly distinguish between any U.S. arrangement and the explicit "social contracts" which exist in several West European societies between the labor movement, the government, and the business community. In those societies the government engages in multilateral bargaining with labor and management over the future growth of wages and prices. In exchange for guaranteed wage and price moderation and a clear income policy, the government frequently makes a commitment to certain tax, monetary, and fiscal arrangements.

This explicit tripartite bargaining is almost totally absent from the U.S. industrial scene. The closest the United States has come to this was during World War II, when government wage-price controls were coupled with a no-strike pledge and other institutional arrangements heavily involving the government in labor-management affairs. Given the decentralized nature of much of U.S. collective bargaining, the structure of the U.S. labor movement, and the large size of the non-union sector, it appears that tripartite social contracts of the Western European variety would be very difficult in this country. (Flanagan, 1980; Barbash, 1972)

In very recent times, the closest the United States has come to such institutional arrangements is various presidential labor-management committees composed of top labor and management leaders. These committees have looked at major issues facing the country and its economy, but all have been merely advisory and have failed to achieve any concrete results (Moye, 1980)

Any discussion of a U.S. labor-management "social accord," "social compact," or "social contract" thus should be clearly distinguished from formal tripartite mechanisms. For all intents and purposes, no such mechanism exists in the United States or is likely to in the near future.

For the purposes of this chapter, we will also avoid an overly broad use of such terms, where virtually anything that occurs is considered "contractual," or where "the people" have a "social contract" with "the corporations." While such a loose usage of language may be useful for certain purposes, it does not lend itself to a great deal of clarity. An example of such broad language is an article by David Kusnet which sees every piece of government regulation over business as a "social contract between the people and corporations":

> From the Progressive Era through the New Deal, businesses were required to pay a minimum wage, end child labor, bargain with unions chosen by their employees. During the 1960s and 70s, businesses were required to maintain health and safety standards in the workplace, provide employees with a minimum level of pension benefits and recognize consumers' rights to product safety and truth-in-packaging. . . . These reforms. . . comprise the social contract between the people and corporate America. (Kusnet, 1987:25)

Arguing for the plant closing bill passed in 1988, Kusnet claims that such legislation means a rewriting of the "social contract".

Under such a broad usage, the term "social contract" would apply to not only institutions but to amorphous entities like "the people," and it would apply to any situation where businesses operated since some regulatory legislation would have to exist on some level, however slight. To have a precise meaning, a social accord or contract would have to embody more than the current regulatory legislation (whatever it is), and it would have to apply to recognizable institutions (such as labor unions and corporations), not merely "the people."

In a similar vein, John Sweeney (president of the Service Employees International Union - SEIU) and Karen Nussbaum (president of SEIU District 925 and executive director of "9 to 5," National Association of Working Women) subtitle their book Solutions for the New Workforce with "Policies for a New Social Contract." They assert that an old social contract worked in the past:

> A social contract between business and labor dating back to the 1930s ensured the sharing of prosperity. Unlike Europe, where laws set standards for health coverage, job training, layoffs, and leave policies, the United States did not rely heavily on government action to make this promise a reality. . . job policies were largely a matter of negotiation between employers and unions or individual workers, negotiation that depended on an implicit agreement with business that the well-being of the work force would be a central corporate goal. And for the most part, major corporations kept their side of the bargain. . . a union job meant security, the opportunity for advancement, and the ability to support a family. . . . In all, the ground rules appeared to be working. Change brought progress and a rising standard of living. (Sweeney and Nussbaum, 1989:6)

But all of this has changed in the 1970s and 1980s, they assert. With declining living standards, a torn "social safety net," and the like, we need a new social contract.

While there is nothing wrong with using the term "social contract" in this loose manner for the purposes Sweeney and Nussbaum intend, it is not relevant or adequate for the issues we are exploring here. The vagueness, imprecision, and lack of the specific features characterizing modern industrial relations means that we will not find here a key concept illuminating the central features of post-World War II industrial relations.

Other claims of a "social contract" have been somewhat more specific but still remain at a level of abstraction beyond that which is desirable if we wish to look at the specific features of a particular era, such as the post-World War II decades. U.S. Senator Daniel Patrick Moynihan, celebrating the mainstream U.S. labor movement's commitment to the capitalist system, has argued that this is a part of a "social contract" from the late nineteenth century to the present:

Its terms were simple and direct:

--First, labor would not seek to transform the American
economic system by posing an alternative system.
--Second, labor would not seek to transform the American
political system by founding its own political party
--But, third, in return, the labor movement would not only be
permitted but would be encouraged to seek to gain within the
American system so constituted a broad range of material and
social benefits for the people it represented.

Stating that this contract has been "scrupulously upheld" by labor,
Moynihan states that labor's choice was right because it has brought
"unequaled well being, dignity, and position to American workers."
(Moynihan, 1980:ii,iii)

There are several problems with Moynihan's analysis. One is
the question of historical accuracy. The labor movement had to fight to
obtain a position of relative permanency in major industries in the
American economic system. It hardly seems adequate to term the Open
Shop Drive of 1903-1913 or the union-busting "American Plan" in the
1920s, or the massive use of the "Mohawk Valley Formula" in the
1930s, the widespread use of spies and provocateurs or private police
forces to stop unionization, or specific incidents such as the Ludlow
Massacre, the Lawrence Textile Strike, or the 1937 Memorial Day
Massacre as encouragement for the labor movement (no matter how
much it restricted its goals to material gain). In fact, prior to the
enactment of the Wagner Act in 1935, the United States had the most
violent labor history of any country in the advanced industrial world.
Even after the Wagner Act, there are numerous examples to show that
unions were only accepted when it was clear that they were here to stay,
like it or not.

Beyond the problem of historical accuracy, Moynihan's
analysis is at a level of generality way beyond that we will be
attempting here. "Compacts" or "contracts" which extend over entire
centuries are likely to be fairly useless as indicators of specific
institutional arrangements of more limited periods. The post-World
War II period did exhibit features of labor-management relations which
were unique and which required implicit agreements and parameters of
behavior on both sides. These are better captured by historically
specific terms which do not become so abstract that they are applied
across broad scopes of history.

We turn now to more specific analyses which are confined to the post-World War II period. A. H. Raskin, long time labor reporter for the <u>New York Times</u> and well-known journalist of labor affairs, notes the post-World War II development of a "live-and-let-live relationship rather than endless confrontations." He calls this an entente cordiale:

> Dominant elements in big business accepted the somewhat heretical notion that strong, secure unions could be of advantage to management by combating wildcat ("quickie") strikes and fostering cooperative relations in the workplace. (Raskin, 1986:7,8)

Noting that management got stability and wage rate standardization from this arrangement, Raskin points out that unions got security through union-shop contracts. The result, he claims, was a "kind of pushbutton unionism, in which employers became for all practical purposes the chief recruiters of new union members and also collected the union's dues under checkoff arrangements." (Raskin, 1986:8)

Another prominent labor journalist, William Serrin, highlights a different aspect of the more cordial relationship. While Raskin sees management stability and union security as the payoffs to each side, Serrin sees management rights and worker economic gain as the respective gain:

> A strengthened management and a weakened labor movement agreed in the post-war years to what became known as the social accord. Under this, workers received predictable wage gains and increased benefits, while management retained the essential prerogatives of ownership; that is, the right to make decisions on the important matters, such as production, pricing, plant location and other investments. (Serrin, 1988:19)

Writing in the 1970s, Serrin had earlier characterized the exchange as one of predictability for the company, with wage gains plus limited job control being given to the union:

> What the companies desire--and receive--from the union is predictability in labor relations. Forced to deal with unions, they want to deal with one union, one set of leaders, and thus they have great interest in stability within the (union) and in a continuation of

> union leadership. They also want to have the limits
> of bargaining clearly understood and subscribed to....
> The union has come to accept this philosophy as
> the basis of its relationship with the companies; it
> will get money, some changes in work procedures,
> usually nothing more. (Serrin, 1973:156-157)

United Auto Workers activist and writer Eric Mann also uses
the notion of a social compact to inform his analysis. Mann argues
that General Motors under the leadership of Alfred P. Sloan moved from
"class warfare to social compact" in its relations with the United
Automobile Workers (UAW). (Mann, 1987:44) The main contours of
the social compact are described as follows:

> The corporation received dependable labor and
> uninterrupted production, while the workers received
> dependable wages and, for the most part, uninterrupted
> work. (Mann, 1987:381)

Mann writes that class conflict in the unionized industries following
World War II was still present but largely attenuated and mostly orderly.
Labor-management relations were characterized by

> collectively bargained contracts; the agreement by the
> union not to strike during the life of the contract; the
> limitation of most of the workers' options during the
> life of the contract to individual grievances solved one
> at a time; the development of the mediation
> arbitration industry to reconcile class conflict; and the
> mutual agreement that the government's National
> Labor Relations Board would be the arbiter of most
> labor disputes. (Mann, 1987:380-381)

Economists Samuel Bowles, David Gordon, and Thomas
Weisskopf also write about a postwar "capital-labor accord" which they
characterize as a "tacit agreement between corporate capitalists and the
organized labor movement." The terms of the accord are seen as giving
the corporations control over the work process ("management rights")
and labor discipline, while the unions achieve legitimacy and
acceptance. Workers would receive income gains, greater job security,
and better working conditions:

> Corporations would retain absolute control over the
> essential decisions governing enterprise operations--
> decisions involving production, technology, plant

location, investment, and marketing. This set of corporate prerogatives was codified in the "management rights" clauses of most collective bargaining agreements. In return, unions were accepted as legitimate representatives of workers' interests. They were expected to bargain on behalf of labor's immediate economic interests but not to challenge employer control of enterprises (much less the legitimacy of the capitalist system itself). Unions would help maintain an orderly and disciplined labor force while corporations would reward workers with a share of the income gains made possible by rising productivity, with greater employment security and with improved working conditions. (Bowles, Gordon, and Weisskopf, 1984: 73)

Jack Metzgar has attempted to expand the idea well beyond the limited sphere of industrial relations. Metzgar believes there is a "social contract" operating in the United States which goes well beyond collective bargaining:

The American system of collective bargaining is but the principal part of a larger negotiated settlement between capital and labor, a settlement that includes the social, cultural, and political realms as well as the economic. This settlement established a social contract between capital and labor, a contract that has determined the boundaries and rules of class struggle in all its reaches since the late 1940s. (Metzgar, 1980:33)

This social contract is claimed to operate in many spheres of life, as indicated. In the economic realm it operates through a system of collective bargaining which has become standardized since World War II. Metzgar emphasizes "management's rights" as the price employers demand for allowing collective bargaining to even take place:

At the workplace, the organized working class negotiates terms of employment (wages, hours, working conditions), but it does not interfere in the way management organizes work, runs its business, or invests its capital. Capital engages in collective bargaining in America only on the condition that labor recognizes "management's prerogative" to direct

> the work force and to run its business as it sees fit. The "management clause" in all union contracts specifies that it is the sole right of the owners of the means of production, and their representatives, to decide what will be produced, how it will be produced, and where it will be produced . . . . Labor's very right to bargain over terms of employment is contingent upon granting capital the right to make the ruling decisions. (Metzgar, 1980: 39)

This acceptance of management rights is seen as extending to the political arena, where government is to leave intact the basic prerogatives of business. For example, the government can seek to alleviate the disastrous consequences of a plant closing decision, but it is not to interfere with management's right to make that decision unrestricted by any external political power:

> This too is part of the social contract between labor and capital: though government has a right and responsibility to protect the citizenry from the overall effects of private enterprise, it has no right to interfere with the basic causes of those effects. And this is exactly what the American working class agreed to in its social contract with capital. (Metzgar, 1980:40)

Expanded to the entire political arena, Metzgar sees the social contract as committing workers to a restricted political role. Workers agree to play a passive role politically, essentially staying out of political affairs:

> Except as an "interest group" with a national lobby and sometimes as a local patronage administrator, the organized working class agrees to stay out of politics so long as it is granted the social space to cultivate its way of life and to look forward to a better tomorrow. (Metzgar, 1980:40)

The exchange alluded to grants workers the expectation of economic betterment and certain social and cultural autonomy.

This leads to the most imaginative part of Metzgar's thesis. The social contract in the collective bargaining and political arenas is merely a part of a larger social contract granting workers their own space culturally and socially, protecting them from domination by other social classes, according to Metzgar:

> The working class has sought to preserve its way of
> life primarily by ignoring the other classes, wherever
> this has been possible. Even in larger cities, the blue-
> collar worker greatly values a sense of power over the
> immediate environment and isolation from the
> disdainful glances of "the better classes." Working
> people do not compete with the other classes, though
> quietly they know their way to be superior, because
> they have been granted the social space in which to
> shape their own values and perceptions of the world.
> (Metzgar, 1980: 37-38)

The union contract, with its wage and working conditions
provisions, is seen as merely a means to this social and cultural
autonomy, the principal goal workers seek through the social contract:

> This freedom to live in its own way within a steadily
> expanding range of choices is the principal benefit for
> the working class of the social contract between
> capital and labor. . .this increase in social autonomy
> is the end for which improvements in wages, hours,
> pensions, and job security are merely means. In our
> society freedom and dignity are purchased with cash,
> and thus the organized worker has made wages and
> benefits the linchpin of the social contract with
> capital. (Metzgar, 1980:38)

Metzgar claims this is not merely the way it has worked out
but is actually the conscious choice made by workers in acceding to the
social contract:

> For over the past three decades it has seemed a small
> price to pay for these increases in social autonomy to
> allow "the company" and "the better classes" to make
> the larger decisions that determine the frameworks
> within which our lives are lived. (Metzgar, 1980:38)

Metzgar's thesis is provocative and and interesting, but it also
is highly speculative. A great many of its particulars could be
questioned. For example, the claim that workers quietly feel superior to
other classes is a very broad generalization that ignores an enormous
quantity of social science literature showing much the opposite.
Sennett and Cobb's The Hidden Injuries of Class is but one notable
example of the evidence that the U.S. class structure has driven many

workers into self-doubt and feelings of inferiority. There are undoubtedly sub-cultures where working class pride predominates, but this would not prove the broad generalization Metzgar makes for all workers, or even for all or the majority of organized workers.

Closely related, the claim that workers choose to "ignore" other classes of people wherever possible is difficult to evaluate. But surely it cannot be true in many of the stronger senses in which this claim might be taken. Working class people, of course, live within their own cultural milieu, but it is likely that they pay more attention to the lives and lifestyles of the professional and upper classes than vice versa.

Even if the previous claims can be substantiated, questions remain. The 1950s, 1960s, and 1970s would seem to be unusual years to pick as ones of particularly great social autonomy for U.S. workers. These were precisely the years when television became the dominant cultural medium for most people in the United States. The three decades following World War II were also years when traditional, usually ethnic, working class communities with a unique culture began to disintegrate at a faster pace due to suburbanization and demographic population shifts. Again, this is not to deny the existence of post-World War II working class communities with a unique culture; rather, the question is whether they were more prevalent than in previous periods and whether they had a more socially autonomous culture than had previously been the case. On the surface, at least, it is not apparent that either is true.

Related to this, and perhaps even more problematic, is the purported tie between an autonomous social existence and a union contract. Metzgar argues that the union contract protected an autonomous way of life "from domination or effective intrusion by the other classes" (Metzgar, 1980:38) because the improved wages, benefits, and job security won from the 1940s through the 1970s were able to buy autonomy. Perhaps; although the vagueness of the formulation makes it hard to tell. An "autonomous way of life" is a slippery phrase. For example, suppose that good union wages for an autoworker or a steelworker allow that worker to buy a fairly nice house in the suburbs plus a motor boat. Yet if this new lifestyle requires long hours of overtime work plus heavy installment debt payments, it is not clear that this can necessarily be considered greater social autonomy.

The above comments have all been directed at the most speculative aspects of Metzgar's claims. Intriguing and provocative as it is, Metzgar's version of a labor-capital social contract is very difficult to substantiate if rigorously questioned. Because my central concern in this chapter is with the less speculative claims of the more restricted versions of a social contract, I have not dealt with these issues in greater depth. But if my later cautions and criticisms hold for the more restricted versions, they would also certainly do so for Metzgar's more expanded version.

A further problem is that we have again moved beyond recognizable institutions (like labor unions and U.S. corporations) into the realm of a "contract" between "capital" and "labor" or "capital" and "the working class" (or at least the organized sector of the working class). While an analysis at that level of generality may be useful for some purposes, here it is more useful to carefully limit the idea of a social accord to specific arrangements between social institutions. Although the claims will be more limited, they will be easier to measure against our knowledge of the period.

II. THE POST-WORLD WAR II INDUSTRIAL SYSTEM

U.S. unions and their corporate adversaries emerged from World War II in an unsettled and somewhat contradictory position. On the one hand, the business community had reasserted its dominance in American life following the disastrous loss of influence and confidence during the depression of the 1930s. Taking advantage of the war effort and its defense contracts, American business used the wartime situation to reduce "New Deal" influence in Washington and to reclaim business control over all aspects of the war effort. After tax profits of $10 3/4 billion in 1944, well over double those of 1940, indicate how financially powerful and successful businesses had become.

At the same time, the institutional labor movement had recorded impressive gains during the same period. The extremely tight labor market, coupled with the urgent need for defense production free from disruption, meant that organized labor had a wonderful opportunity to consolidate its gains from the CIO upsurge of 1936-38 and even to expand. World War II (and preparations for it) had finally pulled the United States out of the Great Depression; labor markets were now more favorable for permanent organizing gains.   Furthermore, widespread U.S. government intervention into labor-management relations (primarily through the War Labor Board) protected union survival.   Although the intent was labor peace to ensure wartime production (not primarily to ensure union survival), the actual effect of the War Labor Board's "maintenance of membership" policy with its corollary, union dues check-off from an employee's paycheck by the company, meant a strong boost to unions' institutional stability and security.

In some unusual cases, government intervention virtually forced unionism on strongly anti-union employers, as with the Wilson meat packing company. More often, government influence was less drastic, but it did favor union survival as long as unions confined themselves to "responsible" roles in keeping with maximum production and minimum disruption. Unions which would accept this limited role and grant the no-strike pledge were encouraged and recognized. As the War Labor Board put it:

> By and large, the maintenance of stable union leadership and responsible union discipline makes for keeping faithfully the terms of the contract and provides a stable basis for more efficient production. (Filippelli, 1984:214)

By the end of World War II, union membership was approximately 15 million. This was over five times its membership only 12 years earlier and also a sizable increase from the slightly less than nine million in the immediate pre-war years. Whether employers liked it or not, unions were undeniably a presence to reckon with in the immediate post-war years.

But there was a third feature to the war years which caused management a great deal of discomfort. Management's "right to manage" had been challenged on many fronts during the war years. The source of the threat was occasionally the official union structure, but just as frequently it came from local unions and leaders acting on their own.

In certain industries, management felt that it was losing control over the workplace, at least to some degree. Although the degree of loss of control can easily be overemphasized--and was overemphasized by certain businessmen of the time--there is clear evidence that "management's right to manage" had been eroded during the war years. One indication was the demoralization among front line supervisors, and the consequent threat that they would unionize. A Foreman's Association of America union briefly made its appearance, causing immediate counter-measures by the corporate community. (Harris, 1982:74-87)

A second indication is the number of strikes, virtually all of them wildcats, which erupted near the end of the war. In 1944 alone, 18.5% of all rubber workers, 20.3% of all steelworkers, and 50.3% of all autoworkers went on strike. This was despite the no-strike pledge of the unions involved. Strikes were also serious in the farm equipment and electrical machinery industries. The extent of the wildcat strikes should not be exaggerated (the bulk were in just two industries and cities: auto and rubber, Detroit and Akron). Nevertheless, they were only the most extreme expression of a much greater restiveness on the part of the rank and file.

Wildcat strikes tended to center on workplace issues, ranging all the way from racist "hate strikes" against the introduction of black workers to strikes over safety. The erosion of management's control went beyond strikes, however. Shop floor union officials sometimes had a a great deal of authority over virtually all major shop-floor decisions. A 1946 survey of management acknowledges that management was not always in control. A rubber industry executive stated, "We recognize that in some of our shops the union committeeman exercises greater authority than the foreman," and an auto executive said, "If any manager in this industry tells you he has control of his plant he is a damn liar." (Brody, 1980:181)

Perhaps these were exaggerations, but they clearly represent a shift in workplace control to management's disadvantage. Weak or peripheral firms such as Packard and Studebaker in the auto industry were particularly vulnerable to rank-and-file encroachment on managerial authority.

Moving from the shop floor to the collective bargaining level, management also worried that unions were unwilling to confine themselves to their "proper" sphere. A November 1945 conference of major labor leaders and organized business only intensified these fears. At that conference, the labor representatives refused to accept any list of the specific functions reserved only to management and not subject to union influence or bargaining.

Thomas Roy Jones, a key figure in the National Association of Manufacturers, sounded the alarm:

> In the labor leader's way of thinking, there is no conceivable concession which the employer should not make, no obligation which he should not assume. Annual wages, private social security systems, early

retirement, twenty-five hour weeks--all are completely within the range of economic possibility. Of course, control of management is possible, too; and so is the distribution of profits; and advertising policy; and marketing and production methods. . . .But there is a limit to everything. The limit here might be the relinquishment of the stockholders' last right--the ownership of corporate stock. . . .If this is not to be countenanced, then some limit has to be set before that end is reached. What is that limit, and who will set it? (Harris, 1982:59)

This is overwrought language of an alarmist nature, but it was only slightly stronger in tone than many management pronouncements at the time.

In fact, most unions were only seeking to control or influence management's rights in very specific areas of personnel policy: those most directly affecting their membership. This meant wages and hours, "just cause" for discipline, and a reasonable or rational basis for layoffs, rehires, and promotions (with seniority playing a prominent role). These were not the revolutionary challenges envisioned by some business spokespersons; in fact; they became commonplaces in virtually all later union contracts.

However, further issues were "up for grabs," or at least appeared to be at the time. Most immediate were production standards, work rules, and the like. In the 1940s some unions were demanding to bargain not only over the setting of these but also their administration. This would have required union approval before these standards could be set, modified, implemented, updated, etc. To management, this was a frightening restriction of legitimate authority. Worse than the actual changes being forced on managers was the uneasiness about "where it all would end"; the feeling of being ever more hemmed in. In practically all industries, the trend had been against managerial control throughout the war years.

Finally, there were the larger fears that some labor leaders were aggressively pushing union control beyond the limited sphere of personnel matters or strictly shop-floor issues. Walter Reuther of the auto workers was the chief villain in corporate eyes, but Phillip Murray of the United Steelworkers and Sidney Hillman of the Amalgamated Clothing Workers also were attacked vehemently for their alleged socialistic inroads on basic corporate authority over business decisions.

There was some substance to these fears, although these leaders were hardly the radicals they were seen as. Reuther and Murray had proposed joint labor-management councils in each industry to oversee defense production. Old line labor progressives like John Brophy, labor intellectuals like Clinton Golden of the Steelworkers, and others pushed "industrial democracy" as the culmination of the CIO upsurge. Reuther's famous reconversion plan to shift from wartime to peace production also contained a large and influential role for labor. All of this appeared to the business community as an alarming incursion on management's basic authority concerning the broader issues of running the business.

The most immediate push was on corporate pricing policy. Unions were putting forth slogans like "Higher Wages Without Price Increases." In the famous 1945-46 UAW strike against General Motors, Walter Reuther demanded that GM "open the books" to prove to the union (and the public) that it could not meet his demands without a price increase. Even worse from management's point of view, union meddling with pricing policy could easily be followed by union attempts to influence or control investment decisions and plant location choices. Yet another union target could be choice of new technology and its introduction if this encroachment was allowed.

Consequently, the corporations in all the major industries in the 1945-1950 period stood determined to reassert management control over all areas of authority it had lost. This meant a sharp reassertion of supervisory authority at the workplace. Authority to discipline disruptive workers and local leaders was one key. In industry after industry, this battle was fought (and largely won) by the corporations in the late 1940s and throughout the 1950s.

As in much else, General Motors took the lead. It took on the auto workers in all areas with a professionalism and determination that would only be duplicated by others more slowly, if at all. In the 1945-46 negotiating round, it took a 113-day strike and tens of millions of dollars in immediate losses to assert its managerial authority and prerogatives. In a letter to the UAW, the corporation laid down the limits of any acceptable bargaining:

> 1) That wages, hours of employment, and other conditions of employment are the only matters which are subject to collective bargaining.

> 3) That the products to be manufactured, the location of plants, the schedules of production, the methods,

processes, and means of manufacturing, the right to hire, promote, transfer, discharge or discipline for cause, and to maintain discipline or efficiency of employees, are the sole responsibility of the corporation.

7) That there be appropriate penalties, including loss of seniority, against any employe (sic) taking part in any strike or work stoppage in violation of the agreement. (Harris, 1982:142)

On all these major points, GM won. Although it was unable to achieve its more extreme proposals, such as total elimination of any union security provisions or elimination of meaningful seniority rules, it reached a compromise that it could definitely live with. The union had been shown the futility of any further attempts to extend union influence or authority into "management's rights."

In the 1948 and 1950 bargaining rounds, GM consolidated its position on the "management's rights" front by extending to the union relatively generous terms on wages and fringe benefits. The pattern was clear: absolute resistance on control issues, accommodation and flexibility on employment costs. This pattern was to be replicated by other major corporations in the 1945-1960 period.

The 1950 GM-UAW bargaining round sealed the direction which had been set earlier. No longer was the union seriously pushing forward on job control on management authority issues; all movements in this area were slight and favorable to the company. Instead the union pressed for the money; management got the rest. GM also got an unprecedented five year contract, ensuring stability and known labor costs for the indefinite future. Dubbing the contract "The Treaty of Detroit," Fortune magazine was ecstatic over the agreement. "G.M. may have paid a billion for peace. It got a bargain," it intoned:

What did the corporation buy for its billion. . .? . . . General Motors has regained control over one of the crucial management functions in any line of manufacturing--long-range scheduling of production, model changes, and tool and plant investment. It has been so long since any big U.S. manufacturer could plan with complete confidence in its labor relations that industry has almost forgotten what it felt like. (Fortune, 1950:53)

Stability was granted to the corporation, its chief aim. The union received hefty wage and fringe benefits improvements for its membership. The trade-off meant that a somewhat stable, modern "mature" relationship between the two had now been forged. Gone were the days of a strong union threat to "management rights." Equally gone were the days of overt union-busting. The union threat had been contained.

Politically, the corporate community also moved to clip the wings of the labor movement. Already in the later war years, the business community had populated many positions in the Roosevelt administration, turning many of its policies toward a conservative direction quite opposite to the "New Deal" liberalism that followed the 1936 election. The 1946 congressional elections were disastrous for the Democrats and even more disastrous for liberals.

A right wing crusade, ostensibly targeting Communism but actually aimed at containment and partial reversal of the New Deal, swept the country. Anti-communism became a bludgeon to use against any and all opposition to corporate goals. The labor movement, particularly the CIO, was one target of this crusade. Loyalty oaths, purges of unions from the ranks of the CIO, purges of individual members and leaders from national and local unions, widespread raiding of members from established bargaining units, and the permanent loss of tens of thousands of members to the labor movement were all results of this anti-communist crusade during the late 1940s and early 1950s.

But the most immediate blow to the labor movement was passage of the Taft-Hartley Act in 1947. The National Association of Manufacturers was directly behind this bill, which banned the closed shop, allowed states to ban the union shop, created unfair labor practices (illegal labor tactics) for unions for the first time, and required all union leaders to sign a non-Communist affidavit if the union was to use the National Labor Relations Board.

Even though the Taft-Hartley Act was clearly anti-labor, it just as surely demonstrated that there would not be a repeat of the post-World War I situation: labor was to be contained, but most of the business community was not prepared to attempt its total destruction. Most of the basic labor rights contained in the 1935 Wagner Act were left intact. Weakening labor both politically and at the bargaining table was important, but few corporations had the will to attempt a bloody all-out assault, precisely at the time when U.S. business expansion abroad was uppermost on the minds of the major corporate decision makers. Practically speaking, organized labor was just too well entrenched; the costs of total warfare against it were too great to justify this course of action.

Corporate political behavior in the 1950s was also designed to keep labor from advancing any major legislative goals. In this respect, the Cold War helped business immensely; the 1950s labor movement was retreating and very much on the defensive in the atmosphere of the anti-communist hysteria of the McCarthy period and its aftermath. Yet, even at this time, the goal was containment and a weakening of organized labor, not its total elimination.

This chapter has focused on the auto industry, and General Motors in particular, to exemplify the trends of the period. So it is important to note that there were wide variations from the GM pattern. Even within the auto industry, Chrysler was different throughout most of the 1950s. It was not until the end of that decade that Chrysler was successful in adopting the more "professional" approach to labor relations pioneered by GM and closely followed by Ford. Throughout the 1950s, Chrysler experienced labor turbulence, wildcat strikes, and shop floor struggles over disciplinary and workplace control issues. However, by 1960 it had "normalized" its relations with the union to the extent that it now resembled GM and Ford. (Jefferys, 1986)

In virtually all industries, real struggles continued over very major areas of authority. Contracting out of work, plant openings and closings, technological change, and especially job standards, job descriptions, operating rates, and the like, were all subject to struggle and negotiation. The struggles were particularly acute for immediate shop floor issues. All told, between 1947 and 1960, approximately 25% of all strikes were over issues of work load, job security, or shop conditions. (Brody, 1980:195)

Different industries followed different patterns. In the steel industry, local union control over local work practices was granted by section 2-B of the contract. Only by means of technological change or some similarly large change in the entire "basis" for a practice could a steel company unilaterally change workplace practices. An eight month strike in 1959 was primarily over management's attempt to reassert authority over this crucial issue. The industry lost; 2-B remained in the contract. Over the next twenty years, the industry accomplished its objective in a "softer" way: technological changes and buying off any jobs lost through changed work rules. But in 1959 the "hard" approach only precipitated a strike which the employers lost.

Other industries exhibited notable conflict. In farm equipment, J.I. Case, Allis Chalmers, and International Harvester all took long and bitter strikes. International Harvester was particularly notable for its anti-union behavior, but the entire industry was far less reconciled to unions and collective bargaining than was the auto industry.

Electrical products also differed. General Electric, which had accepted unionism since the 1930s, felt betrayed by the militance of a 1946 strike by its union, the United Electrical Workers (UE). In the words of historian Howell Harris, GE "went to war" against the UE:

> Under a new vice-president, Lemuel Boulware, it embarked on a successful campaign to divide and undermine its unionized workforce. The corporation became stridently anti-Communist and used the Taft-Hartley law, churchmen, rightist labor leaders, Cold War liberal Democrats, and McCarthy himself--the man, not just the ism--to help it smash the UE. Boulware made many practical and rhetorical attacks on the strength and the very legitimacy of unionism. . . .It showed the hardest face of managerial realism in its determination to confine unionism to the declining blue-collar labor force in traditional industrial districts, to weaken and dominate the blue collar unions it tolerated, and to get rid of them altogether where it lawfully could. (Harris, 1982:157)

Boulware's later collective bargaining tactics in undermining the unions he dealt with were so famous that they became known as "Boulwarism." Westinghouse, although less strident, was hardly friendly to unions. Bitter strikes in 1946 and 1955-56 at Westinghouse punctuated a rocky relationship with its unions.

Other industries never even accepted unionism and were able to prevent unions from ever getting an effective toehold at all. The chemical industry is a case in point. Companies like DuPont remained either union-free or confined their labor organizations to the status of independent "enterprise" unions (often "company" unions or something very close to it). The oil industry likewise fought unions tenaciously, preventing them from ever attaining a strong bargaining position.

To this point, our entire discussion has centered on CIO unions in large basic industries. Outside the basic industries, in localized situations where employers were usually smaller and craft unions exercised considerable workplace power through "control of the craft," the situation was quite different. In construction, for example, the skilled craftsmen and their unions already had considerable influence over many workplace issues all along. The above analysis cannot be applied to this sector of the labor movement because of its many differences in union structure, employers, etc.

Despite all these differences, a generalization can be made about the post-war years. In the "core" industries of the U.S. economy, labor-management relations after World War II stabilized. Unions were grudgingly accepted as fairly permanent fixtures on the industrial scene. However, they were "legitimate" only to the extent that they confined themselves to narrow personnel issues. Accepting this role, U.S. unions in these industries made large monetary gains in the decades following the second World War but lost influence and potential power in the larger areas of corporate decision making.

III. A SOCIAL ACCORD?

If we attempt to summarize the preceding section in the language of a social accord, we could state it as follows: organized labor and management in the major core industries of the United States implicitly (and to some degree explicitly) developed a trade-off in their dealings with each other in the post-World War II decades. In this trade-off, the unions ceded to management its two major goals at the time: (1) stability, or predictability, in its labor relations and (2) control over the major decisions affecting the enterprise (as defined in the "management's rights clause" of the union contract). In return, management granted to the unions their two major goals: (1) legitimacy, or acceptance as permanent fixtures in the industrial scene, and (2) for the membership, relatively good wages and benefits (steadily increasing from year to year), and relative job security.

This trade-off was understood by the two sides as a trade-off, at least implicitly. Hence, a refusal by the other side to live up to its end of the accord would be seen as a betrayal by the injured party. The contours of this social accord were clarified more or less rapidly in the decade and a half following World War II. For some companies it was solidly in place by the early 1950s; for others it took until the end of the decade. But for the vast majority, the pattern was firmly established by 1960.

The union grant of stability or predictability to the corporation meant that contracts would be longer. Instead of one year between bargaining sessions, two years and eventually three became the norm. The union was expected to allow effective discipline over workers engaging in wildcat strikes, slowdowns, or other disruptions of production. In some cases, the union was required to actively intervene to end such disruptions and to help the corporation enforce discipline. Grievance procedures were to be developed and used to cause minimal disruption to ongoing production. "Quickie strikes," shop-floor confrontations, and the like were out; the union was to guide all grievances into specific bureaucratic channels which progressively moved the dispute away from the shop floor and the immediate protagonists.

Closely allied to the stability issue was the control issue. Unions were to stay out of all major decisions affecting the overall direction of the enterprise. On issues not directly tied in to the shop floor the prohibition was complete. Pricing policy, product determination, plant location, investment decisions, financing options, and the like were entirely sacrosanct and off limits to the unions. Other issues which directly impacted on the working conditions on the shop floor were subject to more skirmishes but large issues like technological change were to be left to management with minimal or no union interference.

For the union, legitimacy or acceptance from the corporation meant that blatant union-busting was to be a thing of the past. Corporations were to grant automatic check-off of union dues from employees' paychecks, accept the union shop in states where such a contract clause was legal, agree to the basic features of the union contract necessary for unions to function normally (such as seniority rights), etc. Also, companies would not attempt to operate during a strike or attempt to use a strike as an opportunity to permanently employ strikebreakers and break the union. In cases where a "mature" relationship had developed fully, companies would even grant concessions to specific leaders with an eye toward strengthening the political position or internal stability of union administrations which were more accommodating.

From the union side, the bedrock of any accord with management had to be the delivery of enough significant company concessions to the membership that they would accept the trade-off. This was delivered in the form of steady wage increases, with few interruptions, for close to three decades. Benefits packages followed suit, becoming more varied in content and larger as a percentage of total compensation. Job security also was quite good, especially for workers with significant seniority. A "good" job in a key unionized industry in the 1950s or 1960s meant a job for life in the eyes of those entering it.

Thus the industrial relations system in the decades immediately following the second World War can be summarized in the language of a "social accord." The terms of the accord are summarized in Table 1.

TABLE 1
The Terms of a Possible "Social Accord" Between Organized Labor and Major Corporations in the Decades Immediately Following World War II

Labor was to grant Capital:	Capital was to grant Labor:
Above all, labor relations stability and "management rights"	Above all, legitimacy and economic gains
--longer contracts	--automatic union dues check-off
--effective discipline over disruptive workers	--union shop, where legal
--end to wildcat strikes, "quickie" strikes, slowdowns	--no operation of facilities during strikes
--orderly and bureaucratic grievance procedures	--steadily increasing wages
--free hand in overall policy matters (pricing, product, plant locations, investment, etc.)	--benefits increases, both in quantity and variety
--company control of technological change, direction of the workforce, etc.	--relatively good job security for the workforce

Perhaps a similar "accord" could be constructed for the much less clearly defined political arena. Such an accord would stress the unions' commitment to stay within the established two party system. No third party or labor party would be allowed. A socialist or social democratic direction, as embodied in much of the European labor movement, was to be forsworn. Neither would the unions attempt to turn the Democratic Party into a labor party by challenging the dominance of liberal business elements within that party. Labor support was also expected for corporate goals in U.S. foreign policy. In exchange, the business community was to accept organized labor as a legitimate--if junior--partner in political affairs. The labor movement obtained important (although not dominant) influence within the Democratic Party. And in general, the business community moderated its most extreme right wing, allowing organized labor and its allies a number of social reforms in times of liberal prosperity, such as the 1960s.

Such an accord in the political arena is probably more speculative than it would be on the industrial front, however. In any case, most of the advocates of the notion of a social accord do not extend it to politics. Consequently, we will confine our attention here to the more restricted "accord" in the labor relations field.

The terms of a social accord have been stated. Do they hold up? Was there such an accord? Is this an accurate description of the time? I believe that the social accord analysis pinpoints some very important features of the industrial relations system at the time, but it needs at least four significant qualifications if it is to be upheld.

First, the terms of this accord did not extend to many industries. It was confined mainly to the central "core" industries in the U.S. economy, where the industry was likely to be concentrated to such a degree that "administered prices" rather than competitive pricing policies were possible. The auto and steel industries are perfect examples. Even in industries less oligopolized than auto, the accord's terms were operative only when competition was less intense. Fiercely competitive industries, even if heavily unionized, did not deliver the wage and benefit gains. The men's clothing industry, the shoe industry, the textile industry, and the ladies garment industry are all examples of unionized industries left out of the full terms of the accord. Wages in these industries fell well behind those in the more oligopolized industries like auto.

Even within the more concentrated industries, the terms of the accord only held to the degree that strong, individual unions dominated the field. Wherever industries were fragmented among numerous unions, or where unionization was less complete, employers used their advantage to divide and conquer. The electrical products industry, which had been split among many unions following the red scare purge of the United Electrical Workers (UE) from the CIO, was a clear example. Wages in this industry progressively fell behind those in comparable industries because of this. Any accord in this industry was very partial at best. Other industries where the union failed to establish itself as a strong, unavoidable presence were devoid of any full blown accord. The oil industry, the chemical industry, or the pharmaceutical industry serve as examples.

A second major qualification concerns employer acceptance of unions and collective bargaining. Even though major corporations pragmatically accommodated themselves to unions, this adaptation was never deep or philosophical. At the philosophical level, the vast majority of employers were committed to unions only at the level of convenience. In the terminology of historian Howell Harris, they were "realists" rather than converts to the "progressive" position of harmonious interests between employer and union. This meant that any "accord" would be at best a marriage of convenience. Depending on circumstances and opportunities, large U.S. employers seized upon the opportunities to weaken or undermine (in the long run) the very "responsible bargaining partners" they were supposedly committed to.

Even in the 1950s and 1960s, and with accelerated intensity in the 1970s and 1980s, U.S. businesses relocated production facilities with an eye toward union avoidance wherever possible. The behavior of Ingersoll-Rand, which progressively moved from 100% unionized in 1960 to 80% by 1970 to 60% by 1980 to 30% by 1986, was not atypical. Through mergers, acquisitions, selective plant closings and openings, and occasional decertifications, Ingersoll-Rand steadily freed itself of union dependence. (Knauss and Matuszak) GM's famous "southern strategy"--an attempt to escape the UAW by opening plants in the deep south--is but one more example.

A third major qualification is necessary. On the shop floor, at the rank-and-file level, it is doubtful that any accord ever existed. We have already noted that shop-floor struggles continued throughout the 1950s and 1960s over shop-floor issues such as job standards, line speeds, discipline, and the like. Where management's "control" issues directly impinged on working conditions, unionized workers resisted. Contrary to many of our images of the decade, the "quiet fifties" were not so quiet from the standpoint of the shop floor. Looking at the auto industry, one observer notes:

> Contrary to oft heard claims, the 1950s were not--for this industry at least--a decade of worker quiescence, eclipsed by the shop floor insurgency of the Vietnam era. Rather, the fifties were an era of widespread rank and file protest, of unrepeated levels of wildcat strike activity as workers remained incompletely inducted into the logic of the mature connective bargaining model. Only after a severe industrial contraction extending through the later years of the decade had the shop floors of America's auto plants taken on a manifest calm that would serve as the apparent benchmark against which analysts (misleadingly)

compared a militant resurgence in the late 1960s and early 1970s. (Flaherty, 1988: 270)

The few studies of shop floor relations in the 1950s which have been done seem to bear this out. (Jefferys, 1986) There were too many battles over working conditions in the 1950s to be able to characterize relations at this level as an "accord" or a "truce."

If there was an accord, it was at the level of the collective bargaining system. It was not at the level of shop-floor relations or practice. And by far the most unpopular aspects of that accord were those which gave management a freer hand in discipline and control of working conditions.

A fourth qualification concerns the duration and timing of any accord. In some of the versions of the social accord, it began to disintegrate in the second half of the 1960s because of worker militancy (Bowles, Gordon, and Weisskopf, 1984: 84-91; Naples, 1987). According to this analysis, rank-and-file movements in the late 1960s and early 1970s undermined the social accord by disrupting the stability it had earlier delivered to the corporations. Ultimately, it is claimed, this disruption reached such proportions that corporate profitability was badly undermined.

If the social accord was only fully realized in some industries in the very late 1950s (but in others, earlier), its dissolution beginning approximately in 1966 would make it a very short "accord" indeed. A more detailed examination is likely to show that the terms of the "accord" held in their essentials for widely varying periods depending upon the industry and company studied. For one, it may be from the early 1950s through the mid-1960s; for another, it may be from 1960 until the late 1970s. For yet a third, it may have "held" only through the late 1950s to mid-1960s for five or six years. For many, it may have been operative from the early to mid-1950s up through the mid- to late 1970s.

We lack the sufficient number of detailed historical investigations into specific industries and companies for this time period to be definitive, but what we do know would seem to indicate wide variations. When the accord could be considered "broken" is also a matter of interpretation; the looseness of its terms necessarily make this the case. But it is clear that the patterns are not identical from industry to industry. In steel, for example, the "accord" would seem to have worked best in the late 1960s through the late 1970s; a period when the Experimental Negotiating Agreement (ENA) guaranteeing no strikes was enacted and labor-industry cooperation was at its highest. Yet in the mining industry, the exact opposite was the case: wildcat strikes and major confrontations were the order of the day.

The point is that any "accord" must be considered rather elastic in its application from industry to industry or company to company. Rigid periodization along the lines of a "labor truce" followed by a "labor revolt" will not fit the facts very well.

Four major qualifications have been added to the "social accord" analysis: (1) certain industries were never covered by the terms of the accord or were only partially; (2) the accord did not signify a permanent or philosophical acceptance of unions; (3) the accord was not operative at the shop floor level for issues concerning working conditions; and (4) it was operative for widely different periods and lengths of time, depending on industry and corporation.

Do all of these qualifications destroy the entire notion of a social accord? By the time we are done, has it died a "death by one thousand cuts"? I don't think so. The qualifications merely make it ·more precise. The main features of post-World War II industrial relations and the trade-offs involved are precisely pinpointed by the social accord analysis. Even if its full terms were confined to core industries, and even with all the other qualifications, the social accord exerted a widespread and powerful influence across the entire industrial spectrum. Thus, the idea is too important to be discarded merely because it needs important qualifications. However, the language with which this idea is expressed should perhaps be re-examined.

Because the terms "accord," "contract," "compact," "truce," etc., could be misleading in their implications, it may be wiser to adopt another terminology. For example, Piore and Sabel criticize the notion of a social accord as follows:

> But the notion of an accord is misleading: it is misleading either if taken in the strong sense of a peace treaty setting out the rights and responsibilities of each party or if taken in the weak sense of a cease-fire freezing the positions obtained during past battles and subject to violation whenever the balance of forces changes. There was neither a peace treaty nor a cease-fire; rather, there was a shared set of understandings about the continuation of the struggle. (Piore and Sabel, 1984: 98)

It seems to me that it is precisely the idea of "a shared set of understandings about the continuation of the struggle" that the social accord analysis is pointing to. Yet, misleading implications are read into this choice of words.

If we intend to pinpoint a somewhat stable set of trade-offs and mutual expectations which emerged between organized labor and the corporate community in key industries following World War II, a different wording is perhaps advisable. The parameters of acceptable behavior on both sides could be described as an "accommodation." Given the lack of philosophical depth or conviction on the business side in its commitment to this accommodation, it is even better described as a "provisional accommodation." The terms of the provisional accommodation would be identical to those listed in Table 1 as the terms of the social accord.

The provisional or conditional nature of this accommodation is clearly evidenced by the behavior of the corporate community in the 1980s. In virtually all industries, the economic terms of the trade-off have been broken. Steadily increasing wages and improved benefits packages disappeared. "Concession bargaining" became the order of the day. Even with a long recovery in the second half of the 1980s, negotiated wage and benefit increases failed to keep up with the inflation rate; real incomes were dropping.

The job security provisions were equally abrogated. Massive permanent layoffs and plant closings in one major unionized industry after another made good paying union jobs among the most insecure.

Even the legitimacy of unions as institutions was no longer a given. A strike frequently became a tool to break the union, .^ the company would continue to operate using permanent replacements. "Union avoidance" and "decertification" specialists widely plied their trade, which became a multi-million dollar business. Large employers who were absolutely unable to avoid their unions were more circumspect and avoided blatant union-busting of a confrontational nature, but the overall pattern was clear.

In a word, the accommodation (or "accord") has been broken by the corporate side. A usual explanation for this is the highly competitive atmosphere of the 1980s due to increased foreign and domestic competition. While this is undoubtedly a major factor in the aggressiveness of the assault on unions, it is only part of the story. Ever since the 1950s corporations had been positioning themselves to progressively shed their unions. In reviewing the data on union and non-union plants, Klein and Wanger found that "most of the union plants were built before the mid-1950s, while those plants built since have remained predominantly nonunion." An industrial relations director explained:

> Up until the 1950s we often encouraged cooperative unions to organize within our plants in an effort to avoid having to negotiate with one of the larger international unions. But in the 1950s, we got smarter in our personnel practices and the NLRB handed down a number of rulings which finally allowed us to tell our side of the story during organizing campaigns. (Klein and Wanger, 1984: 77,76)

Much of the progressive de-unionization occurred through selective patterns of plant closings and openings and work relocations, although other devices were employed.

Thus, even at the height of the accommodation, the corporate community was undermining the power basis of the labor movement. When the conditions were ripe for a massive assault on unions (as in the 1980s), it was carried out.

IV. CONCLUSION

The "social accord" analysis of U.S. labor relations in the post-World II period points to a number of the major and important features of the period. However, previous analyses needs considerable qualification. Ultimately, the entire language of an "accord" may be too confusing to be worth using.

However, this should not blind us to the extremely important issues raised by the social accord analysis. The critical point is this: <u>it is precisely labor's retreat on the management's rights issues which has left it defenseless in the wake of the corporate assault on unions in the 1980s.</u> As long as unions have no control (and no legitimate right to seek control) over plant location decisions, investment policy, introduction of technological change, and other key management decisions, they are at a tremendous disadvantage in an unfavorable atmosphere such as the 1980s.

This is not to argue that the retreat on managerial control issues could have been easily avoided. The accommodation was in accordance with the dominant temper of the times. Perhaps it was unavoidable. At the time it seemed to most of those involved to work out well for all concerned, and it seemed to work over a number of decades. Corporations got stability, unions got (conditional) legitimacy, and the union worker got a steadily rising standard of living.

There was minimal or non-existent union rank-and-file pressure in the immediate post-war period for union control over the "bigger" capital decisions, or to contain management direction of all but immediate workplace issues. And any attempt to push forward on this frontier, like Walter Reuther's one weak attempt at influence over pricing policy, was bound to meet extremely strong corporate resistance. Nevertheless, the labor movement's failure to push forward in this area (coupled with its failure to advance in political power or, most important, in organizing the unorganized) has left it wide open to the devastating assault it faces in the 1980s and 1990s.

BIBLIOGRAPHY

1. Barbash, Jack, <u>Trade Unions and National Economic Policy</u>, Baltimore: The Johns Hopkins Press, 1972.

2. Bowles, Samuel, and Herbert Gintis, "The Crisis of Liberal Democratic Capitalism: The Case of the United States," <u>Politics and Society</u>, Vol. 11, No. 1 (1982), pp. 51-94.

3. Bowles, Samuel, David M. Gordon, and Thomas E. Weisskopf, <u>Beyond the Wasteland: A Democratic Alternative to Economic Decline</u>, Garden City, N.Y.: Anchor Press, 1984.

4. Brody, David, "The Uses of Power I: Industrial Battleground", and "The Uses of Power II: Political Action", pp. 173-257 in <u>Workers in Industrial America: Essays on the 20th Century Struggle</u>, New York: Oxford University Press, 1980.

5. Davis, Mike, <u>Prisoners of the American Dream</u>, London: Verso, 1986.

6. Filippelli, Ronald L., <u>Labor in the USA: A History</u>, New York: Alfred. A. Knopf, 1984.

7. Flaherty, Sean, "Mature Collective Bargaining and Rank and File Militancy: Breaking the Peace of the 'Treaty of Detroit'," <u>Research in Political Economy</u>, Vol. 11 (1988), pp. 241-280.

8. Flanagan, Robert J., "The National Accord as a Social Contract," <u>Industrial and Labor Relations Review,</u> Vol. 34, No. 1 (October 1980), pp. 35-50.

9. <u>Fortune</u>, "The Treaty of Detroit," Vol. XLII, No. 1 (July 1950), pp. 53-55.

10. Gordon, David M., Richard Edwards and Michael Reich, <u>Segmented Work, Divided Workers: The Historical Transformation of Labor in the United States</u>, New York: Cambridge University Press, 1982.

11. Harris, Howell John, The Right to Manage, Madison, Wisconsin: The University of Wisconsin Press, 1982.

12. Jefferys, Steve, Management and Managed, New York: Cambridge University Press, 1986.

13. Klein, Janice A., and E. David Wanger, "The Legal Setting for the Emergence of the Union Avoidance Strategy," pp. 75-88 in Thomas A. Kochan, ed., Challenges and Choices Facing American Labor, Cambridge, Massachusetts: The MIT Press, 1985.

14. Knauss, Keith, and Michael Matuszak, "Torrington/Ingersoll-Rand's Shutdown of its South Bend Heavy Bearings Plant," in Charles Craypo, ed., Grand Designs: The Corporate Assault on Local Unions (forthcoming).

15. Kochan, Thomas, Harry Katz, and Robert McKersie, The Transformation of American Industrial Relations, New York: Basic Books, 1986.

16. Kochan, Thomas, and Michael Piore, "Will the New Industrial Relations Last? Implications for the American Labor Movement," AAPSS Annals, 473 (May 1984), pp. 177-189.

17. Mann, Eric, Taking on General Motors, Los Angeles: UCLA Institute of Industrial Relations, 1987.

18. Metzgar, Jack, "Plant Shutdowns and Worker Response: The Case of Johnstown, Pa.," Socialist Review, No. 53 (Sept.-Oct. 1980), pp. 9-49.

19. Moody, Kim, An Injury to All, London: Verso, 1988.

20. Moye, William T., "Presidential Labor-Management Committees: Productive Failures," Industrial and Labor Relations Review, Vol. 34, No. 1 (Oct. 1980), pp. 51-66.

21. Moynihan, Daniel Patrick, "Foreword", pp. i-iii, in Sol Chick Chaikin, A Labor Viewpoint: Another Opinion, Monroe, N.Y.: Library Research Associates, 1980.

22. Naples, Michele I., "Industrial Conflict and Its Implications for Productivity Growth," AEA Papers and Proceedings, Vol. 71, No. 2 (May 1981), pp. 36-41.

23. Naples, Michele I., "Cyclical and Secular Productivity Slowdowns", pp. 159-170, in Robert Cherry, Christine D'Onofrio, Cigdem Kurdas, Thomas R. Michl, Fred Moseley, and Michele I. Naples, eds., The Imperiled Economy, New York: The Union for Radical Political Economics, 1987.

24. Piore, Michael J. and Charles F. Sabel. The Second Industrial Divide, New York: Basic Books, 1984.

25. Raskin, A. H. "Labor: a Movement in Search of a Mission," pp. 3-38 in Seymour Martin Lipset, ed., Unions in Transition, San Francisco: Institute for Contemporary Studies, 1986.

26. Serrin, William. The Company and the Union, New York: Alfred A. Knopf, 1973.

27. Serrin, William. "Cold Warriors Throw an Icy Reception," In These Times, August 17-30, 1988, pp. 18-19.

28. Sweeney, John J., and Karen Nussbaum. Solutions for the New Workforce, Cabin John, Maryland: Seven Locks Press, 1989.

Further Resources

Bowles, Samuel, David M. Gordon, and Thomas E. Weisskopf, Beyond the Wasteland: A Democratic Alternative to Economic Decline (Garden City, NY: Anchor Press, 1984). This book relies heavily on the notion of a capital-labor accord and its dissolution in the late 1960s to explain economic decline. It presents alternative proposals for a more democratic and worker oriented economy.

Brody, David, Workers in Industrial America (New York: Oxford University Press, 1980) chapters 5 and 6. These chapters examine the post-World War II industrial and political labor scene in the United States. Although he does not use the language of a "social accord", Brody does argue that the corporations and the institutional unions had a common interest in containing rank-and-file independent activity in the post-war years.

Davis, Mike, Prisoners of the American Dream (London: Verso, 1986). A leftist analysis of U.S. labor today. Davis touches on many themes which are relevant to the issue of a labor-capital social accord.

Flaherty, Sean, "Mature Collective Bargaining and Rank and File Militancy: Breaking the Peace of the 'Treaty of Detroit'" (Research in Political Economy, Vol. 11, 1988, pp. 241-280). This article analyzes the auto industry from the 1950s to the present in terms which rely upon and relate directly to a "social accord" analysis.

Gordon, David M., Richard Edwards, and Michael Reich, Segmented Work, Divided Workers: The Historical Transformation of Labor in the United States (New York: Cambridge University Press, 1982). This book, which presents a segmented labor market economic theory, relies on the notion of a "labor truce" in the post-World War II years.

Harris, Howell John, The Right to Manage (Madison, Wisconsin: The University of Wisconsin Press, 1982). This book is a very important contribution to our knowledge of the World War II and post-war years concerning labor-management relations. Harris illuminates the "management's rights" issues of the time.

Jefferys, Steve, Management and Managed: Fifty Years of Crisis at Chrysler (New York: Cambridge University Press, 1986). Examining shop floor relations at the Dodge Main plant in Detroit, this book argues against the notion of a "labor truce" in the 1950s, followed by a "labor revolt" in the late 1960s and early 1970s. Jefferys argues that there never was a truce at the shop floor level.

Kochan, Thomas A., and Michael J. Piore, "Will the New Industrial Relations Last? Implications for the American Labor Movement" (AAPSS Annals, 473, May 1984, pp. 177-189). Kochan and Piore outline the industrial relations system of the past fifty years, which they call "the New Deal industrial relations system," and which they argue is now outmoded. They call for a new form of accommodation between labor and capital, one which relies on labor-management cooperation and which has even less room for independent union power than was previously the case.

Metzgar, Jack, "Plant Shutdowns and Worker Response: The Case of Johnstown, Pa." (Socialist Review, No. 53, Sept.-Oct., 1980), pp. 9-49). Metzgar presents a far-reaching version of a social contract between labor and capital. The contract is said to hold in the industrial relations, political, and social and cultural spheres. Imaginative and provocative, but highly speculative.

Moody, Kim, An Injury to All: the Decline of American Unionism (London: Verso, 1988). Moody presents a leftist analysis of American unionism in the post-war period, arguing that business unionism has drained the labor movement of its vitality. Many issues relevant to a social accord are contained in this book.

Piore, Michael J., and Charles Sabel. The Second Industrial Divide (New York: Basic Books, 1984). Piore and Sabel analyze the U.S. industrial relations system in terms relevant to a "social accord" analysis.

Serrin, William. The Company and the Union (New York: Alfred A. Knopf, 1973). Classic account of labor-management relations between General Motors and the United Autoworkers in the early 1970s.

CHAPTER 6

A NEW ENVIRONMENT CONFRONTS TRADE UNIONS IN ADVANCED INDUSTRIAL COUNTRIES

A Comparative Institutional Analysis

Solomon Barkin*

Buffeted by economic turmoil, strong cyclical movements, rising levels of unemployment, unfriendly economic and political policies and hostile employers and governments in the seventies and early eighties, trade unions in advanced industrial states after 1983 faced a markedly changed environment. Only slowly did the nature of the new era become apparent. New economic and industrial structures emerged; the composition of the work force changed; and the balance of power in the labor market had been shifted. Unions began to realize that their position was less secure and their bargaining leverage had weakened. Their membership in some countries had been significantly reduced, while in others it was maintained only with difficulty. Much expansion took place in several countries outside of the ranks of the established national federations, as many new recruits came from the

*The author wishes to acknowledge with appreciation the comments and suggestions on the manuscript offered by Professors Gerard Braunthal, Eric Einhorn, and Stanley Young of the University of Massachusetts, Amherst; and Howard Gospel, Keynes College, Canterbury University, Kent, England.

ranks of professional, managerial and technical employees. They joined independent unions or organizations affiliated with new federations. (The European Trade Union Institute, 1982, and Roberts, pp. 35-6, 98-99, 161 and 194)

In recent years leaders in the movement began to recognize the need for reevaluating underlying principles and operations to recover and maintain the prominent and significant positions achieved in the sixties. Several national federations organized study groups to grapple with these new issues and challenges. The tendency nevertheless was to focus on a select number of questions rather than the full range of incongruities created by the new climate. The problems, although numerous, have not been fully defined. Discussions concerning them were all too recent to present a range of alternatives. The new reports were still circumspect in their recommendations for meeting the new challenge. Internal polemics are too tentative to produce well-rounded programs for reconstruction.

I. TEN STAGES IN WESTERN TRADE UNION DEVELOPMENT

To provide a setting for the analysis of current developments and contrast them with prior   epochs in the evolution of trade unions, we offer a concise outline of the successive stages in their history in advanced industrial countries.

After a century of persecution, repression and judicial and legislative prohibitions (Stage I), the modern labor movement encompassing the economic and political branches crystallized in the three decades before the outbreak of World War I (Stage II) (Dick Geary; Harvey Mitchell and Peter M. Stearns). These foundations provided the base for trade union acceptance, influence and impressive expansion during the War, reaching its peak in the postwar years of 1919-20 (Stage III).

The trade union movement suffered major setbacks during the depression of 1920-21. In the twenties and thirties, it was rocked and weakened by economic instability and the prolonged depression and political turbulence of the thirties. Internal schisms provoked by communist and revolutionary dissenters and secessionists further undermined its structures and diverted the leadership and membership from the battle against external forces. Much havoc was wrought by political restlessness which culminated in the wreckage of unions by the Fascist and Nazi states in central and southern Europe. Out of this struggle emerged a new determination to build highly integrated trade union movements and to create stable collective bargaining systems as well as labor political movements to administer national and local governments. These trends were particularly successful in the Scandinavian countries and in Canada and the United States (Stage IV). (H. A. Marquand and others; Adolf Sturmthal)

During the second World War the leaders of many allied nations recognized the need to link the trade union movement intimately to the war effort. Unions were widely recognized and dealt with as representative bodies for employees; collective bargaining was seen as vital to the achievement of a democratic political system; and union leaders were named to essential governmental posts and as advisors. The collective bargaining systems were further entrenched in these countries (Stage V). Unionists and socialists (including laborites) occupied central posts in the reconstruction governments (Stage VI). (1)

In the fifties, the political scene was dominated in most countries by centrist governments which accepted the collective bargaining system shaped by governments and employer-union understandings during and after the war. Governments and the collective bargaining parties recognized their mutual dependence and the need to actualize the democratic and egalitarian ideals proclaimed during the war. Unions expanded. The collective bargaining system created stability and delivered a series of benefits to and improvements in the well-being and working conditions of the work force. High employment added a sense of security not previously enjoyed. A new spirit of comity led some sociologists to project a "non-ideology" philosophy believing that rational relations would replace the ideological conflicts characteristic of the social scene in prior decades (Stage VII).

But this feeling of well-being and confidence was pricked by a new restlessness in the population, who called for economic and social advances beyond the visions of the thirties (1968-1973) (Stage VIII). The youth absorbed the broadened expectations of political and social leaders and expected to have them realized. New humanistic goals were in ascendancy. Minority groups including women and immigrants sought equality. Employees awakened to this new spirit and demanded higher standards and more rights, particularly participation in decision-making within the economic structure and individual workplaces. Many groups turned to militant action to achieve their aspirations. Stoppages, sit-ins and plant takeovers became widespread in advanced industrial countries. This enthusiasm for change propelled the socialist movement (2) in several countries actively to seek and gain the right to govern their nations. Political reforms to implement these goals became common. Several socialist governments entered into social compacts with the national trade union movements on the terms of basic local and national economic, industrial and social reforms. Union membership during this period expanded to historic heights. The prestige of unions and their leaders grew, and their participation in the social and political fabric broadened.

The optimistic bubble ruptured in the next decade (1973-83) (Stage IX). Initiated by a primary commodity price boom and reinforced by the petroleum price hikes set in 1973 by the oil cartel, a recession emerged in 1974-75. The subsequent recovery was short-lived, followed by another decline and further oil price boosts in 1979 with a subsequent inflationary sweep in 1980. These movements came to a halt with the recession in 1981-82.

Stagflation and high unemployment rates characterized the late seventies. During this era, unions maintained their militant strategy and made substantial gains in wages, hours and benefits. As governments initiated more restraining measures, unions moderated their targets. Socialist governments were displaced in several countries by centrist ones; in others centrist administrations were replaced by socialists. Intellectuals again began a search for new theories but confessed their confusion caused by the new economic behavior. They became less able to forecast developments in face of the vast changes in the economy and society.

In the eighties economic growth became modest, prices relatively stable, but unemployment remained high except in Austria, Japan, Norway, Sweden and the United States (Stage X). Leaders, in all fields, having little success in defining new guideposts for policy and legislation turned to the market place to bring adjustments and realize national goals. (Solomon Barkin, (1983) pp. 1-38)

II. THE PROFILE OF THE NEW ENVIRONMENT

Issuing as the current era of industrial relations and trade unionism has from a recession, it is essential to the understanding of these development and challenges to define the economic, political and demographic profile of the new setting confronting trade unionists.

A. Economic Setting

1. Overall levels: Low activity

In the economic realm the level of economic growth among OECD (Organization for Economic Cooperation and Development) countries has receded. From growth rates of 4.4 percent in the fifties and 5.0 in the sixties, in which cyclical fluctuations were modest, they declined in the early eighties to less than two percent, rising to 3.3 percent in 1987 and 4 percent in 1988. The projected levels for 1989 and 1990 are 3.25 and 2.75 respectively. (OECD Economic Outlook-December 1988) Throughout the period Japan recorded substantially higher rates while Europe, Canada and the United States, experienced lower ones. Currently the United States and Germany are again achieving higher output, but the uncertainties surrounding present conditions cast doubt about their persistence.

In the midst of this modest positive activity, one notes shifts in the growth trends in the individual components. Agricultural employment continued the decline of prior decades. In many countries a shrinkage is apparent in manufacturing. Offsetting the above is the expansion of the work force in the conglomerate services sector, with many countries reporting that more than half their work force is within this sector. (OECD Employment Outlook--September 1988) Both downward and upward trends in employment are visible within the component industries and subsections in this sector. Along with the turbulence among the industries, there are major dislocations in the sites of economic activity. Some communities are expanding and others are contracting in their employment volume, producing major migratory movements of the population and pockets of high unemployment. An even higher turnover rate is observable in individual workshops. The rate of temporary employment attachment is becoming an even more significant, ever-threatening determinant of human behavior.

2. Employment and Unemployment

As unsettling to the work population has been the lower priority assigned to the full employment goal among national targets. For two decades after the end of the war the major test of government performance was its record in this field. But in the last two decades this priority has yielded to controlling inflation. Unemployment rates stayed at about 2.5 percent during the fifties and sixties, even though the American record was about double. In the seventies, the rates began rising, ultimately reaching 8.8 percent in 1983. They subsequently receded to 7.9 percent in 1987, 7.25 in 1988, and are projected to be 7.25 percent in 1989 and 7.5 percent in 1990.   European unemployment rates stayed unusually high at 10.7 percent in 1987, 10.25 percent in 1988, and are forecast to be 10.25 for both 1989 and 1990.   Several countries still suffer from rates above ten percent (Belgium, Ireland, Netherlands, Spain and Turkey). The United States rate dropped in 1983 to 9.4 percent and to 5.5 percent in 1988, a level it is likely to maintain in the following two years.   In 1988 total unemployment in the OECD countries was estimated at 31.5 million, including the European component set at 19.75 million and the United States at 6.5 million. The share of the long-term unemployed (those experiencing unemployment of 12 months or more) remained high particularly in Europe, where they have constituted two-fifths of the unemployed. But the rate dropped in the United States.

3. Price Movements

Another distinctive characteristic of the new environment until now is the maintenance of relatively low rates of price increases. Starting in the fifties and persisting through most of the sixties the rate was 2 percent. At the end of the decade it began to climb, attaining 5.6 percent in 1970. With the dramatic escalation of commodity and petroleum prices in 1972 and 1973, the annual overall increase soared to 13.4 percent in 1974. Price hikes then receded slightly, to ascend again at the end of the 1970s to 13.0 percent. The subsequent recession forced the rate of price increases down to 2.6 percent in 1986. It rose again to 3.2 percent in 1987.

4. Government Economic Policy

Following the war, the industrial nations embraced a package of Keynesian policies. These built on the belief that the government had to occupy the key roles of planner and manager and in some instances operator of the economy through the use of direct and indirect instruments and programs for intervention into the economy to achieve national goals. (Andrew Shonfield) But with the mounting threats of inflation in the seventies, economic theorists recognized the limitations of these measures and began devoting attention to the monetary system. Many economists abandoned their belief that they could fine tune the economy and conceded that the organism was too complicated and involved for effective manipulations by a limited number of instruments or monetary aggregates. Out of this disillusion emerged conservative policies favoring governmental austerity, the privatizing of governmental enterprises, greater efficiency in the operation of governmental services and deregulation. But governments encountered resistance from the electorate to the curtailment of most public services and benefits, hence few were abandoned or seriously dismantled. These measures often failed to take account of the extravagant and oligopolistic practices pursued by private enterprises and thereafter governments reverted to systems of direct intervention and the partial restoration of regulation and control of the private economy in some deregulated areas. (The Economist, January 21, 1989)

In trying to shape national economic policy, the governments learned that they were part of an international system and therefore had to take into account the measures taken by other countries to meet their problems. All nations, including the largest, in order effectively to operate had to coordinate their policies with those of others. Considerable progress then followed in creating new instruments for coordination, despite the resistance from individual governments. While the World Bank and the International Monetary Fund existed from the early postwar years, recent innovations include the organization of the European Monetary System, begun in 1979, requiring member countries to observe defined ranges of fluctuation for their currency and to assure a common approach toward adjustments in values. In 1985 seven leading countries (Canada, France, West Germany, Great Britain, Italy, Japan and the United States) created the Group of Seven to devise common policies on exchange rates and monetary policies and methods of dealing with the huge overhanging Third World debt, particularly in Latin America. On the last issue they considered outright forgiveness, swapping debt for equity, stakes in local companies and assistance in their continuing economic development.

5. Innovation, Productivity and National Competitiveness

More specifically the new environment depends upon the pursuit of programs for technical research, development, installation of new technology and managerial methods and product marketing. They are crucial factors to achieving higher productivity and competitiveness both at the national and international levels. From these fields stem the renewed emphases on innovation and coordination to stimulate output, lower costs and to achieve greater competitiveness by the enterprise and the nation.

While the urgency for achieving faster rates of growth is stressed, the achievements, as reflected in measures of productivity, are not reassuring. OECD countries reported an annual rate of increase of productivity per employee of 3.9 percent for 1960-68, which dropped to

3.1 percent for 1973-79 and 1.6 percent for 1979-86. In the latter period the United States, the established leader in this field, began falling behind Western Europe and Japan in rates of increase, evoking national consternation and frustration. A continuing flow of programs to reverse this trend issued from private and public sources, but overall impressive results are still to be registered.

An inherent paradox in the current debates on raising the levels of productivity focus on national achievement, but the initiators of higher levels in the new competitive countries often are multinational corporations or nationals of these new countries who had been educated and trained in the developed nations. Such corporations in their decision making, moreover, had abandoned the national orientations of their home countries and devoted themselves to the overall interests of their corporations. More and more joint ventures are being organized between organizations and persons of different national origins; consortiums are based on diverse national institutions; other corporations are entering into cross-national licensing and royalty agreements, consultations and participatory managements, establishing joint research agencies with nationals of foreign countries, and making investments in research by foreign universities. The recent upsurge of American acquisitions and joint American and European investme its in Western Europe speaks dramatically of this ongoing process of creating mixed transatlantic and transpacific enterprises. While a dominant domestic goal is still the promotion of national well-being, the overall corporate orientation is that of the international enterprise or economy. Definitive resolutions of these conflicts have yet to be adopted.

With Japanese enterprises forging ahead in the national competitive race, other operators and nations have moved to improve their own levels of competitiveness. One consequence has been a growing interest in production management in schools of management. Top corporate executives have initiated newer techniques including quality control and circles, employee cooperation programs, automation and robotization of production, team systems of employee alignment, just-in-time scheduling, computer-aided design (CAD), computer-aided manufacturing systems (CAM), simulation, flexible machine centers and computerized numerical control. Flexibility in production has joined low cost and quality as tests of effective production.

These alterations in the workplace and reorientation of executive personnel have revolutionized management approaches. Concepts such as management by objective essentially derived from systems of central controls and extensive use of staff are being replaced by pragmatic procedures. Authority is being decentralized, with responsibility shifted to lesser figures in the divisions. The ultimate goal is always the financial result, the bottom line. Price margins and profit results tied in with market valuation of the enterprise as a whole guide judgments on projects. Local managements become the initiators and innovators with the expectation that this orientation would seep down to the lowest levels in the firm. Shared risks and bonuses are tied to financial returns; profit-sharing is becoming more common. Lowering costs is the target for all participants. The clamor is rising for new accounting systems for costs and finances to serve better the production floor and the financial decision-making personnel.

Besides revamping the business orientation, the actual structure of the work force is being reorganized. The objective is to keep the core workforce small and rely increasingly upon peripheral groups who are added or called as needed. Among these types are contractors, self-employed skilled and technical personnel, part-time or short-term employees, telecommunication, cottage industries, and homework. (The European Trade Union Institute, 1985)

In this era of business orientation little or no provision is made for collective bargaining in the administrative system. In a number of European countries, codetermination agencies are prescribed either by agreement or by law. But few of them have registered significant achievements.

6. Business Structure

With the renewed concentration upon and preeminence assigned to the bottom line of the income statement, corporate valuation and competitiveness, business leaders focus on these ends. Diverse arrangements are employed to achieve flexibility and shifting risks without limiting the organizations' capacities for achieving the desired cost and product results. A significant new instrument is the "hollow corporation." (Norman Jonas) While providing the nucleus for a business system, it varies in size from very small to very large, depending on the functions which each assumes. Basically it defines the ultimate products, coordinates production units, services and marketing and, in some cases, finances the components. Such corporations may generate autonomous subsidiaries by providing modest capital investments, and using outsourcing of parts or products, franchising, joint ventures, linked subcontracting, networks licensing and management agreements, particularly with developing countries or other governments. (Solomon Barkin, 1986 and 1987, and Clutterback)

Another major method of achieving this end is through mergers and acquisitions. The current record of such action is impressively high, both inside and outside a country. The trend has produced an ever-rising number of multinational corporations. American capital penetrated Europe in the forties and fifties. With the impending creation in 1992 of a freer internal market, this movement has been renewed and more recently directed to other continents. (New York Times, March 13, 1989) Concurrently corporations in these parts of the world have acquired business enterprises and properties in the United States. The enthusiasm for these efforts, friendly or hostile, continues despite the grave questions raised by research findings as to their value and usefulness to the individual corporations or the national economies (The Economist, December 17, 1988).

This merger movement has been further stimulated by the initiatives of financial groups which saw opportunities for extraordinary fees, commissions and speculative gains. The financial community has been particularly aggressive in pursuing leads and innovative by devising new types of securities, such as junk bonds, which pay high rates of interest. This movement has also enabled managements to gain control of corporations through buy-outs of stockholders, and/or assure themselves lucrative jobs, bonuses and "golden parachutes." While the movement was initiated in the United States, foreign financiers and managers in other countries followed suit.

In surveying these and other developments in the business world, one recognizes a major transformation in the economic world. The representative new business leader is not necessarily an empire builder, though some are appropriately classed in this category. Currently, the key figure is an aggressive builder of international systems of business units which are constantly being reshaped as circumstances suggest through the sale of component units, the acquisition of new ones and the formation of new relationships with other business organizations and governmental bodies. The executive earnestly seeks, develops and applies the newer technologies, and promotes consumer-responsive products. The goal is to design business enterprises which are expanding in terms of volume and profits, which are highly competitive and maintain secure shares of markets and which provide high returns on their capital investments.

7. Globalization and Economic Interdependence

The proliferation of multinational corporations and other forms of transnational business relationships, the multiplication of intergovernmental international agreements and treaties and the formation of institutions which administer them have intensified the process of globalization of the economies. An index of the process of internationalization is the ascending ratio of international trade to gross national product. A study of twelve industrial and less-developed countries shows that this percentage had risen from 12.0 percent in 1960 to 21.7 percent in 1984-85. It is also reflected in the high degree of sensitivity of individual national economies to business developments abroad as reflected in the sympathetic movement of interest rates, exchange rates, cyclical fluctuations, prices and output. (Norman S. Fieleke)

Technological innovations have also facilitated and accelerated these processes. Among the most impressive are those in the telephone and computer fields which use computer-aided designing (CAD) and computer-aided manufacturing (CAM). These developments have evoked such phrases as the "global office" and "global manufacturing systems," increasingly the most characteristic structures of the current era (New York Times, October 18, 1988).

Governmental developments, worldwide and regional, are reinforcing these trends. The Uruguay Round of negotiations under the GATT (General Agreement of Tariffs and Trade) has made faltering progress in current negotiations, but the basic advantages the agreement will offer all interested nations, will presumably produce compromises on disputed issues and an ultimate instrument to remove obstacles to freer trade. A second current effort is that of the European Economic Community to implement its goal of a freer internal market, by creating in 1992 a new setting for the conduct of economic activities with other countries (Michael Calingaert). While these moves toward freer trade are gaining momentum, the people and unions in the affected industries and occupations, anticipating displacements, are raising questions and protesting these steps. When implemented, issues arise about compensation and readjustment for workers.

The globalization process has accelerated the rate of extension of the free trade economy. As a result efforts at national policy-making have become more complex and hazardous for more variables have to be considered than where closed economies are involved, including the effects on exchange rates, balance of payments and competitiveness. Smaller economies such as France have frequently faced this challenge, but now that the United States has lost many competitive advantages, it also must consider these issues in defining policies and measures.

8. Environmentalism

The newest significant force affecting the institutional climate for decision-making in union organization and collective bargaining is the environmental movement, seeking to protect natural resources from depletion or destruction, prevent pollution, eliminate exposure to and use of injurious materials and promote the health and well-being of the population and the work force. Initiated as an active movement in the sixties, it has since gained considerable momentum as well as wide popular and political support. Originally dependent upon youth groups, individual issues have since won endorsement among other strata of the population.

In Germany and Sweden, the Green parties won representation in national and local parliaments and legislative bodies. Now many other parties endorse specific proposals which have gained popularity.

In the early days of the movement, unions and the working population were highly suspicious of environmental controls for fear of losing jobs. But as the threats to life, security and the viability of natural resources became more evident, sympathy for this cause mushroomed. There is now a greater readiness by unions to reason cautiously and to seek solutions by agreeing to reductions or the elimination of materials to minimize their adverse effects as well as propose solutions with reasonable costs and job and employee protection. The reconciliation of the diverse interests of citizens, employees and management on matters of economic costs and human well-being remain to be resolved in each local instance through bargaining, careful regulation and cost assessment (The Economist, December 24, 1988).

9. Distinctiveness of the Economic Environmental Profile

The new economic environment calls for the reorientation of industrial relations. A key figure in this process is the principal business executive who is impelled by many forces in the buying, production, financial, product and service markets. He constantly evaluates proposals for the divestiture and acquisitions of units to improve the organization's national and international competitive positions and to realize high rates of returns. His calculations are likely to be global in character, weighing alternative locations, materials, processes, financial and organizational structures and strategic methods, products and markets, thereby contributing to a high volatility of the global economy. His commanding position makes his views critical in determining the policies and well-being of individual nations and the enterprise business system and the achievement of stable growth within the national and world economies.

B. Political Setting

1. Current State: Calm and Smooth Succession

The current era of relative political calm and smooth succession of governments follows periods of turmoil which persisted from the end of the sixties through the seventies and early eighties. Socialists, centrists and even communists joined together in the period of postwar reconstruction (1945-50) to rebuild the economic, political and social fabrics of their nations. National economic planning and the welfare society were then introduced. For almost two decades (1950-67), the nations were generally governed by centrist parties, occasionally inviting socialists to join them, except primarily in the Scandinavian countries, where socialist parties were in power. These governments supported the reaffirmation of the market economy, the rights of property and the democratic political systems. Many significant economic and social reforms were introduced; foreign policy tended to be patterned by the United States, emphasizing an anti-Russian orientation. Unions enjoyed broad recognition and collective bargaining spread. Full employment prevailed in most years and countries. A feeling of satisfaction pervaded the adult population which had experienced the deprivations of the depression and war. Several labor and socialist parties led by West Germany shifted from a Marxist to a more populist approach, making them people's parties.

Subsequent to this long period of relative stability came one of widespread disquiet, led first by the youth but then other minority and disgruntled groups, including employees (1968-79). The left was reinvigorated. The socialist parties became the principal beneficiaries. In some countries they gained the reins of government. In the eighties, governments lasted for longer periods and had fewer internal conflicts within administrations; the extreme right and left were less evident. Communist influence was largely deflated, particularly as internal factional fights destroyed much of their determination to gain increasing power. Several national parties in embracing Euro-Communism narrowed their differences with the Social Democratic competitors. Similarly differences among most political parties dwindled as faith in governmental action was deflated. The people's preoccupation was with immediate problems. A spirit of acquiescence overtook the population. This moderation in politics is seen in the failure of extremist parties to gain control of any advanced state. The governments of eleven countries are currently in the hands of the centrist (including more conservative) parties--Belgium, Canada, Denmark, West Germany, Ireland, Japan, the Netherlands, Portugal, Turkey, United Kingdom and the United States. Seven countries have governments controlled by socialists--Australia, France, Greece, New Zealand, Norway, Spain and Sweden. And coalitions including socialists and centrists govern six countries--Austria, Finland, Iceland, Italy, Luxembourg and Switzerland. Whereas the eighties began with a feeling of great unease, they are ending calmly but beclouded by uncertainty.

2. Shrinking Role of the Nation State

Our discussions have made it clear that the nation state is now more constrained in handling economic, political and social issues. The bulging power of the multinational companies and international agreements to which the states are signatories contributed to this trend. In the labor and social field, international conventions and resolutions adopted at the annual conferences of the International Labor Office, founded in 1919, are benchmarks for national action. Evidence of the binding nature of these new developments showed up in the experience of the first Mitterrand government in France when it unsuccessfully tried to pursue an independent expansionary economic policy in face of the prevailing trend toward austerity among other governments.

3. Unions and their Political Partners: A Strained Symbiosis

a. Creating the Symbiosis

The bond between trade unions and their political partners, particularly the socialist parties, was born out of a common longing to realize an equality of status and rights for all citizens, particularly the working class, and continuing improvements in the terms and conditions of work and their standard of living. Both were committed to the progressive amelioration of conditions and effective changes in the economic, political and social structures to achieve their ends. Moreover, members of each group had over the years been persecuted and their institutions suppressed. They were hounded by authorities and often by employers. They were considered to be confederates by their foes. The political parties were led by people who believed in the need for unions and assisted in their formation and later in the promotion and establishment of national union federations. In one instance the reverse happened in that unions sponsored the formation of the Labor Party in Great Britain. In all countries, union members or workers generally became the core of the socialist parties' membership. The leadership of both organizations tended to share a common political ideology. They became known as two wings of the labor movement.

Catholic, Protestant and Liberal parties later sponsored unions in response to the formation of the "free" unions to maintain the allegiance of worker congregants. These unions kept their ties with the respective political party's wings, constituting themselves factions within the party, while usually promoting programs similar to those pronounced by the "free union" movements. For decades a spirit of noblesse oblige prevailed among them. Poaching of membership rarely occurred. Seldom did individual members of these unions cross over to the political bodies of alternative movements.

The interchange between the two wings is clear in Great Britain. The organization of the Labor Party was initiated by the TUC (Trade Union Congress), which invited several existing socialist organizations to create one political organization to aid unions seeking support against unfavorable judicial decisions. In 1906 it was named the Labor Party. In the early years the socialist membership gave precedence to the union agenda and leadership, without whom the Party would not have survived. The apex of this cohesion was reached in 1918 with the acceptance of a Socialist oriented constitution by the Labor Party. The groups also agreed to constitute common staff agencies such as in research and information, to service the TUC and the Labor Party. (Clegg, V. 2, p. 231)

During the following decade the two wings (industrial and political) shared a common program, including criticism of the existing economy and society, and pragmatic proposals for improving the lot of the working class. The Labor Party in this period was a class pressure group concerned with "a narrow range of problems, namely those immediately affecting the interests of its (trade union) membership." (Sturmthal, p.5) Despite these political activities, the unions' daily concerns were similar to the bread-and-butter issues of the American trade union movement. While they served similar functions, European unions worked through political parties and representation in parliament and legislative bodies and the Americans, through political lobbying. Both failed to pursue "constructive proposals for dealing with the economic crisis." (Sturmthal, pp. 4-8) Out of this complementary development and behavior emerged a unitary labor movement.

b. The Roots and Evidence of the Strain

i. The Confirmation of the Autonomy of the Two Wings

The evidence of strains became evident early in the history of the movement. Three issues arose. First was the autonomy of the trade union movement from the parties, since the latter in most countries had helped promote union organizations and nurtured them in the early years as their own agencies. In 1906 both in Germany and at the international level, the respective organizations agreed on their separateness and independence. Second, agreements followed to eliminate the prescription that union members or the unions collectively maintain membership in the socialist parties. The requirement was implemented in different ways in each country depending on the wishes of the union's membership and/or national laws concerning such membership. Some call for collective (union) membership and other, individual adherence. Some parties accept its voluntary character, achieving a special form in Great Britain with the invention of the legal requirement of "contracting in" or "contracting out." Other countries followed suit. The third issue, particularly prominent in Germany, originated from the unions' insistence on freedom from the obligation to observe party directives in the industrial field, particularly strike action. This principle was accepted. In several countries socialist parties require their adherents to maintain membership in the unions in the fields in which they worked. In practice unions played a minor role in party policy formulation, but party representatives sat in the meetings of union executive bodies. Union leaders, particularly retired ones, and members have been enlisted as candidates for the parties, though that practice has over time diminished because of the higher priority unions placed on union officials devoting themselves to their professional responsibilities which tended to become more extensive and time consuming. In Great Britain union-sponsored candidates and elected members of Parliament dropped from over 80 percent in 1906 to 50 percent in 1929 and declined further in later years.

Despite these separatist trends, some national federations, particularly those loyal to their association with the communist and denominational movements remained established centers (exceptions are the FTC in France and the NKV in the Netherlands, with the latter merging with the NVV to form the FNV). The number of national federations increased as white collar, professional and technical and government employees in several countries favored distinctive federations to avoid being identified with established ones and their political or economic philosophies.

ii. Causes of Strain

Over time strains developed in the relations between the political partners, again primarily socialist ones, and trade unions. While the tensions rarely led to severance, they produced tensions, debates, misunderstanding and factional conflicts, and reduced organizational effectiveness. Some issues persisted for long periods of time. We shall consider and illustrate some of these strains and their effects.

aa. Maturation of Organizations

One simple cause is that institutional growth has a tendency to produce an insistence on organizational independence and separateness. In Great Britain after having taken in 1919 specific acts to cement their relations, the trade unions especially after the experience of the general strike of 1926 intended to force a settlement in the coal industry, insisted upon their ability and responsibility to formulate policies on problems such as unemployment and industrial issues independently of the Labor Party and Parliamentary Labor Party. The TUC and its agencies held conferences on these issues to which the Party was invited but as onlookers rather than as participants. The TUC insisted on separating the services so the agencies would continue to maintain direct channels with governmental agencies, even when a non-Labor Party government held the reins.

bb. Socialist Parties Broaden Objectives and Institutions

Having acted in earlier years primarily as a pressure group for unionism, it became evident as socialist parties in the twenties gained control of governments in Denmark, Germany, Sweden, and the United Kingdom that other socialist parties had to be prepared to serve as national political parties. They developed views on a wide range of subjects and practical programs for dealing with most issues. They became clearly aware of their failings in the depression of the thirties in not offering effective programs for dealing with current challenges. Some came to look with considerable approval on the venturesomeness of the Scandinavian Social Democratic parties to formulate and advocate new programs for stimulating economic growth, reducing unemployment and defining governmental functions to gain greater social justice and equity. A number of parties in the fifties, led by the Germans, perceived that if they were to discharge their ultimate wish to gain control of the governments, they had to extend their appeal beyond the working class. They began to identify themselves as a "People's Party" and set up machinery and programs addressed particularly to the middle class, professionals, technicians and other social classes. They also saw that new national union federations were being formed of unions among white collar employees in the private and public sectors. If they were to appeal sensitively to them and their needs a new leadership had to be offered.

This development was also fostered by the changing character of the membership of the local constituencies, party organizations and the parliamentary delegations. In paying greater attention to local activity, the party leadership tended to reduce the influence of trade unionists and their spokesmen and to facilitate the access of reformers and left wing politicians. This trend has been visible in most European countries. The major exception is Great Britain where unionists are entitled to a fixed ratio of voting power in the Labor Party. As new personalities multiply in the political activities they tend to encourage interest in a broader range of issues and higher priorities for them. They also emphasize political ideologies, more stress is placed on securing larger delegations in legislative bodies and control of more offices in local and national governments. Up to now the British trade unionists have been able to moderate these trends by maintaining a fixed ratio of representation in the policy making organs and the presence of a large though diminishing number of trade union sponsored members in Parliament. But there is considerable pressure to diminish this ratio.

i. West Germany: A Stand-off

Differences between the two wings of the labor movement in West Germany have from time to time been marked, but the leaderships avoided knockdown and dragout battles even when sorely tried. They continued their close relationship during favorable and/or sorrowful times. Open and private criticism has at times been unrestrained.

In reorganizing the trade union movement in the postwar era, the leaders' first determination was to create a united non-political, non-denominational organization. Several countries have tried to follow this pattern but only Austria and Germany succeeded. The DGB (German Trade Union Federation) defined its position as being independent of political parties and neither "politically neutral nor'non-political.'" Nevertheless, most leaders are identified with the Social Democratic Party (SPD) and the preponderance of DGB membership is generally supportive of it. (Willey, pp. 41-43) The DGB President at the 1954 convention described the relationship by declaring that "a division between the Social Democratic Party and the German trade unions is inconceivable. We are the children of one mother." (ibid., p. 42) The DGB looks to the SPD to be its political advocate and protector of workers' rights, benefits and status. An overwhelming number of the SPD members of Parliament are union members and some are trade union leaders. To have a direct access to unionists' opinions and a funnel for offering recommendations to the SPD on industrial and other matters, the SPD in 1968 sponsored the formation of the Trade Union Council. Later in 1972 the National Association of Workers (AFA) was organized to coordinate the activities of the SPD shop groups formed to recruit and maintain their support for the party and to keep in close touch with them. Chancellor Helmut Schmidt (SPD) appointed five unionists to his first cabinet (1974-78) but overlooked the traditional courtesy to consult with the DGB in these appointments.

Other fundamental cleavages do arise. The SPD at its convention in 1959 replaced its former Marxist workers' party orientation with a view of itself as a People's Party. By broadening its appeal it hoped to extend its attractiveness to new elements in the population and advance its goal of gaining the right to become the ruling party, an end which it realized at the end of the sixties and in the seventies (ibid., p. 53).

While the SPD was in the opposition (1949-66) the relations between the two organizations were very positive; agreements on policy were easily reached. But this rapport, especially as regards economic and industrial issues, was upset when the SPD became part of the governing coalitions (1966-82) either as the junior or senior member. The cabinets at times took positions at variance with those recommended by the DGB. Chancellor Willy Brandt (SPD) in an address before the 1968 DGB Congress declared that divergences in positions were inevitable since "one cannot on one hand affirm the development of the SPD into a people's party and on the other hand expect it, in its activities and internal structure, right up to the sociological composition of its leadership circles, to be an old-fashioned workers party." He added that "trade unions are not the instrument of the party, but the party is not the instrument of the trade unions." In its 1975 long-range program the SPD observed that "trade unions cannot relieve the party of the tasks of political leadership nor the activation and mobilization of members, supporters, or the population as a whole." (Braunthal, pp. 112, 115) In summarizing the situation, the analyst concluded that the "SPD government leaders (believed) that they must represent the general rather than the DGB special interests."

This developing understanding made union leaders realize that "they had to depend more on their own resources, even at times on the support of other parties." (ibid., p. 115) The same analyst noted that after 1969 the SPD could no longer "listen only to the DGB demands but had also to take those of other groups and the FDP (Free Democratic Party, the junior member of the government) into consideration." When it did so "the DGB officers realized that their identity of interest with the SPD was eroding; at times. . ., the two fraternal organizations became sharp adversaries, even though the SPD-led government members knew that in the long run they could not govern against the unions and even though the DGB officers knew that the SPD would support their goals more than any other party." (ibid., p. 115)

The DGB in seeking to assert is independence voiced its frustration with the SPD-led governments because they were disposed to meet FDP objectives, rather than trade union positions. The activist divisions in the DGB urged strong protests against some government decisions. Such initiatives were taken in local areas; one occurred in Stuttgart in 1981 where the IG Metall district organized a "major anti-government rally attended by over 70,000 metal workers." This protest meeting "vehemently attacked" the government's austerity package. (Markovits, p. 132, chapter 3, footnote 163) In face of the prolonged economic crisis and continuing large-scale unemployment, the dissatisfaction with the SPD-led government mounted. It led to the DGB's July 1977 statement entitled "Suggestions Regarding the Restoration of Full Employment," outlining proposals to mitigate the situation. Individual unions conducted at the end of the seventies a series of strikes, and managements responded with lockouts which further strained the DGB relationships with the Schmidt government.

The mood helped crystallize support for a "Strategy of union self-reliance" as unions were "disillusioned with the government in power" (ibid., p. 149). The document pleaded for "unions to pick up the slack where the former structures failed to defend labor's interests." This determination to rely on workers' strength and bargaining power would become "the centerpiece of labor's strategy to combat the hardships of the crisis." The two chief goals were the promotion and use of shop floor power and the 35-hour week. Both were incorporated in the DGB Action program of 1979 and the Basic Program of 1981 which spelled out goals, measures and strategy. For the DGB "codetermination at the enterprise and workshop levels as well as collective bargaining" would be the leverages to gain their ends. Less reliance would be placed "on the state for the implementation of demands as had been the case for decades." (ibid., p. 153)

When the SPD government was replaced by the Conservative one in 1982, both the DGB and the SPD could return to a more congenial mood. But even then individual political leaders intermittently pushed the DGB to make changes in its policies to make them less of an irritant on the public scene and less of a burden for the SPD to carry, including the advocacy of a free market orientation. While these men were usually quieted for a time in the interest of party unity, the differences of approach between party and union interests and between the activists and accommodationists in the union movement caused continuing strife between and inside of the two wings of the labor movement. (Sten Martenson) The most publicized statement was that by Oskar Lafontaine for the reduction of working time accompanied by a loss of pay which rekindled intense resentment among unionists. (Bremen Nachrichten)

The relationship of the labor wing of the Christian Democratic and Christian Social Union parties (CDU/CSU) was even more distant because the party responds primarily to property, business and employer interests. While the labor wing had about one fifth of the party delegation in the Bundesrat, of whom many are usually DGB members, its primary effect is to moderate the essentially conservative positions, particularly on matters in which unions are interested. (Willey, p. 185)

ii. Great Britain: Labor Party: A Pressure Group or "Party of Government"

The departure of trade union members in 1931 from the Ramsey MacDonald Labor cabinet started a new era of rapprochement between the two wings of the British labor movement. Union leaders became more influential in shaping industrial relations and other policies, particularly those relating to public ownership, collective security and rearmament. (Minkin, p. 12) This trend continued through the war years and the Attlee Labor government (1945-51). The TUC was supportive of government programs, endorsed its accomplishments and urged its constituencies to conform.

In the fifties the debates and contests within the labor movement cut across factional lines rather than dividing political and union activists from one another. The latter avoided non-industrial issues, insisting however that joint statements should be mutually arrived at for acceptability and that agreements should support collective bargaining and reject governmental intervention in the bargaining process and union operations.

One of the first acts taken by the Labor Party and the TUC upon the installation of the Labor government in 1964 was to issue a "Joint Declaration of Intent on Prices and Incomes." It spelled out their common positions, and an agreement for the formation of a Royal Commission to examine and recommend changes in the industrial relations system, a target of academic and popular criticism. The statements urged an expansionary demand management policy.

In the sixties, this era of comity ended. The first jolt was registered when a union leader lined up with the left faction of the party in support of a plan for unilateral nuclear disarmament. Though it passed at the 1960 Labor Party Conference, in the following year it was overridden at the insistence of the leaders. Many party leaders began voicing strong views to broaden the party's appeal to include the needs and views of the middle class and white-collar and government employees. Some urged that it follow the German model and become a People's party, but Labor Prime Minister Harold Wilson called for a "Party of Government" to stress its qualifications for heading the government for all people. Modernization and responsibility became the catchwords. The drive was reinforced by the Labor Party victory in the 1966 election. As a consequence, the party's labor origin and orientation were not to be emphasized. Wilson declared that the "government must govern," disregarding the adverse effects on party morale and party-union relations. (ibid., p. 18)

The pendulum however swung back after the party's defeat in the 1970 election. The two wings began consorting to cooperate especially as the new Conservative government's (1970-74) activities outraged the trade unions. They organized demonstrations and political strikes, capped by the 1974 Miners strike. They protested against the new measures, by boycotting some and openly resisting others. A clamor arose among trade unionists for the return of a Labor government. Preparations were then initiated for the next election. To avoid the fracas that had developed under the prior Labor government, the two wings issued a joint declaration entitled Economic Policy and Cost of Living (February 1973), which became the basis for a subsequent document labeled the Social Contract. It called for the repeal of restrictive labor legislation enacted by the Conservative government and outlined new rules for industrial relations to expand worker rights and union opportunities for growth and participation. It endorsed programs for higher welfare expenditures, rejected deflationary policies and condemned income policies. Unions in return offered moderation in their wage demands and participation in investment planning at all levels from the plant and enterprise to the national one.

It proposed labor representation on the boards of corporations. The goal was to realize full employment and higher standards for workers.

The agreement could not eliminate the conflicting points of view of those who would convert labor's political arm into a "Party of Government" and the trade union emphasis on maintaining a labor party which would be the trade union's pressure force. In time this clash became evident in the behavior of the second Wilson-Callaghan government (1974-79). In its first two years the party-union relations were harmonious. The government delivered a legislative program which carried out the agreed-upon program. The TUC avoided steps which might be embarrassing to the government. But by the winter of 1978, the economic crisis deepened. Workers rejected proposals for a 5 percent wage increase norm. "Wage strikes spread. Wage settlements swung upwards and the Labor government's claim to a successful working relationship with the trade unions (which was considered a major electoral advantage) lost creditability." (Goodman, p. 68) To bridge this gap a new concordat was negotiated in February 1979. But the strikes of winter 1979, many commentators argued, were a sharp and disastrous blow to the Labor Party. One writer notes that the strikes disclosed "the limitations of the fading government-TUC alliance." (ibid., p. 61)

The Conservatives in the 1979 elections regained control of the government. The Thatcher regime veered towards weakening the trade unions, largely through legislative measures. Another commentator concludes that "relations between unions and the party were always better during periods of Conservative rule . . . when it was Labor's turn to manage the brittle national economy, the party and the TUC had great and increasing difficulty doing each other anything but harm. The proneness of the economy in crisis made it difficult for Labor governments to provide their union allies with consistent policy rewards for their electoral support. Similarly, the organization structure of unions and their sensitivity concerning their market economy made the TUC an unreliable partner for Labor Governments in difficult economic straits." (Bornstein, p. 72)

The debate over the relation of the Labor party and the TUC continues with great intensity. The editors of The Economist, who call for the strengthening of the Labor Party as a counterforce to the dominant Conservative government declared that the only hope for the party was to "uncouple Labor from the unions." (The Economist, July 25, 1987, pp. 14-15) They urged the party to stop clinging "to the wreckage of the trade unions, which Britons have not yet forgiven for the excesses of the 1970s." (The Economist, January 7, 1989, pp. 14-15)

The Labor Party under its new leader, Neil Kinnock, appears to be moving in the above direction. The 1988 Labor Party Conference voted to limit union influence and that of extreme leftist activists in the designation of local candidates by transferring this responsibility to the membership. The Conference also rejected the proposal to restore the demand for universal nationalization. Other "democratic" measures are likely to follow, both in policy and the operation of the party. A move to reduce the size of the unions' role in the national organization appears to be under way. It is hoped by the protagonists of this course that they would improve the party's profile with the electorate. The TUC leadership appears disposed to accept many changes to help revitalize the Labor Party and improve chances of ousting the Conservative government.

iii. Sweden: The Three-Headed Union Movement

The traditional image of the Swedish scene, the so-called Swedish Model, usually projects a unified, centralized, coherent structure for both management and employees. As for the labor side, it is complemented by a Social Democratic party which is driven by the same orientation and dedicated to the advancement of worker interests. Until the seventies this simplified characterization held true. But with the subsequent accelerated surge in the membership of the two major white-collar employee federations, a more complicated structure resulted which has not yet fully sorted itself out. Three union federations are now competitive, independent and often pursue individual policies and action programs. No longer do the Swedish Confederation of Trade Unions (LO) and the Swedish Employees Confederation (SAF) set national patterns for wages, labor standards and industrial relations. The negotiating process and settlements are more decentralized within each area. The orientations may be sharply different between the industrial and white-collar orbits and within the latter field between the two principal federations.

During World War I and through the twenties, the Social Democratic Party (SAP) was either a member of a governmental coalition (1917-20) or the leader of a minority government (1920, 1921-23 and 1924-26). It promoted social welfare, education and other reforms including women's suffrage (1919), an eight-hour day and forty-hour week. On the third occasion (1924-26), its term in office was cut short as it annulled the parliamentary committee order requiring striking miners to return to their jobs. It ascended again to government control in 1932 with the help of the Farmers Party. It built its appeal on an expansionary economic program. It thereafter maintained this right to govern either as a senior member of a coalition or the governing party until 1976, returning to office again in 1982.

An analyst summarized the nature of the interplay between the two wings of the labor movement when he wrote that "throughout its history LO's strategic outlook has been decisively conditioned by its ties to the SAP. The effectiveness of the party's economic policy when in office has been an important factor in shaping the way the LO has tried to use these resources in the market arena." (Martin, pp. 95-96)

The SAP's rise to power and the ability to maintain its position persuaded employers no longer to expect governments to intervene on their behalf in industrial controversy, a common practice in prior years. The new environment also offered the sense of security which led both labor and employers' organizations in 1938 to enter into an overall Basic Agreement on mutual recognition, agreed upon methods of conducting collective bargaining and the settlement of disputes without governmental intervention. The Agreement accelerated the centralization of authority in the LO. In 1941 the latter's constitution placed the power for allocating strike funds in its hands. Thereafter the strike weapon was subordinated to "the supposed requirements" of the party's economic policy. (ibid., p. 199)

This union-party partnership rested on an accord on economic and industrial relations policies as well as joint activities in education. The first plank was the state budget, which should be used to shape the environment in which the managers make production decisions. Second, industrial peace could be realized through the industrial relations system itself in which unions and management would agree on distributive issues. (ibid., p.203-210) The third plank called for economic and manpower policies through which inflationary demands of a full employment economy could be avoided without resorting to the traditional weapons of wage reductions, high unemployment and deflationary fiscal and monetary measures. Fiscal and monetary measures including sales taxes would restrain price increases, and solidaristic wage policies would promote equal pay for equal work, without regard to a firm's level of profitability. Marginal units would increase their efficiency or close down. The manpower program coordinated by a National Labor Market Board would help displaced persons readjust and secure new employment, one hopes at higher pay levels, through retraining, job transfers, information, counseling, relocation, state temporary jobs and financial support. Manpower bottlenecks would be eliminated and local wage pressures relaxed.

Profitable firms and state insurance programs, particularly the state pensions system, would offer funds for new investment. Unions could then pursue a moderate and solidaristic wage policy. The program was implemented after 1957 through the expansion of National Labor Market Board activities. The supplementary old age pension system of 1959, actively promoted by the LO and the SAP, channeled its surplus funds to the approved investments. (ibid., pp.203-210)

A fourth plank, industrial policy, emerged from the separate and joint studies by the LO and SAP. This policy is to supplement the job-creating activities in the private economy, since the latter is unlikely to produce a job program of sufficient size nor be responsive to the principles of "equality, security and ultimate democracy." (ibid., pp. 228-235)

The fifth plank called for legislation to limit the scope of managerial prerogatives and promote decision making in plant operations. Laws developed during the seventies on employment, security, occupational health and safety, shop stewards' rights and joint determination of work arrangements elaborated on this new employee-employer relationship. In the course of these enactments, the government nullified Section 32 of the Basic Agreement, which had barred local unions from intervening in the conduct of production systems. Unions also gained the right of "interpretation prerogatives" permitting them to offer their interpretations on controversial shop issues and making them binding until superseded by the decision of higher authorities. Dismissal of employees would also be postponed if challenged by unions until ruled on by Labor Courts. Employers were also required to initiate requests and negotiate with unions on all changes in job and operating procedures and arrangements, both in the private and public sectors. (ibid., pp.260-264)

The final plank called for employee investment funds accumulated through taxes on employers to advance economic development. Initiated by the LO, the proposal emerged from prolonged negotiations with the SAP after many revisions and was adopted in 1983 in face of considerable opposition from conservative parties and the business community. The funds are now organized on a regional basis, with union representatives constituting a majority of the boards and with employees exercising the funds' voting rights on company boards of directors. (ibid., pp.268-278, 328-332)

There are critics both inside and outside of the LO who are critical of the ways the funds are being invested, largely to existing rather than new enterprises. This course has in part been followed because the private investment market has grown in recent years and has financed many promising enterprises. Others are troubled by the provision in the final Act, stopping further accumulation of funds at the end of the trial period in 1991.

One analyst concludes that "the interaction of the politically powerful Social Democratic labor movement and Sweden's highly organized and internationally oriented capitalistic class has been crucial in shaping the development of the country's political economy." The main condition for the LO's support has been its insistence that "the policies pursued by the Social Democratic governments be consistent with the LO unions' ability to perform the functions in the labor market on which their claims to membership support rest." At the same time LO's stake in maintaining the Social Democratic control of the government "has given it a strong incentive to devise an economic strategy through which the Social Democratic governments can manage the economy effectively." (ibid., pp.341-342) Incidentally, this analyst credits much of the success of this program to the "power of the LO's economic ideas" developed by its staff of economists.

As indicated, the two major white-collar federations in time gained a substantial independent influence on union policies and conduct. The Central Organization of Salaried Employees (TCO), with two-thirds of the membership of the LO, and the Swedish Federation of Government Employees (SACO/SR), with about one quarter of the TCO enrollment, are the critical forces. Both recruit in the private and public sectors, but the public sector constitutes slightly less than one-half of the former.

Neither organization has formal ties with political organizations, but it is estimated that SAP voters account for a little more than two thirds of the TCO membership and about 15 percent of the SACO/SR membership. (Elvander, p.69) Two other small organizations cover supervisors and syndicalists. A large proportion of the TCO membership constitutes lower income employees; the interests and views of the LO and the TCO overlap on many subjects such as wage solidarity and taxes, which is not true of the SACO/SR. LO efforts to coordinate the bargaining demands and strategy of the union movement were not well received by the two organizations. In pursuit of their competitive relation, the federations keep a close eye on one another and their contract negotiations, occasionally holding up the finalization of their own contracts until the others have concluded theirs to ensure equal benefits.

One practical reason for such alertness is that they compete in recruiting members among technical and other employees where computers and electronic controls have taken over manual tasks. Jurisdictional disputes have become more common in recent years, but many are being resolved with the help of mediators.

Another reason for this sensitivity by the LO about the policies and strategies followed by the two white-collar federations is that they have been more aggressive in pressing their claims. Evidence is the 1966 teachers' strike of 30,000, the 1969 strike of 300 supervisors in the state service, and hundreds of harbor pilots; the 1971 public service strike of 50,000 employees; the 1980 strike of low wage and intermediate wage groups for higher wages, involving 30,000 employees; the 1985 strike of 20,000 salaried personnel to secure a more favorable interpretation of a clause in the agreement relating to wage equity; the 1986 strikes in the public sector affecting about one million employees arising out of the demand for wage parity with the private sector. In 1988 the wage negotiations for the white collar employees in the private sector, primarily the engineering branch, provoked the largest strike for this class of employees in Sweden's history. (Flanagan et al. and Casten van Otter)

One of the major forces contributing to the uniformities among the agreements concluded with the three federations has been the increasing involvement of the government in defining the levels of wage benefits which could be sought. While the prescriptions from the Minister of Finance were most often exceeded, they nevertheless guided the parties. The Minister has briefed the parties on economic conditions and level of settlements which would be consistent with governmental economic policy. This intervention became common with the return of the SAP government. A first conference, referred to as the Rosenbad meetings, was held in anticipation of the 1984-85 negotiations. In fact, in 1985 Minister of Wages was appointed to oversee, though not to participate or prescribe directly, the terms of the proposals and the course of negotiations as well as the final agreement. (Kristina Ahlen)

A current source of controversy within the labor movement centers on the proposed changes in tax policy. The Minister of Finance has recommended lowering income taxes and raising indirect tax rates. Opponents of these ideas object to the reduction of the degree of progressivity in the tax system. Similarly they are troubled by the open advocacy by the Minister of what he calls "market socialism" to achieve greater flexibility and growth. But independent observers are reassuring that such differences have been common and that in time compromises will be devised to smooth the passage of revised measures. (Viklund; LO-Tidningen, February 10, 1989)

iv. United States: Hardly Political Partners

With the tradition of political nonpartisanship and the practice of rewarding friends and punishing foes, it is hardly surprising that the American union movement has no formal alliance with specific political parties. Before 1933 the AFL (American Federation of Labor) leadership fought and defeated factions which advocated this course. Friendship was narrowly conceived as sympathy for or assistance to specific union causes or favors such as contract awards to unionized employers. The national federation even resisted legislative action for setting labor standards or regulations except for workmen's compensation, child labor, working hours, immigration controls, safety and health and in select cases, economic aid to depressed industries.

A slight change in outlook occurred during World War I when unions accepted a series of industrial relations laws and administrative orders. Many unions supported an independent candidate in the 1924 presidential election, but the real breakthrough came with the formation in 1936, by CIO (Congress of Industrial Organization) unions, of the Labor's Nonpartisan League to promote the election of Franklin D. Roosevelt for the presidency. He reflected the sympathy of many disadvantaged groups, which has affected the subsequent coloration of the Democratic party (Lubell). The AFL followed suit with the formation of Labor's League for Political Education. After the merger of the two organizations in 1955, the AFL-CIO established the Committee for Political Education (COPE). On no recent occasion has the leadership proposed the formation of an independent political party. Efforts to do so proved transitory and ultimately these organizations were merged with the state Democratic parties or became their appendages.

So close had the trade union movement in recent decades come to the national Democratic party that in the early eighties several representatives sat on the National Committee and were consulted on many issues. In the 1984 presidential campaign the Republicans made an issue of this linkage, charging that the unions controlled the Democratic Party. The issue became so prominent that commentators attributed the final defeat in part to this charge.

In the 1988 presidential campaign the Democratic candidate and the trade unions submerged their contacts to avoid a repetition of this charge. (New York Times, June 7, 1988) The unions instead followed a multi-candidate strategy in the presidential primaries, encouraging local people to run for positions as delegates to the Democratic convention on the slates of the candidates they preferred or thought most likely to win. The union, observed one writer, "can pursue this strategy because it can live with all major contenders." Moreover, if the selection process proceeded beyond the first ballot, the union bloc of delegates could increasingly act in unison. (Business Week, February 22, 1988)

A major barrier to any close relationship between trade unions and the Democratic party is the very nature of the American party system. The parties tend to disclaim any special ideological attachments and are themselves composed of people of diverse orientations. Party affiliations are the product of many forces, including historical conditioning of parts of the electorate. Individuals' political mobility among parties often increases in periods of shifts of public opinion. At present the differences of outlook among groups within the Democratic party are much grater and sharper than in the Republican, where groups have coalesced and shifted to the right during the Reagan presidency.

Even though the Democratic party has commanded majorities in both houses of Congress during most recent years, labor's powerful and skillful lobbies have not gained significant union legislation. The lobbies have provided critical and effective support and pressure on legislatures and administrations on broad social issues or when it has enjoyed the cooperation of other lobbying groups (Wilson).

As in other countries, the worker constituency has been divided in its voting pattern. Even among union members, those voting for the Democratic Presidential candidate in the 1988 election constituted but 69 percent of the total (AFL-CIO News, December 3, 1988).

cc. Partnerships in Conflict

Illustrations from three countries describe the relations between the trade unions and their political partners when in power.

i. West Germany: Estrangement Deepens

Many issues produced fissures between unions and socialists when the SPD joined the government in 1966. It initiated the Concerted Action program, which had as one of its purposes the promotion of moderate wage movements through discussions among labor, employers and the government. In 1969 spontaneous strikes occurred with the upturn in business profits, which exceeded the projections used in wage agreements. Employees struck and secured substantial increases. Workers engaged in subsequent strikes sponsored by the unions for wage increases and the results exceeded the Chancellor's proposed patterns. (Willey, pp.57-58) The conflict in interests between the unions and government grew so intense that when the managements in 1977 challenged the constitutionality of the Codetermination Law, the DGB withdrew from the Concerted Action arrangements. (Markovits, p.140)

A second controversy occurred when a steel company acquired a non-steel company. The latter then argued that it was no longer bound by the parity provisions of the Codetermination Law affecting the iron and steel industry. The SPD and the FDP cabinet ministers took opposite positions on the issue and the dispute threatened a breakup of the coalition. Finally, the issue was temporarily resolved by ordering the postponement of the company's reorganization to 1987.

A third controversy centered on the DGB proposal to extend the principle of parity representation under the codetermination laws to all industries. After considerable delay and debate between the coalition partners, a legislative compromise was reached for the appointment of a senior salaried employee to the board of directors as a worker's representative (enacted in 1976), thereby depriving the DGB of its goal of parity in representation on the corporate boards.

A fourth controversy emerged out of the wage disputes of 1973 and 1974. Workers engaged in wildcat strikes followed by a three-day general strike among public employees. Ultimately, the agreement provided for an 11 percent wage rise, again exceeding the proclaimed national government standard. The negotiations and strikes during the period further embittered the relations between the DGB and the SPD.

A fifth issue derived from the union proposal for a bill to establish a central investment fund financed by management. This principle was endorsed by the executive boards of the SPD and the DGB, but the Chancellor postponed the issuance of his decision.

A sixth issue dealt with the unions' demand for a 35 hour work week spearheaded by the metal union. It secured the 38.5 hour work week and finally in 1987, achieved the standard work week of 37 hours.

The unions also criticized the government for the very meagerness of its legislative achievement in the face of the many union proposals, but union officials tended to withhold making sharp public comments.

The sense of frustration was intensified by the subsequent experience under the conservative government. In 1986 the government secured a revision of paragraph 116 of the Work Promotion Act which made it difficult for workers to secure unemployment benefits when laid off because of parts shortages resulting from a strike in other bargaining regions, a practice which offset workers' losses in earnings in many strikes. (Markovits, pp. 137-150)

ii. Great Britain: Labor Government Undermined by Industrial Conflict

The TUC found to its chagrin that the Joint Declaration of 1964 had not produced a program sufficient to turn the economic tides for the better. The problems were further exacerbated by a huge deficit in the national balance of payments. Unwilling to devalue the pound, the government resorted to deflationary measures and restricted wage increases to zero. Though the wage freeze of July 1966 was approved by the TUC, local and national unions moved ahead to secure further wage increases. In 1968, the Labor government scrapped its income policy and replaced it with proposals for limiting union bargaining power. In addition the government cut public expenditures and raised prescription costs. Unemployment levels rose to new high levels. The government also gave up its plans for improving the income distribution profile. The death knell for the government was the 1969 White Paper entitled In Place of Strife, which proposed government intervention in collective bargaining including criminal sanctions for violations by offending trade unions. The proposal caused such an uproar both among Labor backbenchers and the unions that it was withdrawn. A new bill produced in April 1970 eliminated the criminal measure and other items. The opposition to this weak revision was also strong and union-sponsored Labor MPs were not pacified. Then followed a rash of strikes. One analyst concludes that there was a "growing awareness of the divergent purpose of the trade unions and Labor governments, a feeling of estrangement from the party on the part of trade union officials." (Minkin, p. 29)

As indicated, the TUC-Labor relations during the first two years of the Wilson-Callahan era (1974-79) were relatively smooth, but the government's subsequent wage policies again enraged the working population and leaders, finally precipitating the strikes of the winter of 1979 which brought the Labor government to its end.

In subsequent years, the recession muted the restlessness among manual workers. White-collar and government employees concurrently became more militant and engaged in serious strikes to gain improvements in their status. Radicalism and frustration spread in the face of the Labor Party and TUC failures. Several moderate leaders of the Labor party, out of distaste for the growing influence of the left-wing groups, resigned from the party and formed their own independent Social Democratic Party.

iii. Spain: The 1988 Confrontation between Unions and Socialist Government

With the establishment of a parliamentary democracy after forty years of General Franco's dictatorship (1936-75), unions in Spain emerged from the depths of the underground and the state-sponsored works councils developed during the Franco period. The principal labor organization became the General Workers Union (UGT) associated with the Spanish Workers' Socialist Party (PSOE) and the Workers Commissions (CC.OO), associated with the Communist Party of Spain (PCE). However, the CC.OO became increasingly autonomous of the party in face of the numerous splits in the left political movement. Other minor federations included the Solidarity of Basque Workers and Union Labor (USA) and the National Federation of Labor (CNT).

The national collective bargaining system evolved from its beginnings in 1977. The initial "Moncloa Pacts," endorsed by all parliamentary parties, set the pattern for future agreements. They have been the 1979 Interconfederal Agreement with employers, the 1980 Interconfederal Framework Agreement, the 1981 National Agreement on Employment and the 1983 Interconfederal agreement, and the 1985 Social and Economic Agreement.

Several of these agreements involved commitments by the national government to create jobs. The principal union negotiating partner was the UGT, which was joined in individual cases by the other federations, whether singly or together or neither, as in the case of the 1985 agreement. Beginning in 1984 governmental wage patterns in the public sector provided a guide for the private sector. With these national agreements as a base, special contracts were negotiated for the individual industries and plants.

The UGT endorsed the government's general economic policy when it considered the policy in the workers' interest, but where it disagreed, it voiced its criticism. An example of this relationship is its opposition to the proposed pension reform bill introduced by the government. (European Trade Union Institute Info 17 Spain, pp. 57-62)

The unions' acceptance of governmental guidelines until 1987 set the limits for labor negotiations. But in that year a series of demonstrations and prolonged strikes reflected the depth of disappointment with the wage ceilings set by the government. Subsequently the UGT leader resigned in protest from his parliamentary seat in the Socialist bloc. The unions charged that the government was abandoning the Socialist commitments and yielding to pro-business counsel. Strikers and protesters rejected the government's call for austerity. One direct consequence of this dissatisfaction was the loss of Socialist seats in the June 1987 municipal elections.

As the rate of economic growth rose and business became more prosperous, the restlessness spread particularly in face of the continuing high rates of unemployment despite the mounting number of jobs. When the next government wage guides were announced, the resentment heightened and provoked even more discontent. Moreover in 1988 the government proposed subminimum wages for youth to induce their employment by companies. The opposition to the policy was so great that the UGT and the CC.OO called a joint one-day protest strike on December 14, 1988. Eight million workers of a total work force of eleven million walked out; an impressive number given the union penetration rate of less than 20 percent. The strike was conducted in a disciplined manner, and people returned to work on the next day in the same fashion. Following this effective strike, the government indicated a willingness to negotiate with the unions and employers. But the unions insisted that the initial discussions be conducted solely with them, to which the government agreed. A Socialist Party Congress in January 1989 endorsed the government's policy and at the same time supported the proposal for negotiations for fear of the adverse effects of these events on the national election in 1990. But further negotiations, both in December 1988 and January and February 1989 had not produced a general agreement. The government did qualifiedly cancel the controversial youth employment scheme, but the Prime Minister on February 14, 1989 declared no concessions would be forthcoming. (New York Times, Paul Delaney dispatches; Peter Bruce; The Economist, March 11, 1989)

dd. OECD Countries

As the preceding analysis dealt with five countries, a more generalized image is therefore appropriate of the relationship between trade unions and their political partners in the twenty-four advanced industrial countries encompassed by the OECD. This summary is necessarily limited but will provide further insights.

1. In most advanced industrial democracies the national union federations are associated with a political partner. Their intimacy and degree of collaboration vary greatly, ranging from those where they are relatively distant to those in which the cooperation is intimate, continuous as well as established, having functioned for several decades. Nevertheless, there are federations which shun such formal or informal contacts. This aloofness developed because of the diversity of political commitments of union membership, the leaders' determination to achieve a consolidation of independent federations, each of which had such past affiliations, or the need to avoid choosing among the disparate political factions among members of the left, or the desire to escape affiliation with a communist party.

2. The trade union federations are primarily associated with the socialist or communist parties, the Christian Democrats, or other political parties such as Liberals.

3. In some instances the parties exercise substantial influence on federation policies and strategy, arrange for a continuing interchange of officialdom, collaborate in the formulation of education and public relations policies, and conduct joint activities such as demonstrations. Political partners in the early postwar years often subsidized the establishment and expansion of the trade union associate. But these links have declined in importance, particularly among the communist group as factionalism multiplied. Some federations have maintained a steadfast tie with their national Christian Democratic or Communist parties or their equivalents.

4. The political partners have served as advocates of union positions though on some issues they have modified union proposals to adapt them to party views and immediate political situations.

5. The socialist parties in particular have sought to broaden their appeal to the electorate, hoping thereby to extend their following, and raised their ambitions from being a union pressure group to becoming a realistic alternative government to the traditional parties. They added many planks to their platform and altered their positions to satisfy the newer non-worker constituencies. The Christian Democratic parties, representing primarily a constituency composed of members of the middle class and higher income groups, have in the postwar years accented their centrist positions. Labor factions in such parties sought

to amend policy statements or secure endorsements for specific union measures.

<u>6</u>. When in power, the socialist parties have experimented with economic measures growing out of their ideological orientation and the needs of their constituencies. When the parties proved inadequate or deficient in reaching their goal, the spokesmen shifted to mainstream economic practices and programs in the hope of achieving growth, stability, full employment and the establishment of new enterprises as well as in dealing with cyclical, monetary and fiscal problems. Often the result was to provoke outright opposition, strikes and deep dissatisfaction among their followers. This, in turn, produced a decline in electoral support and the end of socialist governments.

<u>7</u>. The socialist governments have tended to abandon their ideological orientation as an overall framework and emphasized instead individual measures. Few have ventured as far as the Scandinavian movements to devise new comprehensive approaches to economic and social issues, thereby defining new roads for economic and social change.

<u>8</u>. In some countries, socialist parties stuck by their doctrinaire positions and refused to compromise them, thereby eliminating themselves as potential participants of coalitions for which programmatic compromises are often essential. In these instances the protection for workers and incremental gains were often forfeited.

<u>9</u>. Trade union federations have benefited substantially from the association with political partners by securing benefits and advantages for their constituency and expanding their roles in the national economy, political system and society, thereby enhancing their image and facilitating their appeals for new members.

<u>10</u>. In the last few decades trade union federations have increasingly had to define independent positions on many individual economic, political and social issues to express their own interests, expertise and goals. These have frequently enriched the party's programs and accomplishments as well as advanced thinking in their societies, as witness the outstanding contributions by trade unionists to the economic and social thinking in Italy and Sweden.

<u>11</u>. Only a few countries pursue organized efforts to fashion policies, strategy and proposals to accommodate the respective viewpoints and needs of both wings of the labor movement. In these cases the results have been mutually profitable.

12. The degree of cooperation among federations in countries with a multiple number of them, and the political parties and governments varied considerably. In some countries the federations evolved the practice of preparing and presenting joint positions, whereas some are antithetical to such efforts.

13. In no case can we find trade union federations withdrawing completely from the political scene, for those without direct associations continued on their own to follow legislative developments and to seek influence bills, administrative decisions, and judicial orders. They found it imperative to make their own views known and useful if not indispensable to find a voice for their interests in the administrative, legislative and judicial halls.

ee. Observations

Among the most serious direct external effects on trade union behavior and policies has been the relations with their political partners. The intimate connection created when both were struggling for a foothold in their respective economies and societies has generally weakened. Their attitudes to one another have in many countries become more reserved, particularly as their immediate objectives diverged, and on these occasions the political partners experienced significant electoral victories or seriously began to court the possibility of taking over the reins of government. The parties then moved to a less exclusive role of being a pressure group for the trade unions and in some cases advocates for more utopian social arrangements, to that of becoming the agent of the people, a "people's party" or the "party of government," frequently bent on achieving economic, political and social change through the political process. In their new position the parties shouldered the responsibility of formulating policies on a broad range of political issues while on occasion subordinating their own priorities. Nevertheless, being fully aware of their dependence upon trade unions for their most loyal supporters and active campaign workers, the parties continued to pay obeisance to the union component of the alliance. A modus vivendi had to be designed to balance these two courses, which on occasion impaired relations. But acknowledging the ties was indispensable to the parties while they designed policies and appeals with which to gain broader sources of support while at the same time being dependent upon the unions for financial and manpower help. Crude subordination of the unions served neither group, as is well illustrated by the German and British experience.

Unions needed to continue their connection with the parties, for governments played an important role in assuring their existence and securing advances or curbing restraints upon them. Only a few countries have seen the two wings elaborate formal workable and satisfactory systems of relationship to minimize the frictions and open up opportunities for discussion, and ultimately, accommodation. In assessing programs and strategies for the future, union leaders must necessarily consider the individual national and local political profiles.

Effective arrangements between the two wings have evolved in Austria, Norway and Sweden. They produced common measures and strategies. Capable spokesmen have offered defenses and explanations for their proposals based on their ideological outlook. They have offered evidence of the practicality, soundness and usefulness of their approaches in face of the declared deficiencies of traditional mainstream policies. These spokesmen assailed those policies as being invariably designed at the expense of the working population and in defiance of the principles of equity and humanistic goals which the labor movement espouses. These explanations have also assisted in orienting the electorate in the objectives of the labor movement and building up confidence in the party and trade union movement.

The above model points to one of the great gaps in the arsenal of measures employed by many trade union and socialist parties. A need exists not only to explain and relate proposals to their own constituencies but also to the general society. The arts of communication in an open society demand that the parties address the general public and electorate in the terms of both their own assumptions and mainstream thinking.

C. Population Setting: Demography of Work Force

Significant changes have occurred in the labor force in all countries. These must be carefully analyzed to determine the changes needed in union policies and strategies for recruitment of new membership and in the administration of the organizations.

1. The proportion of the population in the labor force has risen in OECD countries, expanding from 43.5 percent in 1960 to 46.4 percent in 1986. In the United States it rose from 39.6 percent to 49.5 percent and declined in OECD Europe from 44.9 percent to 43.4 percent.

2. The female active proportion of the total female population in the work force grew in this period from 28.7 percent to 36.7 percent whereas those for males slipped from 59.0 percent to 56.6 percent. (OECD Historical Statistices 1960, 1986. pp.32-33)

3. The age of the work force has advanced with the drop of the birth rate, the extension of the life span and the aging of the baby boomers born in 1945-64.

4. Alien and foreign-born labor continues to constitute a high proportion of the work population. Estimates place the total above eight million. The principal host countries are France, West Germany, Great Britain, Switzerland and the United States. But the ratios of these people to the total work force is often higher in specific smaller countries. The decade of the sixties is known as that of the age of the guest worker; the seventies, the age of family reunification; and the eighties, that of the refugee. (OECD SOPEMI 1988 p.1) Shifts have occurred in the relative importance of the deporting countries due to the changing influence of various economic, historic, legal and personal considerations. Unions in several European countries and U.S. cities maintain active programs for helping foreign workers to adjust both in the workplace and community; the unions are also strong proponents for employer and public adaptation services.

5. Part-time and atypical work schedules are becoming more common. Involuntary part-time work has become particularly high among adult males. Shift workers are estimated to constitute 10 to 15 percent of all workers, either on a regular or occasional basis. As flexible work schedules spread, the proportion of employees on atypical schedules is likely to expand. (OECD Living Conditions pp.50, 64-66)

6. The educational level of the work force is also reported to be rising, and the rate of increase is "accelerating...in OECD areas since 1950." The number of years in the educational system spent by women: "is approaching the male levels." (ibid., pp.48-49)

7. Multiple-earner families are growing in number, and their proportion of national household no doubt is expanding.

8. Multi-ethnic work forces are also increasing, and their composition is changing significantly.

III. ONSLAUGHT ON UNIONISM

The seventies and the eighties witnessed an upsurge of diverse organized attacks on unions by academics, employers, national and international governmental organizations and the media. Not only was this movement designed to weaken unions but also in some cases to effect their complete elimination. The goal was to recapture for management the so-called rights of controlling the enterprise. Unilateralism was to prevail. The program involved either measures initiated by management, the government or both in concert. Academics were sure to follow, outlining rationales for submerging bilateral decision-making and the independence of the unions. The new drive was a direct reaction against the ascendancy of unions and their growing influence in the late thirties, through the war and early postwar years. For instance, in the United States, management accepted long and bitter strikes to change these trends, but the social militancy of the sixties and seventies offset this pressure particularly in Europe and provided added impetus to the union movement.   Thereafter managements' counterattack began again to have its effects. These efforts were reinforced by new management techniques designed to win over the work force and detach them from their union allegiance.

A. Unilateral Counterattacks

We shall sketch counterattacks in five countries, emphasizing particularly the respective roles of management, government and academics.

1. Great Britain: Government Is Initiator

The principal initiator of programs to curb union influence in Great Britain was the government. Public opinion had been inflamed against unions particularly from the sixties onwards by conservative management and academic circles.   Even the Labor governments responded to these attacks and offered legislation for curbing union power. The Heath conservative administration (1970-74) initiated active restraints. The ascendancy of the Thatcher administration in 1979 brought this movement to a new peak. With its control of the House of Commons it had a relatively free hand at securing restrictive legislation. Laws were passed in 1980, 1982, 1984, 1986 and 1988 repealing pro-union legislation adopted during the Wilson-Callaghan administration and introducing restrictions. Union efforts to stop this movement were largely futile. Significantly the government's attempts to enlist management as a copartner in this drive were hardly effective. The associations would not engage in direct attacks and open warfare with unions though they favored individual pieces of legislation. Few employers took advantage of the openings in the laws to sue unions through the courts of law. They were reluctant to antagonize their work force or pursue class struggles. Instead the common practice was to negotiate with local unions and seek their cooperation in effecting changes and economies to increase enterprise efficiency. Gains through such improved local relations appeared to be a higher priority. The anti-union movement did reinforce employers' resistance to union demands though the gains actually received exceeded the norms pronounced from time to time. More and more academics joined in the ranks of union critics. (Solomon Barkin, 1986; David Soskice) The debates surrounding the government's legislation as well as the supporting opinions from employers, academics and the media ranks reinforced an unfriendly public opinion. Unions were on the defensive. They were, however, able to adapt to many legal restraints or requirements and still pursue traditional practices. Votes by members supporting closed shops, union political action funds and strike action legalized these measures.

In evaluating the era, the editors of the Financial Times concluded that "the lines and details of any new emerging system of industrial relations are far from clear and coherent at this stage, a result that is hardly surprising under nine years of Thatcherism which is more a matter of attitudes and instincts than a thought-out philosophy in which policies fit together in a coherent intellectual framework." (Financial Times, "The Thatcher Years,"1987, p. 85 quoted by Beaumont) The actual numerical and proportional decline in union membership was attributable more to an adverse economic climate and public attitudes, and the declines of unionized industries than to the government's attack and hostile legislation and action.

2. The United States: A Collaborative Attack by Government and Management

A major factor in labor-management relations in the United States has been the continued management opposition to unions. Vigorous organized anti-union programs have been conducted from the beginning of the century. With the adoption of Section 7a of the NIRA in 1933 and the later passage of the Wagner Labor Relations Act in 1935, the unfriendly attacks became organized. The sequence has been very clear. It moved first to criticism of the National Labor Relations Board, to the promotion of the Taft-Hartley and Landrum-Griffin Acts to demands for shifts of the Board membership toward the right and the dilution by Board decisions on the National Labor Relations Act that had been helpful to labor organization. Symbolically the attack reached its peak with the discharge of the airport controller strikers by President Reagan (1981). In the course of time the Right-to-Work Movement became a spearhead of this anti-union drive.

The onslaught was directly carried on principally by individual companies through opposition to unionism in their plants, the movement of existing production units to "union free" areas (such as the Southeast, Southwest and rural communities) and the rampant discrimination against individuals who showed an interest in unionism. Where union efforts survived these moves, employers fought the organizations in plant elections and applied pressure to discourage employees from voting for unions. When the unions won, they capitalized on all means for delaying union certification and, when certified, made negotiations difficult and prolonged. Unions at the worksite had a difficult time even when they had surmounted these hurdles.

Another managerial approach was to modify personnel policies and practices to wean workers away from unions. During the postwar years managements introduced programs entitled human relations, then organizational behavior and currently human resources management programs to weaken workers' attachment to the unions and introduce substitutes for union institutions such as grievance machinery and arbitration but without affording workers real independence and resources for the pursuit of these opportunities. Like company unions in the thirties these institutions remain essentially company controlled, building on a unilateralist philosophy and approach.

Finally, academics joined this unilateralist movement. Industrial relations experts and authors, such as John R. Commons, and Richard Ely have from the very beginning in the 1880s rationalized unionization and collective bargaining as instruments to humanize employer-employee relations and to assist in managing enterprises more effectively. They abandoned unions when they became militant. Summner Slichter published two major surveys in 1940 and in 1960 in which he analyzed collective bargaining practices. He supported the existence of unions, but he opposed "a laboristic society" and warned management to set up defenses to protect its rights. In the 1960 volume he offers a code of conduct to strengthen management rights in the plants. These authors confined union functions to those dealing with direct relations to employers and identified them, as economic institutions, neglecting their other functions in the political and social fields. In recent years a number of academics have favored and secured the substitution of human resource management courses in colleges for those on collective bargaining. (Solomon Barkin, 1986)

3. West Germany: Management Masterminds Propaganda and Strategy

West Germany has evolved a dualistic system of collective bargaining. One is conducted through unions and deals with industry standards, levels of wage and benefits including prescriptions for health and safety and some shop conditions; the other, through works councils prescribed by law which deals with local personnel, social issues and the enforcement and application of the basic industry agreement to plant conditions. The delegates on the works council consist substantially of the designers of the DGB elected by the employees in the working unit. By law these councils are committed to advance industrial peace and the interests of the enterprise and are prohibited from initiating or conducting strikes. Disputes arising in the deliberations of the councils may be referred by the unions to the labor courts. Individual councils may also invite union representatives and experts to their meetings to help them consider technical issues. Under the codetermination law, the principle of parity of representation on the supervisory boards is compromised by an amendment designating a managerial employee as one of the labor representatives and the law allows the management chairman to cast the deciding vote in case of a deadlock. The codetermination arrangement has contributed to the humanization of corporation decisions without changing the basic power structure within the enterprise.

In the sixties when the militant spirit among workers developed, management initiated through the BDA (Federal Union of German Employers Associations) a deliberate propaganda program to downgrade the power and status of the unions. The basic charge was that the DGB and SPD constitute threats to the democratic state. Privately, it introduced in 1965, as was later disclosed, a CATALOG OF DON'TS (Tabu Katalog) which was recurrently revised. One specialist writes that it "enumerated the BDA's strict guidelines for its members proper behavior concerning their dealings with labor in the process of collective bargaining...(It set) detailed parameters and strict limits for every BDA member regarding such issues as working conditions, work time and work content. The document's firm guidelines clearly aimed at maximizing the employers' control over every phase of their interaction with labor. (It) also served as a concise handbook for the employers' strategy of coordination and centralization in their bargaining with the unions during the crisis." It "represented more than a mere proposal as was demonstrated by a controversy involving working time reduction." (Markovits pp. 146-7) This determination to provide central direction reflects a change in basic management attitudes and the desire to make wider use of the lockout as an answer to the unions' increasing use of strikes and as a determination to halt the further extension of the principles of codetermination.

As part of this aggressive move against unions, employers persuaded the government to cancel the workers' rights to unemployment benefits where layoffs were due to shortages of materials following strikes in other states of the country.

The tense antagonistic relationship has continued to the present. The unions' sensitivity to this belligerent management mood was further heightened by a drive by "certain radical leftist--particularly communist--tendencies among some of its member unions." (ibid., p. 155) To ward off the offense from both sides, the DGB leadership initiated its own counter propaganda moves.

4. Sweden: Management's Criticism of Bargaining System Stimulates Moves toward Decentralized Bargaining

Further evidence of the employer countermoves in facing union entrenchment is discerned in Sweden. The Swedish Employers' Confederation (SAF) under pressure from its constituents sought to change the climate on the bargaining front. It was encouraged in this effort by the rising influence of the non-socialist parties which gained control of the government (1976-82). The SAF initiated a study project for examining the problems and developments of collective bargaining and unions in other countries. The resulting report gained much attention in the country. The chapter on Sweden outlines many common employer complaints about its system. One was that unions had turned to political action and legislation and abandoned collective bargaining to realize their objectives. They sought a voice in management decision making over matters which the collective agreements had hitherto reserved to management. In the process of centralizing decision making in the collective bargaining process the local union lost its crucial function and had compromised the relationship between the individual employee and company management. The author finds that the "system undermines the rights of the individual and his or her general position." He concludes that these changes have led to the "disintegration of the old order."

Beginning from the year 1983 the employers' campaign was effective in getting negotiations decentralized, but the pendulum has swung back to more centralization in later settlements. The full effects of decentralization had not yet been experienced and a workable reconciliation is yet to evolve. One major influence favoring centralized or at least standardized and coordinated agreements has been the Ministry of Finance, which has sought to restrain wage settlements to minimize their inflationary impact. (Anders Leion, "Sweden", in Roberts; Scott Lash and Casten van Otter).

5. Australia: A Surge of Propaganda

The trade union movement in Australia reports the appearance of an anti-union drive to secure restrictive legislation similar to that enacted in Great Britain under the influence of the Thatcher Administration. Groups of employers, conservatives and intellectuals are seeking the repeal of social legislation and the destruction of trade union organizations. Among the leaders in this movement reportedly are the Premier of Queensland state and the newspaper magnate, Rupert Murdoch.

B. Advocacy of a Flexible Labor Market

As significant in many advanced industrial states is the drive to challenge the premises of union activity. A popular cry is for a flexible labor market. It is an outgrowth of the current fashion to call for deregulation as a solution of economic troubles. The protagonists are calling for the removal of provisions in collective agreements which restrict management's discretion over the terms and conditions of employment. No heed is paid to the reality that these regulations are born out of the desire to prevent unfair, abusive and inequitable practices. The United States has been a leader in this move and has been joined by conservative groups in other countries. The OECD has become the intellectual workshop for the promotion of this policy. Despite the fact that many studies made by the organization over the years have called the assumptions into question, its advocacy continues unqualified. The author has examined this subject and concluded: "Critical examinations of the arguments and data do not support the oversimplified generalizations underlying the position of the advocates of flexibility. They ignore available statistical and empirical evidence accessible in OECD publications. No simple relationship exists between general occupational wage levels and mobility and levels of employment. Wage differentials do not necessarily impel the migratory movements posited by the policy pronouncements. The direction, volume and time of labor movements are affected by a complex of factors. Deterrents to voluntary job changes are numerous and often very strong. This welter of conflicting forces is present in periods of high economic activity, recessions and on occasions of major structural change, though their respective impacts vary considerably under different circumstances." (Solomon Barkin, 1987)

IV. UNION RESPONSE

A. Country Reviews

The trade union movement has been sensitive but not fully responsive to the developments outlined in this chapter. Some perceived the fundamental nature of the new reality and the challenge it presents. But others have preferred to consider the reverses as temporary, a function of the business and structural cycles. Some have addressed specific individual problems without considering the fundamental questions. Others have recognized their own future was at stake.

We shall consider a number of answers provided in individual countries.

1. Great Britain: Facing a Declining Membership

The TUC has recognized the seriousness of the issue and appointed a Special Review Board to consider the future role of unionism. The first report by this Board was offered to the 1988 TUC Congress. It primarily considered the question of the decline in membership. The recommendation was that the TUC seek to eliminate the interunion conflicts in organizing new sites and establish a code of practice for unions for the recruitment of members at such places. Other suggestions call for prior notification of the entry of single recognition agreements, no strike clauses and arbitration and inward investment and the general level and terms and conditions involved in such agreements. Significantly, the parties to the first union agreement which would have been covered by the code failed to comply with the pre-notification provision. Still other recommendations call for greater contacts with national employer organizations, a pilot scheme on labor market intelligence and union membership, the expansion of the roles of the TUC in regard to union services, greater organizing efforts for women and younger workers, and a pilot scheme on joint union campaigns at the local level.

It is important to note that the pioneer in the negotiations of single-recognition no-strike agreements was the EETPU (Electrical,

Electronic, Telecommunications and Plumbing Union), which was expelled in September 1988 from the TUC.

Other recommendations offered for the reconstruction of the trade union movement and the reversal of the decline include the following: reelection of a Labor government, union mergers, concentration of organizing efforts, particularly aimed at women and younger workers; a pilot project on joint union campaigns at the local level, concentration of organizing growing industries; and increases in services particularly in the financial and legal fields. (Beaumont: Trade Union Congress)

2. West Germany: A New Stress on Self-Reliance instead of State Action

A significant change in orientation of the DGB is reported in the Fifth Action Program of 1979, replacing that of 1972 and the third Basic Program of 1981, supplanting that of 1945 and 1963. The new statements set forth basic beliefs about the German economy and society. Most prominent are the concerns for the unemployed and the large volume of unemployment and the disappointment with the record of the SPD governments. The programs therefore underscore the need for "self-reliance" rather than the traditional resort to the state. The DGB demands the abolition of the employers' right to use lockouts. "Qualitative collective bargaining" is added to the current stress on economic benefits. Experience had taught the DGB that it was necessary "to accentuate the growing interdependence among work, living conditions and the natural environment including" worktime reduction, particularly the 35-hour week. (Markovits pp.63-4) The movement has to accept its "industrial and unitary character," thereby rejecting factionalism of all kinds. (ibid., p.155) The German Constitution, it held, should be viewed as endorsing "an economic and social system which recognizes the social responsibilities and collective obligations of capital vis a vis the community as a whole." It forms "the very essence of a democratic and social state based on the rule of law." (ibid., pp.155-6)

3. United States: Hold and Attract Membership through Expanded Services

The AFL-CIO in 1982 was willing to acknowledge the seriousness of the reverses suffered by the organization. It appointed a Committee on the Evolution of Work to study its problems. After reporting in 1983 on conditions in the labor market and job changes and highlighting the seriousness of the unemployment problem it called for

"comprehensive action in a wide range of problems." It expressed the
conviction that "much could be done through collective bargaining.
But the federal government has a key role." (AFL-CIO Committee on
the Evolution of Work, 1983 p.16)

In its second report in February 1985 on "The Changing
Situation of Workers and Their Unions" it deals with the need for new
union organization and for encouraging more active membership
participation in union activities and internal decision-making. It
appeals, probably with little hope of fulfillment, to management to
engage in "a cooperative approach to solving shared present and future
problems." (AFL-CIO Committee on the Evolution of Work, 1985
p.6) It adds that "until the time our desire for cooperation is fully
reciprocated, unions must maintain the ability to meet employer
confrontation." (ibid., p.6) But its optimism is reawakened by
reporting that it has found evidence of the existence of "the seeds for a
resurgence of the labor movement." (ibid., p.14)

As for new organizational drives it offers the maxims of
established good practice and urges "union leaders and rank-and-file
members (to) be more involved in organizing efforts." (ibid., p.27).
The Committee feels it necessary to underscore the union purposes and
their members having "a say in the how, why and wherefore of their
work."

The novel guide it urges is for unions to speak in terms of the
workers' own cares and concerns. In some bargaining units workers
may not desire to establish a comprehensive set of hard and fast terms
and conditions of employment but may nonetheless desire a
representative to negotiate minimum guarantees that will serve as a
floor for individual bargaining, to provide advocacy for individuals or to
seek redress for particular difficulties" (ibid., p.18), an established
practice in professional union contracts.

Special "consideration should be given to establishing new
categories for workers not employed in an organized bargaining unit."
These groups as well as the established membership would be attracted
by union services and benefits provided outside of a collective
bargaining structure. This system of benefits would include invitations
to a credit card scheme. Individual unions, it may be added, have
elaborated on this idea by offering other services.

Other proposals relate to increased communication with the
membership and the merger of small unions.

The program fastens on administrative improvements and closer relations with the membership without expanding or defining the functions of unions both in the collective bargaining system and in American society and politics. (Solomon Barkin, 1985)

B. Trade Unionist Consensus

This review of the national federation statements on the policy and reforms needed to revitalize the trade union movements in a number of companies, a goal which must be sought by most of them, indicates that major challenges lie ahead. It is appropriate to offer a distillation of the prevailing views on a number of the key issues in the new environment which union leaders and membership face.

Before proceeding to this summary one may note that most leaders have been conditioned by their own experiences in the postwar period and the movement's record of achievement and the great respect it gained. They have truly played an important role in the development of their respective nations and have significantly shaped the outcome. It is this success they wish to repeat.

Trade unionists share a significant basic outlook. They believe that employees can only by collective action secure remedies for their complaints, realize their ambitions, play a significant function in the industrial world and in society as a whole and achieve the humanization and equity in industry and in society they espouse. In this respect their credo contrasts sharply with that of other groups in advanced industrial countries which rely in their ideology upon individual competition and action, yet such groups have organized themselves into collective units, such as corporations, cartels, associations and political parties, to safeguard and advance their individual rights, to ward off attacks and to implement their own action programs. As unions extended their coverage to professional, technical and artistic employees, they have modified their instruments of agreement to open up opportunities for individual advancement and recognition of individual competences and bargaining powers without sacrificing group interests.

1. General Principles

a. A fundamental assumption of the unionist's outlook is that no matter how strong his utopian visions may be, actual improvements have to be realized incrementally through progressive gains in standards of living and recognition of his other individual rights in the enterprise and society. In the economic society common rules are essential for orderly conduct. Individuals must be respected, their opportunities safeguarded and their contributions recognized and fittingly rewarded.

The disposition toward radical economic change has been considerably weakened. It is commonly accepted that gains will be slowly and methodically achieved. This conviction has been reinforced by the outright confessions of the shortcomings and failings of the Soviet system by many of its leading spokesmen. (Andre V. Kozyrev [Chief of the International Relations Administration of the Soviet Foreign Ministry] New York Times, January 7, 1989).

b. While the open free market system contributes substantially to advancing our well-being, it creates many pitfalls, abuses, injustices and inequities. Regulations by governments were introduced to curb such undesirable consequences. Experience with deregulation has revealed that such negative consequences are regularly forthcoming and invariably call new regulations into being. Public enterprises make significant and useful contributions but they are in need of innovators, entrepreneurs and good administrators. Regulations in the labor market either by law or collective agreements are provoked by abuses and violations by the management of an enterprise, and their repeal very often invites new and old types of misconduct.

c. Trade unions perform an essential function in promoting a humanistic and equitable economic and social system, which seeks to realize the goals of economic growth, stability and smooth transitions. The goals include provisions to aid individuals to make the most appropriate transfers to new activities when their older ones fade out. Individuals should not be asked to carry costs of sickness, unemployment disability, and retirement.

2. Internal Issues

Many serious internal issues have cropped up among unions. Some are more pressing in individual countries than are others but most have to face them.

a. New Organization: Unionists believe that employees need collective instruments to establish parity in bargaining power with management. Countervailing power is an essential instrument in an open market system for those who seek equitable and just treatment. Unions seek to present this message to employees at every level and adapt their policies and institutions to the ever-changing characteristics of the working population.

b. National federations: Many countries have had a multiplicity of national federations. Several successful integrations have taken place to constitute unitary confederations. Otherwise, consultation and cooperation are essential and systems of coordinated bargaining are critical for realizing economic and legislative and administrative demands.

c. Structure of national unions: Some are based on craft, others on industrial and still others on "general" principles. Many different solutions have been designed to avoid strife and destructive competition among unions.

d. International cooperation: With the emergence of the multinational corporation the need for cooperation among national unions is clear but the answers to date have been few in number and essentially inadequate. Corporation bargaining or industry union councils exist, but they have been largely mechanisms for the exchange of information and occasional mutual help. Management has generally resisted bargaining at an international level, but to foster stability and employee interests such bargaining is essential as it has been at the national level.

e. Centralization or decentralization of policymaking and negotiations: They seek different goals. Different accommodations have been invented to obtain the optimum reconciliation of the respective aims, but more efforts and patterns are essential. They must be locally shaped.

f. Innovation versus repression: Internal union conflicts on structure and principles have been and are now common. They involve the consideration of institutions, such as craft versus industrial versus general unions; or new areas and forms of negotiations and bargaining; new principles for negotiations such as single plant no strike agreements; jurisdictional differences; flexibility in the management of auxiliary institutions, such as insurance funds to respond to the changing industrial environments. While protective attitudes are common and often essential to survival, the movement must be alert to new needs and innovations, for they must establish experimental ventures for testing new forms, principles and practices to achieve the basic ends. To reject them outright is to invite new competitive institutions.

g. Principles: some guideposts in bargaining such as the solidarity wage in Sweden have aroused opposition and produced interfederational and intra-federational conflicts. The resulting battles are destructive. Older doctrines will ever be under attack. The advantages and merits of continuing to adhere to or abandoning them must be tested and examined for the benefit of the trade union movement as a whole.

h. Independent trade union evaluation of public policy: Traditionally the political partner has tended to monopolize this function. Unions have increasingly recognized that they have a responsibility and should examine these problems on their own to bring their point of view and expertise to bear on these issues. Their proposals must also allow for the public interests to be protected or advanced.

i. Communication and participation of membership: many new means of communication have been devised. Their use by unions is essential.

j. Type of ownership and management: public ownership and management, or private in both areas. These questions are as serious as the recognition of the limitations of current public administration. Advantages and disadvantages to unions of each form vary among countries; choices have to be carefully made and changed with new circumstances.

k. Political or industrial solutions of problems: The question is when, how and where should unions seek governmental rather than industrial answers for industrial problems. Choices may be changed as circumstances alter.

These questions have been raised in recent years. Many others may be discerned and need careful answers.

3. External Issues

There are four areas of external relations on which we can find considerable consensus.

a. New Organization: There are many groups of employees or enclaves in the population to which union organizations have devoted attention to develop membership and to assist groups in their accommodation to economic and often social life. These include professional, academic, technical and managerial persons. Unions in the past, because of their preoccupation with manual workers, have remained distant from these groups. As previously noted approaches and demands on their behalf have to differ markedly from those which unions are accustomed to make. Such persons focus on individual opportunity and reward for specific contributions which unions in these fields have implemented. The first challenge is to find ways by which organizations in these occupational areas are brought together into confederations with the existing national union organization. A second area requiring special examination relates to the organization of women and youth. With unions in the past concentrating primarily on their male constituency, demands to develop special sets of demands suitable to women and youth needs have grown in recent years and increasingly been reflected in collective agreements. A third group are aliens, internal migrants and groups of disadvantaged people. Aids for facilitating their adjustment are called for so that their integration into the economy and society are promoted. Unions have played an active role in this field of service and cooperated with social service agencies in assuring the appropriate aids. Among the many problems are those relating to the homeless and poorly housed, for which a number of initiatives have been taken by unions.

b. Relations with political partners: Unions have not only perceived the need of offering special proposals to advance their interests and those of their constituency but also to design them so that they also contribute to the national public well-being. The Swedish trade union movement offers a model for these activities.

c. Public and governmental policy: This area has been substantially expanded as unions have made substantial contributions to its development, particularly in economic and social fields. Unions have played significant roles in the promotion of area and regional economic development. As the significance of education and training has grown in the preparation of the workforce, the unions' constant insistence upon adequate schools and universities for the preparation of a qualified workforce has proven most prescient. The entire population has to be given opportunities not only as a right of citizenship but also because the economy is dependent upon the fullest development of its human resources. Unions' focus on the human and social aspects of the nation's development has been most rewarding for the creation of building a more egalitarian society.

d. Collective bargaining: Unions have sought for several decades a role in the operation of enterprises and the development of appropriate policies. Management has designed an increasing number of new programs seeking to encourage employee cooperation and contributions. The great test is how each country designs institutions which integrate the two drives stripped of the antagonistic aims of subduing the adversary. Because employees and unions have been suspicious of many management proposals, they seek intermediary arrangements which would progressively advance to more elevated arrangements of cooperation. The public must support the concept that unions have a responsibility and obligation in their own self-interest to monitor and develop enterprise operations to advance their effectiveness as business ventures and as members of a cooperative work force represented by unions.

C. Prospectus

Some national union federations have taken initial steps to identify the causes of the decline, stagnation or slow growth of their membership. These inquiries considered the sources of external and internal friction. The accent was on urgent measures and immediate institutional issues. Ahead of them lies the more profound challenges of broadening the scope of the inquiries, evaluating their appeals, functions and services and clarifying their roles as spokesmen for specific, and the total, groups of employees, a major segment of society. They must remain independent human and social critics, monitors and participants in the governance of the economic, political and social systems on behalf of their constituency and the citizenry as a whole.

References

1. The term "labour" is spelt "Labor" throughout the text.

2. The term "socialist party" is used to refer to parties which are officially known as Socialist Party, Social Democratic Party and Labor Party in various countries.

BIBLIOGRAPHY

1. AFL-CIO Committee on the Evolution of Work (1983), The Future of Work a Report, Washington D. C.: AFL-CIO, 1983.

2. AFL-CIO Committee on the Evolution of Work (1985), The Changing Situation of Workers and their Unions, Washington, D.C., AFL-CIO, 1985.

3. [AFL-CIO Executive Council at its February 1989 meeting was unable to reach an agreement on a proposal for "unions (to) represent non-union workers, not in a collective bargaining role, but as ombudsmen." (N.Y. Times, February 23, 1989)].

4. AFL-CIO News, "How Union Members Voted," December 3, 1988.

5. Ahlen, Kristina, "Recent Trends in Swedish Collective Bargining", Part I, "Heading Toward Negotiated Income Policy," Stockholm: Swedish Institute (1988), publication no. 358 pp. 8; Part II, "Collapse of the Swedish Model," Stockholm: Swedish Institute, publication no. 359, 9 pp.

6. Barkin, Solomon, editor, Worker Militancy and its Consequences, the Changing Climate of Western Industrial Relations, 2nd edition, N. Y.: Praeger Publishers, 1983, 440 pp.

7. Barkin, Solomon, "An Agenda For the Revision of the American Industrial Relations System," Labor Law Journal, November 1985, pp. 857-860.

8. Barkin, Solomon, "The Current Unilaterialist Counterattack on Unionism and Collective Bargaining," Relations Industrielles (Laval University), v. 41, no. 1, 1986, pp. 3-26.

9. Barkin, Solomon, "The Flexibility Debate in Western Europe: The Current Drive to Restore Management's Rights over Personnel and Wages," Relations Industrielles, Laval University, v. 42, no. 1, 1987, pp. 12-43.

10. Beaumont, Phillip, "The Thatcher/Reagan Administrations Approaches in Labor Relations." Paper read at Annual Meeting of the Industrial Relations Research Association, New York City, December 29, 1988.

11. Bergmann, Joachim, and Walter Müller, "The Federal Republic of Germany: Cooperative Unionism and Dual Bargaining System Challenged," in Solomon Barkin, 1983, pp. 229-277.

12. Bornstein, Stephen, and Peter Gourevitch, "Unions in Declining Economy," in Peter Gourevitch et al., pp. 15-76.

13. Braunthal, Gerard, The West German Social Democrats, 1969-82. Profile of a Party in Power, Boulder, Colorado: Westview Press, 1983, 334 pp.

14. Bremen Nachrichten, "LaFontaine's New Look for the SPD," February 22, 1988, reprinted in German Tribune, March 6, 1988.

15. Bruce, Peter, "Spain: A Political High Wire Act," Financial Times, February 24, 1989.

16. Calingaert, Michale, The 1922 Challenge from Europe, Development of the European Community's Internal Market," Washington D. C.: National Planning Association, 1988, 148 pp.

17. Clegg, H.A., Alan Fox, and A. F. Thompson, A History of British Trade Unions Since 1889, v. I 1889-1910. Oxford: Oxford University Press, 1964, 514 pp.

18. Clegg, Hugh Armstrong, A History of British Trade Unions Since 1889 v. II 1911-1933, Oxford: Oxford University Press, Clarendon Press, 1985, 619 pp.

19. Clutterbuck, David, editor, New Patterns of Work, New York: St. Martin's Press (1984), 135 pp. See review by Solomon Barkin Journal of Economic Issues v. XX No. 4, December 1986, pp. 1163-1167.

20. The Economist
        "Labor's German Lessons," July 25, 1987.
        "Do Mergers Work?," December 17, 1988.

"The Greening of the Invisible Hand," December 24, 1988.

"Thatcher's Non-Opponents," January 7, 1989.

"The Regulatory Two Steps," January 21, 1989.

"Who Speaks for Spain? A Survey," March 11, 1989.

21. Elvander, Nils, "In Search of New Relationships: Parties, Unions and Salaried Employees Associations in Sweden," Industrial and Labor Relations Review, v. 28 no. 1, October 1974, pp. 60-74.

22. The European Trade Union Institute

The Unionization of Professional and Managerial Staff in Western Europe, Brussels (1982), 152 pp.
The Flexibility and Jobs: Myths and Realities, Brussels (1985), 157 pp.
The Trade Union Movement in Spain, Info 17, Brussels (1986), 68 pp.

23. Fieleke, Norman S., "Economic Interdependence between Nations: Reasons for Policy Coordination," New England Review, May-June 1988, pp. 21-38.

24. Flanagan, Robert J., David W. Soskice, and Lloyd Ulman, Unionism, Economic Stabilization and Economic Policy. European Experiences, Washington D. C.: The Brookings Institution, 1983, pp. 301-362.

25. Geary, Dick, European Labor Protest, 1848-1939, New York: St. Martin's Press, 1981, 195 pp.

26. Golt, Sidney C., The Gatt Negotiations, 1986-90. Origins, Issues and Prospects, British North American Committee, Washington D. C.: National Planning Association, 1988, 106 pp.

27. Goodman, John F., "Great Britain: Labor Moves from Power to Constraint," in Solomon Barkin, 1983, pp. 39-80.

28. Gourevitch, Peter, et al, <u>Unions and Economic Crisis: Britain, West German and Sweden</u>, Boston: George Allen and Unwin, 1984, 394 pp.

29. Jonas, Norman, "The Hollow Corporation--The Decline of Manufacturing Threatens the Entire U.S. Economy," <u>Business Week</u> March 3, 1986., pp. 57-85.

30. Lash, Scott, "The End of Neo-Corporatism: The Breakdown of Centralized Bargaining in Sweden," <u>British Journal of Industrial Relations</u>, v. 23, no. 2, July 1985, pp. 215-239.

31. Leion, Anders, "Sweden," in B. C. Roberts, pp. 204-221.

32. LO <u>Tidningen</u>, "Regeringen Overger Utjammingspolitiken," February 10, 1989.

33. Lubell, Samuel, <u>The Future of American Politics</u>, New York: Harper, 1951, pp. 189-197.

34. Marquand, H.A., and others, <u>Organized Labor in Four Continents</u>, New York: Longmans Green and Company, 1939, 518 pp.

35. Markovits, Andrei S., <u>The Politics of the West German Trade Unions</u>, Cambridge: Cambridge University Press, 1986, 599 pp.

36. Martensen, Sten, "SPD Rejects call for Return to a Policy of Nationalization," <u>Stuttgarter Zeitung</u>, January 16, 1989, reprinted in the <u>German Tribune,</u> January 20, 1989.

37. Martin, Andrew, "Trade Unions in Sweden: Strategic Responses to Change and Crisis," in Gourevitch et al., pp. 190-348.

38. Minkin, Lewis, "The British Labor Party and the Trade Unions: Crisis and Compact," in <u>Industrial and Labor Relations Review</u>, October 1974, v. 28, no. 1, pp. 7-37.

39. Mitchell, Harvey, and Peter M. Stearns, <u>Workers and Parties, The European Labor Movement, The Working Classes and the Origin of Social Democracy, 1894-1914</u>, Itasca, Illinois: F. E. Peacock Publishers, 1971, 350 pp.

40. New York Times, Paul Delaney dispatches: "Spain's Chief Tries to Placate Unions," December 22, 1988; "Spanish Officials Meet With Union Leaders," December 30, 1988; "Spain Boom Fuels Dispute on Sharing Wealth," January 22, 1989; Andre V. Kozyrev, "Why Soviet Foreign Policy Went Sour," January 7, 1989; Steve Lohr, "The Growth of the Global Office," October 18, 1988; "AFL Shuns '88 Endorsement," June 7, 1988; Steven Greenhouse, "U.S. Corporations Expand in Europe for 1992 Prospects," March 13, 1989.

41. Organization of Economic Cooperation and Development (OECD)
Continuous Reporting System on Migration (SOPEMI) 1987, Paris: OECD (1988), 80 pp.
Economic Outlook December 1988, Paris: OECD (1988).
Economic Outlook Historical Statistics 1960-1986, Paris: OECD (1988) 166 pp.
Employment Outlook September 1988, Paris: OECD (1988) 220 pp.
Living Conditions in OECD Countries: A Compendium of Social Indicators, OECD Social Policy Studies no. 3, Paris: OECD (1986), 165 pp.

42. Roberts, B.C., editor, Industrial Relations in Europe. The Imperative Changes, London: Croom Helm, 1985, pp. 277. See review by Solomon Barkin Relations Industrielles, v. 41, no. 2, 1986, pp. 417-422.

43. Shonfield, Andrew, Modern Capitalism. The Changing Balance of Public and Private Power, New York: Oxford University Press, 1965, 456 pp.

44. Soskice, David, "Industrial Relations and the British Economy 1978-83," Industrial Relations, v. 23, no. 2, Fall 1983, pp. 306-322.

45. Sturmthal, Adolf, The Tragedy of European Labor, 1918-1939, New York: Columbia University Press, 1943, 389 pp.

46. Tarp, Aage, "Denmark" in B. C. Roberts, pp. 5-44.

47. Trade Union Congress 1988, Meeting the Challenge, First Report of the Special Review Body, London: Trade Union Congress, 1988, 38 pp.

48. van Otter, Casten, "Labor Reformism Reshapes The System," in Solomon Barkin, 1983, pp. 187-227.

49. Viklund, Birger, "Industrial Relations in Sweden in the 1990s." Paper read at Annual Meeting of the Industrial Relations Research Association: New York City, December 29, 1988.

50. Willey, Richard J., "Trade Unions and Political Parties in the Federal Republic of Germany," Industrial and Labor Relations Review, v. 28, no. 1, October 1984, pp. 38-59.

51. Wilson, Graham K., Unions in American National Politics, New York: St. Martin's Press, 1979, 165 pp.

52. Windmuller, John, "European Labor Politics: A Symposium," Industrial and Labor Relations Review, v. 28, no. 1, October 1974, pp. 3-6; v. 28, no. 2, January 1975, pp. 203-207.

Further Readings

1. Bean, Ron, <u>Comparative Industrial Relations: An Introduction to Cross-National Perspective</u> (London: Croom Helm, 1985), 261 pp. A selective thematic presentation of central topics in a comparative analysis, stressing uniformities and diversities among countries both in advanced and developing countries, of trade unions, employers' organizations and collective bargaining, with special treatment of industrial conflict, workers' participation in decision making and multinational corporations.

2. Bennett, John and Julian Fawcett, <u>Industrial Relations: An International Comparative Bibliography</u> (London: Mansell, 1985).

3. Cook, Alice, et. al., editors, <u>Women in Trade Unions in Eleven Industrialized Countries</u> (Philadelphia: Temple University Press, 1984), 327 pp. Nationals write about development of female membership in unions and feminist issues and union reactions and positions.

4. Doeringer, Peter, et al., editors, <u>Industrial Relations in International Perspective</u> (London: Macmillan, 1981), 425 pp. Essays on main theories developed by academics in eight countries.

5. International Labor Office, <u>Collective Bargaining in Industrialized Market Economies, A Reappraisal</u> (Geneva: ILO, 1987), 333 pp. An updating of a 1973 study dealing with methods and practices in collective bargaining in ten countries, but not with public service. ILO has separate volumes for the latter field.

6. International Labor Office, <u>Collective Bargaining: A Response to the Recession in Industrialized Market Economic Countries</u> (Geneva: ILO, 1984), 275 pp. A review of bipartite and tripartite agreements in industrialized market economies relating to recession, inflation, unemployment, and international competition.

7. Lange, Peter, et al., <u>Unions, Changes and Crisis: French and Italian Union Strategy and the Political Economy, 1945-80</u> (Boston: Allen and Unwin, 1982), 295 pp.

8. Lindemann, Albert S., A History of European Socialism (New Haven: Yale University Press, 1983), 385 pp. A chronological review of the socialist parties and theories primarily through World War II.

9. Poole, Michale, Industrial Relations: Origins and Patterns of National Diversity (London: Routledge and Kegan Paul, 1986), 285 pp. Charts multiform patterns of industrial relations. The major themes are industrial conflict, industrial democracy and distribution of economic rewards.

10. Sisson, Keith, The Management of Collective Bargaining: An International Comparison (London: Basil Blackwell, 1984), 230 pp. The volume describes the development of employers' organizations and multi-employer bargaining arrangements in France, Germany, Great Britain, Italy, Japan, Sweden and the United States.

INDEX